VERONICA'S VEIL

Spiritual Companionship for Survivors of Abuse

A Guide for Integrating Faith with Recovery

by

Rev. Lewis S. Fiorelli, O.S.F.S.

T. Pitt Green

Copyright © Rev. Lewis S. Fiorelli, O.S.F.S., and T. Pitt Green 2014

All Rights Reserved

First published by Dog Ear Publishing
4010 W. 86th Street, Ste H
Indianapolis, IN 46268
www.dogearpublishing.net

ISBN: 978-1-4575-3414-0

This book is printed on acid-free paper.

This work is not a substitute for medical or mental health care intervention or protocol. The contents of this work are based on personal experience of the authors, are intended to advance understanding and public dialogue only, and should not be relied upon as recommending or promoting a specific method, diagnosis or treatment as is the purview of physicians, specialists and mental health care professionals. The authors and publisher are not engaged here in rendering legal, medical, psychological or financial counsel and make no representations or warranties thereto. If expert assistance is required or wished for, the counsel of a professional should be sought.

No part of this publication may be reproduced, stored in any retrieval system or transmitted in any form or by any means (electronic, mechanical, photo-imaging, scanning, recording or otherwise), except as permitted by United States Copyright Law or applicable international laws unless, however, the authors' prior written consent has been obtained. **For permission to reprint, photocopy or otherwise reproduce portions of this work, contact T. Pitt Green at herself@teresagreen.org.**

Except where otherwise shown, all Scripture texts are taken from the New American Bible, Revised Edition Copyright © 2010, 1991, 1986, 1970 Confraternity of Christian Doctrine, Washington, D.C. and are used by permission of the copyright owner. All Rights Reserved. No part of the New American Bible may be reproduced in any form without permission in writing from the copyright owner.

Requests for articles, workshops, retreats or other support for your program of outreach to adult survivors of abuse may be addressed to either author and sent to herself@teresagreen.org. The authors welcome your inquires, suggestions and ideas addressed as noted, or visit **www.restoringsanctuary.org**. Video training sessions are posted on YouTube at Restoring Sanctuary (channel).

Nihil Obstat: Rev. Paul F. deLadurantaye, S.T.D.
             Censor Librorum
Imprimatur: + Paul S. Loverde
             Bishop of Arlington
             November 19, 2014

The *Nihil Obstat* and *Imprimatur* are official declarations that a book or pamphlet is free of doctrinal or moral error. No implication is contained therein that those who have granted the *Nihil Obstat* or *Imprimatur* agree with the contents, opinions or statements expressed.

St. Teresa Benedicta of the Cross

Do not accept anything as the truth if it lacks love.
And do not accept anything as love which lacks truth!
One without the other becomes a destructive lie.

FOREWORD

A Survivor Ministry
Rev. Mark Mealey, O.S.F.S, J.C.D.
Vicar General, Diocese of Arlington

Parishes across our diocese, in turns, offer Mass with our bishop to pray for healing and reconciliation in the wake of the child sexual abuse scandals that rocked our Church. They pray for adult survivors of child sexual abuse, their families, our Church, and abusers. Prayer services are similarly hosted; brief services are easier for people who grow anxious quickly. Survivors and family members recount arriving doubtful, only to discover welcome, solace and acceptance. These events mark the beginning of thriving relationships among survivors and our diocesan staff. This book marks a milestone in our efforts to respond with knowledgeable care to survivors and their families—and, in a way, to all Catholics wounded by the scandal of abuse.

For ten years now, I have had the honor of leading our diocesan prayer services. At the request of survivors, we often read the Easter account of women who encountered angels at the tomb of Jesus. One of our survivors calls it "The Stone Story." The three Gospel accounts of Easter morning open with the misconception that Jesus is dead. His followers are overcome by grief; their world has been shattered. They are terrified by seemingly triumphant evildoers, yet the women set out to go where they last encountered Jesus, to care for Him if only in a tomb. Theirs was a deep and lonely burden. They might even have felt foolish, for they surely knew a huge stone barred them from accomplishing their task.

Survivors whom I know have a similar courage. Any sense of safety they experienced in childhood has been shattered by the abuser. They have spent years grieving many losses, including the loss of their childhood. They must grapple with shame and confusion, and sadly they often feel isolated from God, even rejected or abandoned by Him. While nothing could be further from the truth, survivors describe feeling an immovable obstacle between them and God. For those abused by someone with authority in the Church—an adult who seemed therefore favored by God—this isolation and sense of rejection can be particularly powerful. Yet, despite these obstacles, many survivors still venture forward, tentatively, even testily, but nonetheless attempt to begin a faith inquiry. It is finally time to reconcile their experience of the evil of abuse with an inexplicable longing for our all-loving and all-powerful God.

Drawing closer to the Son of God, the women had the benefit of angels who rolled back the stone, revealing the marvel of the Resurrection. Until that moment, the women had been blind to the new life Jesus won for all of us. Who similarly will serve survivors of abuse? Opportunity is there. Again and again, I listen as survivors describe a startling turning point in their darkness occasioned by a religious or lay person who was able simply to listen with kindness and without judgment. Like angels with the Easter message, these unnamed helpers have given many survivors safe home in the Church and with God. This book provides insights for both sides of that encounter in the future.

All around us, adult survivors of child sexual abuse need help finding the new life Jesus reveals in the Resurrection. They are doing so often while facing challenging psychotherapy and even difficult family circumstances. Many carry fear in their hearts and doubts in their minds that they can reach the love of Jesus, while others don't even know their search can find rest only in him. All of them seek a dialog about faith not knowing if the obstacles will ever be removed. Considering the broken trust at the core of abuse, this courageous exploration is astounding and can only be accounted for by the action of grace. Are we prepared to help?

As helpers of others, we too need the help of grace. Working within the Church, many of us have been horrified to learn of the abuse of children who were entrusted to the care of our Church. Most of us simply have not known how to proceed. Many people, including Catholics, recoil from the difficult fact of child sexual abuse, assuming care for its wounds falls solely in the realm of health care professionals. Conversely, some well-meaning people have made the effort, only to say or do the wrong thing. Many of us keep trying, and listening, and learning. We have embarked on a journey not to replace appropriate therapies with spiritual care, but to foster spiritual health. We have been working together, seeking reconciliation without a clear idea how to roll away the stones.

In this diocese we had no idea if survivors would even trust us when we began to reach out to offer sustenance, comfort, and spiritual companionship. It was hard to imagine why they would. And, yet, we ventured out, relying on God's grace to lead us, trusting God would send us helpers to remove obstacles. As we worked against stones blocking survivors from receiving the new life Jesus offers, they began to remove stones blocking us from helping other survivors. This book, written as a partnership between a priest and a survivor of child sexual abuse by priests, is a testimony to the fruitful partnership between survivors and us.

These efforts are not new. Even while some in our Church were failing to protect children from abusers, there were others, ordained and lay alike, who were finding ways to help survivors and their families. But something new and powerful began in 2002 when the United States Conference of Catholic Bishops issued the *Charter for the Protection of Children and Young People* and the *Essential Norms*. Here were standardized guidelines for the entire country which committed to accountability, safe environment, codes of conduct, and the review of allegations—as well as healing and reconciliation for victims, their families, friends and parishes. It did something else. The *Charter* and the *Essential Norms* gave us clarity on our next steps as a Church, as a diocese, and as servants of Christ. It marshaled us in solidarity. The Catholic Church in the United States could begin with new focus.

As we began to implement the *Charter* and the *Essential Norms* in the diocese of Arlington, we really had no idea how to provide meaningful assistance to victims. We needed advice, and we needed workers. To help us, our bishop, Most Rev. Paul S. Loverde, formed an Advisory Board comprised of specialists from law enforcement, psychology and other related areas of expertise. Their goal was to offer counsel in best practices for many initiatives defined in the *Charter* and the *Essential Norms*, including outreach to survivors. As staff, we benefited from contributions made by several committed Catholics who worked brief tenures. I also started a fact-finding process with the help of Mrs. Pat Mudd, at that time a social worker with Catholic Charities. Together we interviewed accomplished specialists in Child Protection Services, in psychotherapy and psychiatry, and in law enforcement dealing with child abuse and survivors of abuse. These professionals generously offered many good ideas. With the help of all, our diocese developed a plan for our program, which is now, just a decade later, flourishing.

A top priority established by the *Charter* and the *Essential Norms* was to see that no children suffer what these adult survivors of sexual abuse endured as children in the Church. Survivors in our program often explain that, more than their concern for their own care, they need to know these corrective measures are not window-dressing. And, indeed, this work is quite real. Now, in our Church, children and young people can worship, study, or take part in parish activities in carefully developed safe environments. Because of the Charter and the *Essential Norms* there is clarity about accountability and prevention. There is routine training as well as background checks with tougher criteria than most public school districts and many governmental security clearances. Having participated in this nationwide initiative for over a decade, I find it surprising how few people, especially Catholics, know that the operations of the Church in the United States were overhauled or that the Church has become a leading model in child-protection best practices in the world.

For example, for the past ten years, every adult in the Church—including priest, employee and volunteer—who has regular contact with children or young people has undergone a background check. Adults who work with children and youth receive training in abiding by Church policy, in observing signs of child abuse and in responding to potential cases of child abuse. They also must agree to comply with a clear code of conduct in their interactions with children and young adults. Training is repeated every few years.

Our fact-finding gave way to a strong plan. Pat Mudd joined as our full-time Victim Assistance Coordinator. With her dedicated work, our diocesan program has evolved and matured. This success is thanks to a warm partnership with many of our survivors who offer advice on how best to serve them. With their input, we have created a mix of ways to support people who have suffered abuse in this diocese and in other dioceses before relocating here. Our program is inclusive. From the start, our bishop was uncomfortable refusing help to survivors simply because their abusers had not held authority in the Church. Our survivors agreed, wishing to share their program with all adult survivors of abuse.

Our program offers different starting points from which survivors may choose based on their comfort level. As mentioned, several times each year our bishop offers a Mass for healing from abuse. These are attended by many Catholics, including survivors. Annually, we also offer several prayer services to welcome survivors in a more casual setting. We offer retreats and other gatherings for mutual support. For discussions, survivors themselves created guidelines so that what one person may share does not trigger any other survivor's memories. These are prayerful settings where we who minister simply listen, hearing stories of remarkable faith. Here we share the wonder of companionship with survivors as they explore unique ways of healing, of reconciling with family and others who have failed them, and of connecting with the Church.

Our diocesan website posts excerpts from some events for those who are not—and may never be—comfortable joining in person. It also posts articles written by our survivors about their individual faith stories and how they became free to experience God's love without the restraining impact of child abuse. Some of our survivors have progressed to a point when they are able and happy to meet with various groups curious to learn how to support a person's faith as they heal from child sexual abuse. For example, we host presentations for therapists who want better to support their Catholic patients. Regularly we offer workshops to priests, deacons, seminarians, sisters and lay ministers about how to offer spiritual guidance to survivors as they integrate their faith lives into overall recovery and psychotherapy.

We also hear from our survivors a deep concern about their grieved family members, current and childhood friends, and former or current parishes. Many of our events are open to these people whose wounds have been inflicted by one degree of separation from the abuse. Family members and friends are welcomed at our Masses and prayer services. Many of our discussion groups invite survivors to bring a support person who may, in addition to helping the survivor, benefit from the evening's fellowship.

Most importantly, we endeavor to create safe places where, at every point, our survivors find each other. In this diocese, the survivor community is thriving, rich with mutual regard and ready to share experiences. Family members and friends find similar comfort and wisdom among support people. What is emerging here in Arlington and elsewhere in our Church is a ministry of listening, affirmation and encouragement.

This book arose out of these diocesan gatherings, presentations and workshops which typically combine psychological presentations, reflections on Catholic ministry, and a survivor's testimony. Requests for invitations to these sessions have increased, especially from priests, deacons, sisters, and therapists. To respond to this growing interest, I asked Teresa Pitt Green and Fr. Lewis S. Fiorelli, O.S.F.S., to imagine a book that would offer help to spiritual companions for survivors of abuse who are seeking to integrate their Catholic faith with their therapy and recovery process.

Knowing the authors' dedication to this ministry, it was no surprise to me when the full manuscript was finished within ten weeks. A long-time member in the Arlington survivor program, Teresa has been on a faith journey for over thirty years. (She has chronicled this journey and its many helpers in a book entitled *Restoring Sanctuary*.) Among his many leadership appointments and teaching responsibilities in the Oblates of St. Francis de Sales, Fr. Lou has been a spiritual director, and teacher of spiritual directors, for over forty years. Both have written and spoken extensively, and both have worked in the Arlington program doing exactly what they have accomplished here—presenting the survivor experience and offering approaches in Catholic ministry and therapy that permit integrating the two.

There is little I can add to what has been accomplished here. One point worth emphasis is how important it is to reassure a survivor that "It isn't your fault." This statement is always true. Abuse betrays a child or young person's need to rely on adults for protection, guidance and security. Every victim's trust has been broken. In reaching out to them, we must strive to be trustworthy. That means we cannot echo the many messages—heard both inside and beyond the Church—telling victims they caused or invited abuse. This falsehood hurts all victims, but especially child victims who suffered usually in isolation with little or no context for what was happening. We need to give voice to what Our Lord says to the innocent: he is their safe refuge and their light in darkness.

It's also important to understand that a survivor's recovery cannot be rushed. Jesus does not rush survivors to heal any faster than they can handle. Indeed, He is far gentler with survivors than the world around us is. His grace sustains them as they endure the difficulties involved in therapy and recovery. Often others push survivors to "move on" or "forget about it." Please remember that if survivors *could* "just get over it" they *would*. Patience is critical for anyone who is wounded, especially for these adults who were wounded while very young.

Survivors' experiences, reactions, and pacing vary. Some survivors are high-functioning and seem like they are living "normal lives," while carrying a heavy and private burden. Other survivors have been wounded in such a way that "normal" life is difficult, even impossible, for long periods of time. For any survivor, some days are good, some days not. A day that may seem "just" downcast in the adult's life can unloose, for an adult survivor, darkness that reaches far back into a childhood agony. Even in such darkness, however, many survivors assure each other there is hope. Their faith stories offer compelling testimonies for the new evangelization. For one thing, the power of prayer can maintain a guiding ray of Light even in the darkest life.

Let me return to The Stone Story. Sometimes our prayer services are what people would call "well attended." La Salette Lay Associates and some of our sisters join us with a special charism for healing and reconciliation. Parishioners join us. Survivors already in our program may join us. Most importantly, two or more newcomers appear, sometimes alone or sometimes with a companion. They come to explore what we are about. At the reception or in the parking lot they may stop to speak to our victim assistance coordinators or to one of our survivors. But, other prayer services are different. The service may be scarcely attended, with just five people gathered near the altar—our two victim assistance coordinators, the hosting pastor, the one survivor who attends to speak and me. Somewhere in the shadows at the back of the church we usually spy at least one person observing from a distance. They disappear before final prayers are said, but often they call within the week. Large and small, our prayer services have been a success—one survivor at a time. Every prayer service is crucial, for God is there as we meet to pray and help remove the power of the stone.

We all know how The Stone Story ends, or how the story of every Christian begins. The immovable stone is rolled away. Jesus Christ is victorious over evil and death. All the worst that human beings have heaped on each other—and so onto the shoulders of God—has failed to destroy our life with God. Laws and institutions that rationalized the death of the Son of God only seem to triumph on Good Friday. On Easter they surrender their power.

Either Jesus has risen, or our faith is folly. We have reason to hope because, despite our failure as a Church in the past, our Savior has risen and offers new life. We are made bold to pursue our own continuous conversion. This is the case with serving survivors, in particular those who have been abused by clergy or others with authority in the Church. What has been born from this change is a relatively young ministry of listening, affirmation and encouragement for survivors which is, in some ways, very old. It joins the testimonies across the all ages about how the impossible stone dividing us from God and from each other has been moved.

This book has been written for many. It has been written to help people of faith know how to care spiritually for adult survivors of child abuse. It has been written for priests, deacons and sisters who are the ones to whom survivors typically first turn, often in confession but also in casual or other formal settings, such as RCIA, the Come Home or Landings programs and the Marriage Tribunal. This book has been written for lay ministers, especially for victim assistance coordinators to enrich their tireless, uncelebrated work. This book has been written for therapists or non-Catholics who work with Catholics struggling to integrate faith into the therapeutic process.

In particular, this book has been written for those who have been abused—within the Church and beyond the Church. It is written for their family members and friends. You may find it useful as part of your therapy process. It may become one of your go-to books as you do the work of recovery. Through the authors' words in this book, may you receive grace. Inspired by this book, may you grow to understand and to share your faith story as a way to heal and a way to help others heal.

Closing, I encourage each Catholic to consider ways to respond to survivors of child abuse whether sexual or otherwise. As many as one child in every six is suffering sexual abuse at this moment. No matter how heartbreaking this truth is, we must not avert our eyes. The problem of child sexual abuse is rampant beyond its terrible history in our Church. As we work to create safe environments for children and for survivors and their loved ones in the Church, our work cannot be limited to our faith community. We are called to bring Christ's healing to the whole world, one encounter at a time. This book is about helping all readers know how to roll away the stone between any adult survivor of child abuse and Our Lord and Savior.

CONTENTS

Foreword 5

Contents 19

Introduction 23

Using This Book 31

Welcome 37

1. First Steps 41

     A Survivor's Reflection 42
     A Spiritual Guide's Reflection 45
     A Psychologist's Reflection 49

     Why Me? 52
     Why, God? 54
     Mirror 57
     Safety 61
     Lies 64
     Choice 67

　　　　Price 71
　　　　Spiritual Guide 74

　2. Listening & Dialogue 79

　　　　A Survivor's Reflection 80
　　　　A Spiritual Guide's Reflection 82
　　　　A Psychologist's Reflection 86

　　　　Shame 89
　　　　Isolation 93
　　　　Secrets 98
　　　　Trust 101
　　　　Abandoned 108
　　　　Rage 112
　　　　Depression 117
　　　　Numb 122
　　　　Self-Wounding (Suicidal Thoughts) 125
　　　　Losses 129
　　　　Grief 131
　　　　Defensiveness 134
　　　　Perversion 136
　　　　Delayed Responses 142
　　　　Worry 145
　　　　Control 149
　　　　Habits & Obsessions 152
　　　　Boundaries 156
　　　　Relationships 160
　　　　Broken Bonds 164
　　　　Hurt 167
　　　　The Caricature 171
　　　　Insomnia 175
　　　　Mantras 178

3. Turning Points 181

    A Survivor's Reflection 182
    A Spiritual Guide's Reflection 184
    A Psychologist's Reflection 186

    Deciding to Heal 189
    Breaking Silence 195
    Redefining Safety 198
    Believing Self 202
    Being Believed 205
    Asking for Help 212
    Gathering Support 215
    Affirming Boundaries 219
    Relating to Family 222
    Fostering Intimacy 226
    Finding Balance 231
    Trusting Self 234
    Opening Up 237
    Simplifying Life 240
    Detaching as Needed 243

4. Reconciliation 247

    A Survivor's Reflection 249
    A Spiritual Guide's Reflection 251
    A Psychologist's Reflection 254

    Prayer 256
    Creation 260
    Job 262
    Bondage in Egypt 267
    Exodus 269

    Walking on Water 272
    Baptism 277
    Gethsemane 280
    Judas 284
    Holy Thursday 288
    Good Friday 292
    Holy Saturday 294
    Easter 296
    Pentecost 299
    Mary 304
    Rosary 311
    Lourdes 314
    Sin 319
    Confession 324
    Cross 329
    Saints 331
    Forgiveness 335
    Praise 338
    Eucharist 341
    Storytelling 344

Prayers 349

Resources 356

Index 363

Acknowledgments 401

Authors 403

INTRODUCTION

This book is about a difficult topic. Shortly, however, the reader will discover it is a practicum for integrating faith into the arduous process of recovering from child sexual abuse. So, ultimately, this book is about hope, even joy, in very practical terms.

Here, we offer a tested language of healing for spiritual dialogue between survivors of abuse, their families, and those seeking to minister to them. This book can open the eye of the heart to the revelation of God's wondrous beauty in survivors of abuse. This is our hope in publishing it for you. But, before the inspiration sets in, first consider the context for the relevance of this book to charity, ministry, and evangelical outreach.

The American Psychological Association (APA)[1] published a white paper that notes about 300,000 children are abused every year in the United States. That is, three million children are sexually abused every

---

[1] All data in this introduction, except data related to abuse by clergy, are drawn from The American Psychological Association white paper entitled "Child Sexual Abuse: What Parents Should Know" at http://www.apa.org/pi/families/resources/child-sexual-abuse.aspx.

decade. The APA paper cites another statistic from the Centers for Disease Control: one in six boys and one in four girls are sexually abused before turning 18 years old. Sadly, incidents are increasing in the proliferation of social media, which serves as a conduit for predators. The APA questions the validity of all these data not because victims lie but because victims and their families continue to *underreport* abuse. The APA concludes the incidence rate is higher than you see here.

Catholics are painfully aware that this abuse hit critical proportions in our Church. A research team at John Jay College counted, through 2002, approximately 10,500 reports of victims abused by Catholic clergy. After that, the Center for Applied Research for the Apostolate tracked reports, whose frequency declined to 25 percent or less of the rate prior to 2002. Both accountings confirmed the same pattern, however. The annual number of incidents of abuse by Catholic priests "increased steadily from the mid-1960s through the late 1970s, then declined in the 1980s" and thereafter.[2]

The downward trend in reported incidents of abuse by clergy was amplified by radical reforms in the United States Catholic Church. An operational overhaul began in 2002 when the Conference of Catholic Bishops issued guidelines for nationwide change. Those reforms are now in place protecting children, standardizing transparent reporting, and

---

[2] Data pertaining to incidence of abuse within the Roman Catholic Church has been drawn from "The Causes and Context of Sexual Abuse by Minors by Catholic Priests in the United States, 1950 to 2010, A Report Presented to the United States Conference of Catholic Bishops," by The John Jay College Research Team, Karen J. Terry et. al., 2011 copyright © USCCB, pages 2-3.

caring for survivors.[3] This book was born in related pastoral care for survivors in the diocese of Arlington, Virginia.

From inside and beyond the Church, many survivors yearn for a healing beyond established therapies. They are seeking healing in relationship to Jesus Christ. This is not to say that psychotherapy is not needed, but rather to say that psychotherapy is sometimes not enough for survivors whose faith plays, or played, a central role in living. Each survivor, especially if abused by clergy, resolves the past trauma in relation to God, to Jesus Christ, and to faith differently. However, the longing to make peace with God and Church in personal terms is quite common. What is true of survivors is often true of their family members, who are wounded by a single degree of separation from the abuse. Many seek, at some point, to take their complaint and grief before the Lord.

Only in a safe dialogue can the wounds of faith heal. In an enlightened dialogue, faith can be integrated into each survivor's unique recovery journey. The problem is that, to date, this dialogue has occurred in isolated instances with scattershot preparation. Many people were eager to offer spiritual sustenance, but pastoral tools were lacking. This book is a practical solution to that problem. It seeks to expand the healing dialogue more broadly in our Church—and in our society.

---

[3] For more information, see the United States Conference of Catholic Bishops' *Charter for the Protection of Children and Young People* and its related *The Essential Norms* which changed canon law as well as Church operations, at usccb.org.

By studying ways to have a safe discourse, people can bring their full capacity for creativity to bear. They find unique ways to create rich bonds of faith in grace. This possibility applies to survivors and family members along with priests, deacons, sisters, brothers, consecrated or lay ministers, indeed with every Catholic. Participants learn words and ways to speak that neither re-traumatize the survivor nor vicariously traumatize others. Here is a book that helps each person know how to listen, teach, learn, share, and grow together in grace.

This process is, first and foremost, about restoring trust. Most children are abused by someone they know and trust. In its white paper the APA reports that about 30 percent of abusers are family members, such as fathers or uncles. An estimated 60 percent of abusers are not family members but known to the child. They may be family friends, babysitters, pediatricians, childcare workers, teachers, coaches, neighbors—or clergy. Although only 10 percent of abusers are strangers, a significant portion of abuse by strangers still involves appealing to a child's trust. Indeed, the abuser's proclivity for grooming is all about captivating a child through trust, thereby facilitating abuse in secret.

Adult survivors who have endured sexual abuse as a child or teen will likely offer trust sparingly, if at all. This emotional reticence is not a flaw. It is reasonable. Child victims learn forever lessons in trauma, becoming adults on high alert for danger. People who offer care gain credibility only through a personal commitment to being reliable, honest, and sensitive. In time, survivors may be willing to believe their spiritual companions that, while there is no beauty in abuse, there is beauty in the reflection of God's image in their suffering, tenacity, courage, and resilience. This is the unexpected image that outshines all other images when caring for survivors, and it is why this book came to be called *Veronica's Veil*.

For a fleeting moment Veronica used her veil to soothe our Savior's burning and unrecognizable face. Anyone reaching for this book is likely someone who wishes to offer, or to receive, such a moment of relief. These pages offer that comfort by showing what helps, and what hurts, in a comforting spiritual dialogue. They also reflect an image of survivors few people recognize, until it is returned as a gift in spiritual friendship. It's quite one thing to know the image of God is in every face of every person, but another thing entirely to recognize that image and its beauty in survivors. This is the gift, not the work, for those who seek to offer spiritual companionship to survivors of abuse. It is the gift, too, that awaits survivors who, leafing through these pages, may wonder whether faith has any effective role in the hard work of psychotherapy.

Reaching out of that solitude to seek spiritual companionship can be awkward, even painful, and sometimes ill-fated. Survivors are wisely turned off by well-intentioned people resorting to the glib two-minute pep talk to "get over it" or "move on with your life." Or, sadly, they encounter recrimination and rejection born of the long-debunked idea that victims are somehow complicit in their own victimization. In the idealized victim or other media caricatures they confront not their own image, but a reflection of hopelessness quite distinct from their own recovery journey toward wellbeing.

On the other side of this nascent friendship, Catholics, both ordained and lay, wish to help but are often unsure how best to do so. Priests often encounter survivors, who not infrequently come to confession to reveal the secret of abuse. Confessors naturally explain this grave sin is not the survivor's to confess, but what to say next to help foster healing? Survivors seek out nuns as persons devoted to the Church but of a different gender than the abuser, but how to help guide someone to a greater sense of safety in the larger Church? Pastors and deacons receive families turning to them in crisis after a survivor bravely reveals the long-kept secret of abuse. How do family members begin to heal—and to help? This book is a guide for how such awkward, even painful first steps can begin a rich spiritual companionship for all involved.

Caring for survivors has many gifts. One is that their tenacious journeys have a great deal to teach about caring for others who struggle with similar problems for different reasons. Some survivors struggle with addictions or self-abuse. Others attempt suicide. Many grapple with short-term or chronic mental or physical illness, including post-traumatic stress. Many remain practicing Catholics. Others reject the Church in a reaction against what happened. Most rage at God; some reject God. These profound human struggles are not limited to survivors of abuse. By addressing them, this book helps you help people in crisis from trauma beyond abuse. It comforts—and helps others comfort—people in the grip of grief, people with chronic mental illness, survivors of domestic violence, and troops managing bouts of post-traumatic stress.

As it teaches a soothing language, this book also permits something wonderful to happen. As the image of survival comes into focus, the shame created by abuse is eclipsed. Spiritual friendship, with its credible witness of God's face revealed, is then a witness to each survivor's beauty. When Veronica gathered her veil from the pained brow of our Savior, the image on the veil in her hands was a beginning. As spiritual companions to survivors quickly discover, the wondrous miracle reflected in each survivor's story is a revelation of God. Inspired ourselves by astounding stories of survivors and family members whom they know, the authors now turn to the practical work of shedding light on how to foster dialogue and spiritual companionship for healing and reconciliation among us.

USING THIS BOOK

Organization

Veronica's Veil may be read from start to finish, but it is intended for a less linear approach because recovery from childhood trauma is not a linear process.

The book opens by providing brief historical and social context. It closes with suggested resources and prayers. Mainly, *Veronica's Veil* covers over 70 topics which are loosely organized in four sections. Each section features a phase in recovery which is described, first, in three companion essays; the first is written by a survivor, the next by a spiritual guide, the last by a therapist. Then, related topics are presented in point and counterpoint, survivor then spiritual guide. This style has been used successfully by the authors in joint speaking venues.

Section 1, "First Steps," addresses obstacles to seeking help. These topics tend to appear early in the dialogue about faith and healing from abuse. Understanding the obstacles works much better than challenging them. Each person will need to grapple with them in their own way and on their own timing.

Section 2 compiles many issues common in the therapeutic process. One of the longer sections, its title, "Listening and Dialogue," reflects listening as a priority. The dialogue runs parallel to therapeutic or other programs in which survivors have participated, are participating, or will eventually participate.

Section 3, "Turning Points," addresses watersheds in a life of healing. Such leaps forward are worth noting and offer inspiration for difficult junctures. Both uplifting and realistic, this short section forms a picture of what wellbeing may become over time.

Section 4, the last section, is not for all readers. "Reconciliation" gathers reflections on sacred topics for when (and if) survivors want (or are able) to delve into the Catholic faith. It emphasizes a double-edged sword in holiness for those who have been abused, for sacred things may be fraught with memories of danger. This section sensitizes clergy, sisters and all Catholics who are talking about faith to survivors of abuse. All such people should read this section in its entirety before working with a survivor of abuse, especially where at least one abuser was associated with faith.

The table of contents and index are designed to help peruse the pages either by seeking a particular topic or by being open to what ideas grab one's attention.

Scope

Veronica's Veil seeks to foster understanding, reflection, informed listening and also dialogue about spiritual dilemmas faced by adults who have survived child abuse, whether sexual or otherwise, whether by clergy or other authority figures.

By making no reference to any details of abuse, the book attempts to avoid re-traumatizing survivors and vicariously traumatizing others. The authors recommend a similar approach be taken in spiritual guidance. A deep-dive into abuse really should be confined to the care of a trained professional. This practice ensures that survivors have trained professional help when processing difficult psychological and emotional issues. It also helps participants not confuse spiritual support with professional counseling.

Uses

Anyone offering formal spiritual guidance to survivors should be familiar with all the topics in this book. They may share the book with survivors, or use the book as part of the program of guidance. However, readings should be selected by survivors; only they know what topics they feel emotionally ready to discuss. Readings might instead be reserved for private reflection and journaling. Essays have already proven useful for groups, including spiritual support groups provided by diocesan programs for survivors.

Veronica's Veil is also written for anyone who is in a position to support and care for survivors of abuse and their family members. This is a large circle. It begins, of course, with parish priests and ministry teams. There also are staff members in Virtus, the Catholic child protection training program; here attendees occasionally decide, in a safe faith setting, to seek help for past abuse. There are Catholic educators and school administrators. There are therapists working with Catholic patients, and there are Catholic therapists, social workers and hospital workers, all of whom are approached for guidance balancing recovery and faith. Among the greatest circles of ministry are the friends and family members of abuse survivors.

Above all, *Veronica's Veil* is for survivors. Your tenacity and courage and spiritual depth have long been obscured by abstract debate and ignorance among those who suggest your voice is less than equal to that of abusers and enablers. This book is, by the way, also for family members of survivors, for you bear the wound of abuse by a single degree of separation. Here for all of you is encouragement and sustenance. Here is the accurate image of your beauty. May *Veronica's Veil* serve as a means for a fresh start in dialogue with those who have not yet understood; such as, for the treasured friend who mistakenly relies on the two-minute "get over it" pep talk; or for the non-Christian counselor who can benefit from insights into the faith aspect of your struggle; or for your parish priest.

First Principle

Veronica's Veil offers this first principle in working with adult survivors of child abuse. Each survivor is God's remarkable creation. Each will leave a distinct image on the veil which you may raise for comfort and relief. Do not compound injustice already done to survivors by treating them as a simplistic caricature, even if gleaned from the pages of this book. Look closely at the image they may dare to show you. You will see suffering, resilience and triumph. Serving this image, you are serving the many faces of God.

WELCOME

Teresa's Welcome

Faith stories are as unique as every child of God. This is true as well for the faith stories of every survivor of abuse. This is true for me as a survivor of sexual abuse by clergy as a child and teen. Here, in our faith stories, we integrate our Catholic faith into a broader recovery process which includes able professional care.

For the survivor of abuse within the Catholic Church, practicing our faith has often continued, in some sense. This work offers a way to deepen that connection. For other survivors, practicing this faith may be possible only after a time, from a distance, or not at all. Still, exploring the distinction between true faith and the perversion of faith by the abuser(s) may help you find peace with the faith setting in which such trauma has occurred—and free you to deepen your relationship with God. For all, this may offer some ease, including for those helping survivors of abuse integrate their Catholic faith in therapeutic and personal recovery work.

For Catholics, and for Catholic counselors, my essays are little more than tiny windows into the great resilience among survivors of abuse. These comprise my best effort to open the imagination of Catholics and others who wish to help survivors change the way they relate to their own faith stories. In this effort I have been blessed by the companionship and great faith of Fr. Lou. He is, as many other gracious priests I have met in my work serving survivors of abuse, what the predator priests, whom I knew in my youth, could never be.

As a last word, my heart and prayers remain with those survivors of clergy abuse who remain estranged from the faith of their wounded childhoods. Every time I receive Eucharist, I receive for you. God bless us, every one.

Fr. Lou's Welcome

As a spiritual guide, I identify with St. Peter. In many ways he is my hero. He who is now a pillar of the Church was, early on and fairly frequently, an imperfect, even broken earthen vessel. Despite his good intentions, brave words, and best efforts he was often a disappointment to Jesus. Yet, Peter never strayed far from Jesus, and Jesus never left Peter. Although weak and wobbly, Peter gained the strength for discipleship from the presence, grace, and friendship of Jesus. In that way, he became an increasingly worthy vessel of the Lord's grace for others while never losing sight of whose gift it really was.

Because of a clear-eyed awareness of my own weaknesses, I strongly believe that whatever gifts I have for spiritual guidance are the Lord's gifts, not mine. I rejoice that He seems to prefer the use of clay vessels in order to make it abundantly clear to both spiritual guide and those in spiritual guidance that the gifts are His, and the graces as well.

Belief in Providence assures me that my gifts, however few or limited, are just what are needed for the one who comes to me for guidance. I believe that in His wisdom God has matched the two of us. For this reason I am convinced that the "Salesian Bread" which nourishes my own spiritual life will nourish those who come to me for guidance as well. I pray that every spiritual guide and every person seeking spiritual guidance will enjoy a similar trust in the caring hands of Providence.

I am convinced that God Himself has begun this good work of spiritual guidance in each of you. My prayer, my conviction, is that He Himself will bring it to perfection!

FIRST STEPS

Overview

The first step toward a conscious effort to recover from the wounds of child sexual abuse involves a great act of private courage. Beyond that watershed moment, each survivor begins and proceeds in their own unique way. Recovery itself varies greatly among survivors. No one reacts the same way, endures using the same defenses, seeks the same doorway out, experiences therapy in the same way, or needs the same patchwork quilt of support. Yet all survivors begin with a first step.

A few issues involved in the first step toward healing are worth considering in terms of the intersection of faith and other recovery work. For example, what are the first issues survivors face at the outset as obstacles to a first step forward? And, what are ways different survivors might experience just the beginning, just the inklings, or nudges of the Spirit, to imagine healing? These are chaotic, even traumatic junctures for many. Certainly God is waiting to offer sustenance and guidance.

To help the work of grace in these moments of a survivor's personal upheaval, it is important to learn about psychological underpinnings and to prepare with prayerfulness on one's own. The essays in this section have been selected as a way to help prepare guides but also to help survivors come to believe, even before they reach out, that they are not alone.

First Steps: A Survivor's Perspective

There comes a time when the defenses stop working. No matter what clever mix of defenses you created as the cocktail to get you through the hell of childhood and the aftermath of abuse, at some point in adult life it fails. That is what first inklings were like for me. And, being stubborn, or tenacious, I wrestled against the inevitable for decades.

What matters is that, at some point, in some way, the pretty smart defenses you developed to survive those peculiar circumstances of trauma and grief and secrecy are no longer suitable for the world you grow into as an adult. And, that's when the trouble begins, maybe small, maybe big, but trouble, and it gets to a point at which you can no longer go on as you have been all along. That's how first inklings can look like disasters.

Recovery, for me, was the beginning of a process of sorting through what was healthful behavior and what was not, who were helpful people and who were not, what was my fault and what was not. My recovery was a long process of making distinctions between maladaptive and resilient, and, ultimately, looking at the memories honestly, that is, accepting the distinction between good and evil.

The beginning of my recovery happened many times, at many different points in my life. I'd graduate from one era of working hard on what the therapist called "issues" and would return to on-going professional success. Then, in the middle of a life crisis, the bottom would drop out and I'd be faced not only with the wounds of childhood freshly opened but also the stubborn fact that my adult life was still hobbled by them in many ways.

There were very real life crises. There was the violent attack and near-rape by a gang of over eighteen men, and then there was the first benign brain tumor, and then there was the second benign brain tumor with something like a stroke, and then there was the divorce, with an assortment of comparatively minor personal skirmishes. There's no small body of research that would link my type of brain tumors to childhood trauma, and there's no doubt my exposure to the kinds of dangerous settings in which a gang could attack me was in large part due to my inability to protect myself.

But it was before all of that, three decades ago, when I first went to therapy. My life had gotten out of control, and I was young enough to believe therapy would work like a car mechanic. We'd make some changes in the alignment and I'd drive around smoothly for years. So, there I was. My life had gotten out of control and I was blaming myself. If I could fix myself, everyone else would fall into place. Life could still be what I wanted it to be. As a high achiever, I was accustomed to negotiating my way to what I wanted. In my unresolved childhood grief, I was doing the same with God.

My first year of therapy was especially helpful, quite possibly because I had staked so much hope in erasing my past. I was, as usual, driven, including years of reading—even working in—self-help recovery literature. The problem was that, as a survivor of child abuse by priests, I could not finally integrate the rich process of recovery in the secular world with the estrangement I felt from the faith of my childhood. And, for me, recovery would not progress beyond a certain point until I could.

I wonder sometimes what my life would have been had the Church been as caring to me then as my current diocese is to me now. How much less strife would my life have faced? It's a question I have found it wise not to ask. Enduring PTSD is like a life lived in a game of chutes and ladders. Recovery has been, in part, learning what ideas not to entertain as a way to avoid a dangerous slide into suicidal thought. So I seldom permit myself to wonder what life would be like now if I had never been abused. Sometimes I must daily reject asking that question, because it returns more temptation to despair than rumination. Therapy has given me many tools for contending with this invitation to darkness and for adapting to my life circumstances. What has provided comfort beyond measure has been to know that, at least, I did not lose the true jewel of my upbringing—my Catholic faith. Catholicism is not something I thought I would ever be free to embrace safely, or return to without a moral conflict, and yet here I am.

First Steps:
A Spiritual Guide's Perspective

Like everybody else, the sex abuse scandals have affected me in many ways and on different levels. As a priest, the first effects of the scandals clustered around the Church. I was amazed, first of all, that it existed among the clergy at all and, then, by its incredible scope and time-span. After that, I became in turn dismayed, saddened, and angered as I learned, over time, how poorly many Church authorities had handled accusations against pedophile priests. More often than not, they sent them off for a few months of psychological treatment and spiritual renewal and then reassigned them to another parish. With each new accusation, the same pattern was repeated, often over many years. I tried to make excuses for this early behavior. After all, I reasoned, until recently nobody had any idea about the high rate of recidivism in sex abusers. The common early practice of the Church, therefore, seemed to make sense: not only could pedophile priests be forgiven in confession but they could also be rehabilitated and healed by treatment. Seen as naive today, it was thought to work then.

But then accounts kept coming out about the ways many victims had been treated by Church authorities when they finally began to come forth with their accusations. Either their stories were challenged or disbelieved altogether, or they themselves were made to feel guilty for the abuse they suffered. Some were accused of just wanting to get into the deep financial pockets of the Church or to embarrass her outright. In the end, when neither guilt ("Do you really want to expose the Church to this?") nor intimidation ("The Church will take you to court for falsely accusing a priest.") worked, they were either paid off for as little as possible or were reimbursed only for counseling and therapy. In either case this was done only on condition that they would never again speak of these accusations to anyone. Rarely, in any this, was there a ready willingness to listen to their stories of abuse or to admit that past practices by the Church in handling accusations were perhaps misguided. There was no apology, either, for the fact that in most cases pedophile priests were not dismissed outright from ministry. Most importantly, however, was the fact that the Church failed to minister pastorally to adult men and women who, as sexually abused children, had had their faith radically shattered and their lives thoroughly ruined by the sinful actions of priests.

Like many of my fellow priests, I was gradually beginning to feel increasingly guilty and ashamed simply by being in the same ministry as those now accused of such horrible crimes against innocent and vulnerable children. Were people wondering about me too? Doors of our offices now had to have a window in them. At every new assignment, our fingerprints had to be taken and checked against the database of sexual offenders. We could never meet with children for, say, altar server training, without the presence of at least one other adult. The list could go on and on but the picture is clear. Because of the actions of a few priests, no priest is now ever fully trusted.

But along with my embarrassment and shame at past Church practice in handling sex abuse cases and my feelings of guilt by association, I began to wonder whether the Church could ever be part of the spiritual healing of those whom some in the Church had violated so grievously as children and then had failed so miserably to help when they came forward seeking justice and redress.

I told myself that I would be there if any victim ever came to me for confession, counseling, or spiritual guidance. Beyond that, I was not sure what else I could do or how I could help. In my work since those days I see that many priests, sisters, lay ministers, and educators feel a similar sense of wanting to help but not being sure how to help beyond prayer. Then I was offered the opportunity to give victims of abuse a day of recollection, about which I will speak later. The encounter opened a door for me to help. And as is so often the case, I was far more enriched by that ministry to brave and good people than I could possibly have imagined. It is just one more instance of the "hundred fold in this life" promised by the Lord!

My prayers were answered each time I was asked to participate in different aspects of the highly successful and pioneering Victims Assistance Program of the Diocese of Arlington, Virginia. It seems my many years offering and training others to offer spiritual guidance in the Salesian tradition was helping survivors integrate faith into their recovery programs.

How my conversations with these remarkable people, with their tenacious faith, enriched my life you will soon discover, as you read this book.

As potential spiritual guides of victims yourselves, you may be as apprehensive as I was in rowing into such uncharted waters. Burdened with the now often negatively perceived baggage of Church affiliation, you may fear, as I did, the possibility of triggering negative reactions in victims simply because of who you are, what you wear, or where you meet. Then there is the fact that there is no play-book for any of this, no sure guide as to what to say, how to react, or what approach to take. Whereas you can presume a certain desire for spiritual growth on the part of others whom you direct, such may not be the case, at least not at first, with victims. Still, there may come a moment for you, as it did for me, when you are invited to assist in the recovery of victims of abuse. So, until the opportunity comes your way to help in some concrete manner in this important ministry to the abused, how can you best prepare yourself for it? That is a question that many of you reading this book are probably asking yourselves.

First, never underestimate the power of prayer. Pray for all those already engaged in this ministry—victims, therapists, spiritual guides, and for all those who administer the programs established for this purpose. Familiarize yourself with the psychological, emotional, relational, and spiritual issues that cluster in the adult lives of victims of abuse. This book is a good start in that regard. Discuss what you hear from the Spirit in prayer with your own spiritual guide. Seek counsel there. And, when possible, be proactive. Dare to take a first step. The Lord will do the rest. Trust that.

First Steps: A Psychologist's Perspective
Frank J. Moncher, PhD

Counseling or psychotherapy is personal. It is a place where people share intimate secrets—at times thoughts, feelings, and stories that have never been told. Therein lays both its power to facilitate healing, as well as its potential as a barrier to those who seek support. Oftentimes the survivor of abuse approaches me with ambivalence and trepidation: discussing trauma and abuse is tricky business, especially since a survivor of sexual abuse by any authority figure has often been compelled to silence by threats. Yet a point is reached where circumstances, destructive coping mechanisms, or relationships (both failed and those with hopeful futures) compel an opposite response, a need, even eventually a desire, to stop hiding, to stop pretending that what happened was somehow unimportant or not really impacting life. The adult survivor wants, and begins to know, they deserve more, deserve better.

"Will I be believed?" "Was it really such a big deal?" "Did I deserve or somehow ask for the abuse?" These are common concerns that create a barrier to making that first call to the therapist. Many times it is only with the support of another, a friend, spouse, or yes even a trusted priest with whom they are beginning the work, that contact is made. In my experience this type of healing rarely occurs individually, but rather is fruit born of some relationships which plant the seed with the survivor that they are worthy, and that it might be possible to consider trusting another.

Trust: Nothing is more necessary for therapeutic success, and nothing is thornier to foment. The therapist's primary duty in the first session, and perhaps many following, is to address the issue of safety, allowing the survivor the control and space they need. Without an experience of a safe place, trust will not grow, and without trust, sharing the secrets from which the survivor needs release is too difficult. I believe that the obligation for establishing a trusting relationship, while reciprocal, has a developmental aspect. That is, when a survivor summons the courage to request therapy, the therapist must meet them more than half-way, and proactively address the common fears that are experienced when one has been wounded in an intimate way by a person in a position of authority and presumed trust.

Therefore, when a survivor experiences these first inklings and seeks therapy, the therapist's stance must be one of patience and gentleness. I would like to share from my first encounters with two particular young adult survivors some years ago: I recall week after week of "placing one's toes in the water," stories unfolding with more or less details, usually less. The sharing was difficult for these survivors, who seemed only able to provide isolated black and white snapshots of their history, while I knew healing would require they produce a motion picture, full color, emotions and all.

And that was OK.

I waited, affirmed where I could, reflected on the struggle, appreciated the sharing that was possible, respecting that these young adults were indeed "running as fast as they could." After all, this was their story and needed to be told in their time.

Before any sharing occurred, I made plain the ground rules: this was on their terms, and I would never force or compel. They were free to ask guidance on how to proceed, and for whatever support they felt was needed. Working with trauma that involved unwanted and abusive touch is delicate; yet touch was eventually part of healing, part of removing that which separated them from others (knowing also that this separation was essential to their safety in the aftermath of such intrusive boundary violations). Guiding survivors through their ambivalence about touch is critical, be it a handshake, gentle pat on the shoulder, or chaste embrace, and most often it is a role that the therapist or spiritual guide cannot fill, given the way in which boundaries had been violated in the past—and the prohibitions diocesan policies clearly outline. Still, we can be present. I listened and waited; months passed with weekly contact. More detailed sharing emerged, though still not all, some memories too painful to share just yet, and some memories not yet fully formed and accessible.

Over time, trust building, a risk taken, new beginnings to the work occurred with each deepening of the connection. To be sure, for some the process differs, family members, friends, and spouses provide the primary emotional connections. But for all, these early stages of the journey to recovery are marked by intense periods and times for retreat. Patience is essential for the therapist with the survivor, for the survivor with themselves. There is a season for everything, a time for every occupation under heaven.[4]

Why Me?

Many of us prayed before and during and after abuse for deliverance, and then we waited, but we were not saved. The Almighty must have had reasons not to intervene. I'm not worth saving, or so the child concludes.

Not chosen by God for rescue, we were indeed chosen by our abusers, with dire consequences. God created us human. The experience of abuse is dehumanizing. That can be more than a feeling. It can become an identity.

To achieve their own ends, abusers and their enablers confuse what victims meekly know. Insisting we want to be abused, they isolate us in their deceit, and we have no alternative to their authority. It can seem like no one else considers this a crisis. Maybe it doesn't matter.

Here begin the shame, confusion, fright, self-recrimination, anger, grief, distrust and other aspects of the

---

[4] Ecclesiastes 3:1 as translated in the NAB: "There is an appointed time for everything, and a time for every affair under the heavens.

heavy burden we will shoulder into adulthood. As their impact accumulates, we may feel worse. Sometimes we believe we are uniquely undeserving after all, making it more not less difficult to refute abusers and their enablers.

Compared to this psychological rip tide, religion can feel shallow and, given the Church's response in my early life, ineffective. Yet, I kept encountering remarkable people who believed in something stronger than the evil that had secretly triumphed in my life. It was impossible (though I did try) to reject their claim that we are called by name and saved at a great price. Perhaps I might not be worthless after all. Such was the great gift of psychic dissonance which would anchor me in Jesus Christ.

"My God, my God, why have you abandoned me?"[5] "Father, into your hands I commend my spirit."[6] Abandonment and entrustment: these sentiments are, on the face of it, mutually exclusive. Yet they exist in one and the same Jesus as he hangs dying in the most excruciating pain.

Victims drawn back to God and back to Church know that these two sentiments can and often do coexist in the same person and at the same time. Rage at being once abandoned by God and Church can be joined with the now comforting and present knowledge that they are loved and cared for by God, and

---

[5] Matthew 27:46; Mark 15:34
[6] Luke 23:46

even by Church. On the psychic level the simultaneous presence of two opposing sentiments can appear to be a form of schizophrenia. But on the spiritual level the co-presence of the two is made possible by the healing and transforming power of grace.

Jesus was like us in all things but sin.[7] His feeling of abandonment by God was real, sharp, and very painful. Yet, somehow he managed to climb out of its dark depths and speak a most heroic act of total entrustment. He trusted that somehow the Father would bring life out of his death and make the Gospel of a crucified Messiah abundantly fruitful.

The rage is real. So is the grace. Each victim knows the pain of the one and believes in the power of the other. In Jesus, victims not only have a friend; they also have a fellow victim. Jesus entrusted everything about his person and his mission into the hands of His Father. Victims can as well, if only one small step at a time. The spiritual guide will help them discern—and take—each next step.

Why, God?

Adult life may become safe enough to rage at God for failing to stop the abuse. Or, life may reflect the tumult of childhood, leaving our feelings buried alongside our unfinished business with God. In time we may forgive people who failed to protect us, but

---
[7] Hebrew 4:15.

resentment toward God can still simmer. After all, most adults will acknowledge other adults fall short, but God? Perfection has no excuse for failure.

Age compounded my complaint toward God. I met more and more people who, worthy unlike myself, still suffered unjustly and terribly. Why, God?

The Church had lost credibility by abandoning tens of thousands of child victims for decades. Religious people, psychologists, legislators and attorneys had participated in ignoring or blaming and silencing us en masse. These were the holy, the ordained, the credentialed, and the educated elite. They were the pillars of society. Why, God, why?

My therapist listened with compassion. While helpful, therapy fell short. Its medical model defined what I had experienced as pathology, but I knew it was evil. In the ascendancy of evil, only faith—with or without the Church—would do.

In faith, there is a truth no abuser can pervert. No stupidity among the powerful can harm it. Professionals and experts and scholars cannot revise it to protect their artful rationalizations. It cannot be twisted by enablers and sympathizers. Here is that from which evil recoils. It was only here where I could rebuild my life safely, starting by unearthing my buried grief and unresolved questions.

When people think of the spiritual life they often imagine that it has to be handled in some artificially pure manner. When, for instance, they speak to God in prayer, they feel that they must use only holy and edifying words. Surely, they can't complain to Him or yell at Him. When I sense any of that thinking in people to whom I am offering spiritual guidance, I remind them of "the prayer of expostulation." It was a favorite of the ancient prophets. They had no problem complaining to or arguing with God. They knew that He could handle it and felt comfortable sparring with Him as did Jacob.[8] They also knew that as long as they kept speaking with God, no matter in what manner, that was in itself an act of faith in God. The love between them was strong enough to see through the pain and the hurt that provoked the complaint to the heart that continued to love and to trust anyway.

This kind of prayer is freeing. It lets the victim confront the God who, though so near now, seemed so distant then; so caring, loving, and present now but then seemingly so aloof and even indifferent to the terrible hurt and the humiliating pain being inflicted on one of His little ones and often by one of His trusted ones.

Sometimes victims still believe in God's true heart; sometimes it's hard to believe in the middle of grieving. Many know that there was no part of Him in any of this. Although He seemed not to be there at those times, there is a sense of His justice and rage on behalf of all victims. Some victims are even somehow certain that He was there and that His heart was as broken as theirs. No matter how victims begin to grapple with the spiritual aspects of their abuse, all

---

[8] Genesis 32:23-32

victims eventually confront some version of these questions: How is it that the all-powerful God could, at that time, appear so weak and so vulnerable? Is human freedom so precious that God must respect it even in such horrendous circumstances?

Where do the discussions move from here, from what we call the theodicy issue? What we say is secondary to our presence. Any explanation is secondary to our ability to witness the injustice, to acknowledge each victim's innocence of abuse. From there, we start to open ourselves to how victims' love can be so strong and truthful that it sounds like cries of complaint before God while seeking to love and be loved still. It is not for us to silence these cries nor to hush these complaints. This reaction is healing and freeing. And at bottom, it is an act of faith.

Mirror

We are most often people of shame. We hide the truth of ourselves, almost all of ourselves, in particular that we survived being victims of abuse. We can feel today as ugly as the abuse made us feel decades earlier. We emerge from a childhood of abuse into an adult world where we, at least in part, hide behind false personas or dangerous chemicals or compulsive behaviors, or we hide in isolation. Our disguises are artful as our hearts ache for loving kindness.

Now and then, we venture to share our story with someone who seems to be compassionate or wise, people most often are silenced, or look away, or avoid us out of their own sense of lack or horror. Or, they react and tell us to "get over it" as if we can flip a switch on our healing. Or, they try to meddle and fix us with advice, mostly to relieve their own anxiety encountering such pain or evil. Or, they invite us to pick up the fight to confront the broken system, before we have even mastered the shocking difficulty in making good, healthful choices in our wounded lives. Such reactions can reinforce our sense of shame, our experience of pain, and our need to hide.

In media, where abuse victims at least are not ignored, we see images of ourselves mostly as pathetic or devious people driven to violence or dissolution. The message is that victimhood is destiny and despair. To preserve how people see us, we work doubly to avoid being associated with these caricatures. There seems to be no image of hope for us.

Along the Via Dolorosa, Jesus was dragging his Cross—and our redemption—on the torn flesh of his abused and wounded body. Veronica slipped out of the crowd to wipe His face with a moist cloth. The image He gave her was formed in blood and dirt and sweat. She beheld that image with her broken heart and saw beauty.

To be a spiritual guide who is fully active and empathetic, you need to be on the lookout for certain topics or situations that may prevent you from listening to the voices and stories of survivors who turn to you. Victims often have a difficult time telling their stories in such a manner that provides a real release or freedom from the bondage of harm left by the abuser. Indeed, some tend to tell everything to anybody at any time, hoping thereby to obtain some release from the painful hold it has on them. Still, there are others who cannot speak of it at all. The reasons for this reluctance are many. Yet, the very thing that may help victims get a healthy distance from the shame they still feel is to speak of it to someone who can listen with a receptive hearing and a nonjudgmental heart. To tell their story to someone in a bond of faith is to expose evil to the purifying effects of sunlight. The spiritual guide needs to take great care not to elicit the particulars of the abusive situation until or unless the victim is ready to disclose them. Nor must he show any discomfort, distaste, or emotional distancing when they are finally disclosed. Psychotherapy has many models and methods that can help victims process the memories and should be a part of how victims move through their recovery. Our listening compliments this therapeutic work. Our listening is about being a Christian witness to injustice and evil.

How do we do that? One of the highest compliments that can be given to any person is to say of them: "What you see is what you get." This implies a complete congruence between what they show of themselves to others and what they are in fact within themselves. Everybody desires such transparency, but is there anyone who is ever fully there? In this life complete congruence between outward appearance and inner reality is always a thing in process, on the way, becoming. If this is true of people in general it is even more so of victims. Until such time as grace has touched and begun to heal the roots of their shame, confusion, and self-loathing, their true selves will be hidden to some degree from themselves and others. And that is okay. What matters is how we remain transparent to victims, who will recoil from what is hidden or false.

An important principle in spiritual guidance is to begin where the person actually is, not where you would like them to be, and not even where they would like themselves to be. To get from where they are now to where God wants them finally to be is the whole journey of spiritual guidance. On any particular day, they need only be where God wants them to be on that day. When tomorrow comes, it will be another "today." With God's help, they can tend to it then. This is very important for victims of abuse as they move into recovery. It's not about being a changed person; it's about being a healed person. It's not about driving forward to a goal; it's about being with God as they are that day—even if that day is a particularly dark or difficult day. God is still there, waiting to be a companion on the healing journey.

Are you able to welcome victims where they are now and to guide them, one step at a time, to the "then" of their tomorrow? Are you able to do this without any hurry, pressure, or discomfort? Here is where you rely on God for your own transformation into what another person needs. He will guide you as you guide them in this work which is often just about waiting in quiet expectation for what God has in store.

SAFETY

Sometimes we have picked up where the abuser left off destroying our very person. We self-harm to continue the destruction and pain of our bodies. We are drawn to attempt suicide to complete the murder of self the predator began. Or, we abuse substances, or replace the abuser with dangerous people and situations in our adult lives. As the life-and-death crisis continues, healing begins with sometimes no more than a longing or desire to escape.

One helpful tool in adding safety to our recovery is some advance work. We can make a phone list of people who are safe to call when we need help. Different people are right for different needs. The number we call for help when we are confused is very different from the one we call if we become suicidal. Having all our numbers listed and available in several places is a smart safety measure.

Knowing who to call for what kind of help is about roles. Roles are about expectations. With a damaging figure dominating our early lives and eclipsing others' roles protecting us, sorting through roles and expectations can get confusing. So, making out a phone list is a great exercise in understanding the different roles different people play as unique pieces of a quilt we are stitching together a little at a time.

It also helps us grapple with how everyone to whom we turn will be limited, because everyone is human. The exception is God, Who is the only sure footing for our long-term recovery.

Grace builds on nature. It is therefore sometimes necessary to tend first to what may be broken or short circuited in our emotional, relational, or psychological lives before we can make any real progress in our loving union with God and the embrace of His will for us. Once healed or healing in those areas, we can then begin spiritual guidance whose emphasis is on growth, particularly on the growth of one's relationship with God.

The ultimate goal of spiritual guidance is to help someone find their way to a state of continual and loving union with the Lord. The path along which you are guiding a survivor is one that leads to an ever-greater embrace of God's will for us as life unfolds day by day. But before that can happen in practice, the victim must first be in a safe place, ready to move out of a crisis mode and prepared to take the steps that lead beyond healing to union. Progress will have its fits and starts. It may even stop at times and begin to slide backwards. Although a victim must be working with a qualified counselor to grapple with these impulses, it's a good second check for the spiritual guide to have a list of emergency numbers and referrals to give to the person in whom we recognize the need for help.

To prevent confusion in the one you are guiding, you will want to be sure that the approach of other professionals is compatible with the tenants and principles of the spiritual guidance you are providing. It's important for you both not to be working at cross-purposes to needed therapy, and for the survivor it's important to consider, when the time is right, how their efforts in therapy relate to their faith. Some dioceses have lists of therapists who embrace spiritual direction in parallel. Catholic Charities may offer referrals and affordable options. In our dioceses, some therapists have joined in workshops with other ministers to listen to survivors describe what worked best. This spirit of listening and cooperating for the sake of each survivor can be very warm and inspiring.

In this process, survivors are naturally quite vulnerable to feelings of desertion or abandonment. It is therefore important to assure them that you will be there for them even while they are obtaining help from other professionals. You need to be able to set guidelines for how spiritual guidance can help, and for what belongs in therapy. Indeed, what they share with therapists may be the same as what they share with you. The difference will be the perspective and approach that each professional brings to what is shared. As spiritual guides, we do not second guess the lead of psychotherapy in dealing with processing the past. Instead, we help the victim through the process as through anything in life, with grace through faith.

Linking Gospel accounts of Jesus's healing miracles with the healing power of grace may be a helpful tool in dealing with any brokenness the victim feels. But it must not remain on the abstract or general level. St. Francis de Sales strongly urges that we personalize these connections. Jesus loves me. He wants to heal me, to hold me, to protect and to care for me. Between meetings, ask them to take a particular Gospel healing account to quiet prayer and to listen with the "ears of their heart" to what Jesus may say directly to them by "first and last name," that is, in a very personal way. At the following meeting, ask them to share with you what the Lord has said to them.

All this implies that survivors have a comfortable and safe relationship with you. This will not happen quickly or easily, especially with someone who has already been betrayed and harmed by one in authority and perhaps even by a priest or a person like you. But, they have chosen to trust you for some reason as the Spirit draws them closer to God. To some extent they will find a way to trust you, and when that does happen you will be privileged to "overhear" the conversation between God and the survivor whom you are guiding. God Himself will give both of you direction as to the next helpful step forward. Trust that it is always the Holy Spirit who leads while the guide and one being guided follow in faith.

After a survivor's first steps to trust a therapist or to trust a spiritual guide, there are many steps to follow in a long path, but already this person has claimed a portion of God's healing power. They have moved from being a victim toward being a survivor. You can both begin to hope for them to move further, as well, to a sense of thriving in a new, well life.

LIES

It was like a shroud, how lies were wrapped around the truth of our suffering—for years, sometimes forever. The predator was more powerful and more credible. Some of us even tried to tell our truth while the abuse was going on, but we were not believed. We have been called the liars, while we watched a world full of enablers support the liars as they flourished. Words have been perverted, except for one Word. He is Truth, and He is the first word in which some of us can gain new trust.

There were parents and teachers and other adults who, for whatever reason, did not protect us. Their authority was not true in the presence of the evil of abuse. There was the Church hierarchy, which silenced our truth or denounced us, or whose attorneys attacked us as liars. There were lay Catholics who dismissed us as litigious or pitied us as if we were hopeless. Yet, there we were, with a truth burning in our hearts to be revealed so it could be healed. We knew better than those who failed us that we cannot heal ourselves. Though our stories are very different, we, too, have the same need for a Savior.

Survivors have encountered the Lie under the guise of truth, and Darkness under the appearance of light. Before that graced breakthrough when someone finally listened and believed, it must have seemed that evil had the upper hand. Yet, during the whole period of abuse, long or short, the priest in Church, the parent at home, and the teacher in school were likely teaching that good always triumphs and that Jesus is always victorious. Survivors as children saw otherwise. Each such assurance, therefore, must have given another psychic blow, another sharp stab to the heart. As child victims, survivors talk about feeling crazy. Maybe black really is white and maybe bad truly is good! Through the person of the abuser, the "father of lies" had turned everything inside out, up-ending their belief in God, in themselves, and in others. Perhaps the worst lie was to make these vulnerable children wonder whether they were the source of the evil and as worthless as the abusers made them feel. If the world was all wrong-sided, what about this child? Was her reality a lie? Was he evil?

Most commonly, the victim was not protected; the abuser was. Authority took his side, not that of his victim. Now the adult survivor is in the presence of another authority figure—you. It would be a mistake on the part of the spiritual guide to forget how another authority figure like you harmed this person. The abuser's words deceived and his actions corrupted. His words, though false, others accepted as true. You may not always know what words will help, but you must always speak words that are true. You must always believe, and must always respect the feelings and perceptions of this person in your care even if they are confused or unpleasant.

There is always more art than science to spiritual guidance, and this is even more so in this situation. Never forget that the goal of spiritual guidance is deepening one's relationship with the Lord. One of the most important bridges to that deepening relationship with the Lord is the relationship between the one who guides and the one who is guided. A survivor's relationship with the abuser was demeaning; it was constructed on a sweet-talking and mind-confusing Lie. The survivor's relationship with you must be built on transparency, honesty, simplicity, and truth. You must be reliable. This is not a person for whom your missing an appointment will be a simple scheduling matter. Is a relationship of trust, mutuality, and perhaps spiritual friendship even possible? Hopefully it is, but certainly not quickly or easily. It will take much time and patience and perhaps only at one small baby step at a time. In living through this process, you must rely on God to work with you as much as with the survivor. Here is where there are great gifts for both of you waiting.

Grace heals. But, because of the entropic legacy of the Fall, the healing process is always a slow and uneven one under the best of circumstances. It may move at even a glacial pace because of the heavy emotional baggage and psychic scarring that stem from abuse. Recovery is messy, so is the spiritual path through recovery. Is this survivor willing to even try, and are you willing to be patient? That's what matters. Will you let the authority you wield as guide be expressed in a gentle, kind, welcoming, and unthreatening manner? Most of all, will you be as open to this person and as life-giving as the Spirit? For, representing God, you are speaking on behalf of the Spirit. Caring for this survivor, you are showing them how you rely on the Spirit as a way for them to rely more fully on the Spirit of God for their own faith journey.

CHOICE

Choice is the first thing a predator destroys. Before the abuse actually begins, grooming methodically blurs judgment for a child and for his or her caretakers. Before the first recovery book is opened or the first therapist office is dialed, there is a choice inside. It's often a ferocious "No!" to an entire lifestyle or relationship or compulsion. It has to be strong enough to counter all the ingrained resistance inside one's heart and in the company of family, friends, and society. This is for many a true life-and-death choice to choose not to be a victim any longer.

Emerging from a victim's life to a survivor attitude can be daunting. It's very clear we have to learn new rules for living in some or all areas of our lives. After we learn them, we must choose them, sometimes again and again and again. Rejecting the past becomes an immediate matter—as we consciously begin to make daily choices for life and not for more of the death of abuse. That is the very freedom of choice the abuser destroyed; we are grown now, and able to choose against the brutality. We can choose to seek a new life.

After exile, God does bring His people back to a safe place and a new life to flourish in the good, right order He is restoring. And he gives us a choice, "I have set before you life and death, the blessing and the curse. Choose life ...."[9]

———

One of the cruelest aspects of abuse is its domination. The child is forced to submit to the will of her abuser, often many times over the course of months and years. There is neither freedom nor choice in this, only dread and submission, feelings for which children do not yet even have words. Robbed of the precious gift of

---

[9] Deuteronomy 30:19

childhood, the survivor has thus missed out on the many small everyday opportunities to try their own wings, to choose this or that, to be playful, spontaneous, and carefree—the joy of just being a kid. They lived not in the pleasant forgetfulness of innocence but in fear, confusion, shame, and loss. Defenseless, alone, and powerless, the abuser took everything from them. Survivors often talk about their personalities having been "killed" or having their childhood "murdered." It's not hard to understand why.

In the survivor of abuse who now seeks spiritual guidance, the great gifts of choice, freedom, and self-actualization have probably not had the opportunity to fully develop and mature—even after years of therapy. Many of life's simple managing tools may be seriously short-circuited. In the verse from Deuteronomy quoted above, Moses urges the people to "choose life." Survivors in spiritual guidance desire to do just that, but they may need much help in going about it.

We are talking in this book a good deal about approaches I've used in giving spiritual direction for many years. Yet, I try not to use the expression "spiritual direction" because the word "direction" may inadvertently connote another form of domination to the survivor. From my work with survivors of abuse, I've learned how powerful words are, because for survivors, truth is a signal of safety. In practice, many survivors do not want somebody else "directing" them, aside from God after perhaps a period of time learning to trust Him again. So, here, I prefer expressions such as "spiritual guidance" or "spiritual companionship or accompaniment." In the Salesian tradition, the expression, "spiritual friendship" is often preferred. This connotes the cordial warmth and mutuality that St. Francis de Sales valued in his renowned guidance of others. The problem with even "spiritual friendship" is that it might easily discomfort a survivor whose abuser employed similar terms of endearment to seduce and then violate them. There are many such potential and unintentional slips that the spiritual guide of a survivor needs to be aware of. As you are patient with survivors, be patient with yourself, too. The slow pace of this work can help your own efforts to be diligent in how you speak and act.

As was brought out above, often a survivor has to learn how to choose to do even little everyday things that the rest of us take for granted: brushing her teeth, combing her hair, dressing in a clean and neat manner, and so forth. This can be a sign of depression, which is another example of why psychotherapy is very important. In spiritual direction, a great deal of patience is called for on the part of the spiritual guide as survivors restructure life in psychotherapy. It's possible to offer suggestions, encouragements and gentle persuasion, but it's critical to respect that change is not always the first priority. Sometimes love is what's needed. Trust survivors in their work to find their own voice, which may have been silenced for years. Help them learn to listen to themselves, so they can hear their own longing for life. Moses's great challenge to "choose life" is a beautiful goal, but for the survivor it will probably have to be realized one small step at a time. It may seem forgotten, or even clouded over by difficulties and grief. As guide or companion on this journey, be creative, patient, unhurried, and gentle.

God will take care of the rest. The Holy Spirit is the agent of change, not you.

Price

For most of us, there's a price to choosing healing, and even a price to returning to the Church in any way—even exploratory ways. Scars of abuse on family systems and friendships respond, like any scar, inflexibly, even rigidly. To seek help is to expose the secret. To seek help is to acknowledge one or more abusers along with people who enabled them. Some abusers made victims of all family members, but some were explicitly enabled by another adult as well.

To seek help is to threaten the system of relationships built on hiding the real workings, and indeed can challenge a family to confront the fact that an abuser (e.g., grandfather, priest, uncle) is still roaming freely at family functions with access to children. In the case of the undetected priest abuser, we have faced their presence at family gatherings, funerals, and weddings. The sicker the system, the higher the price will be exacted from the victim who dares to seek healing, which requires truth to long for and truth to proceed.

Too many survivors will walk into therapy for the first time or into spiritual direction having been denounced or persecuted by their own families for this brave step. Our first step can feel dangerous because it is. While we are no longer children in the hands of abusers, we may be taking steps to upend our world of relationships as we know them—as well as a wounded reality that is, if nothing else, familiar.

———

When adult victims finally reveal the secret of their abuse, there are many ripples, some of which, as suggested above, are very negative and painful. They lost their childhood at the time of abuse. In telling their secret, they may alienate some or all of their familial support system as well. Thus, when they first come to you, they may not need so much spiritual guidance as help in understanding why the high cost of revealing the truth is nevertheless worth the great pain that follows.

Listening and encouraging are always the first priority. When it comes time to develop a spiritual dimension in these stories, a useful source of reflection made be found in the familial rejection, harsh persecution and great suffering experienced by the first disciples, especially as recounted in the Acts of the Apostles. From those accounts, we learn that the price or cost of Christian discipleship has always been a high one. Still, there are the many conversions, even of whole families, the continuing comfort and guidance of the Holy Spirit, and the incredible joy even in the midst of great suffering which was experienced by all those first disciples.

Most especially, there is fellowship among them—the comfort that comes to each disciple when the first Christians come together in community to praise God, to read Scripture, and to break bread. While family support may diminish or disappear, what are other support systems available to adult victims who come to you? Does your diocese offer survivor services, prayer gatherings or discussion groups? Once again, it is import to have a list of them on hand. What are other support groups that may be available? Survivors may be reorganizing their lives in a very painful process that includes finding new people to support them. Until that process is well progressed, you may be one of their few support people, a sure anchor in emotional waters that are still rough and in relationships that are often frayed, fragile or broken.

Take the advice of Jesus at those moments. Let the Spirit work to transform this person from their pained state into a thriving state. Your role remains to be present. Don't worry about what you are to say. The Holy Spirit will give you the right word or, more likely, the comforting presence and will help you to be the safe haven they need. Remind yourself and them that when the two of you meet there is always a community of at least three, for Jesus is always there as well, and so is the communion of saints and the presence of the angels. As each survivor finds a new "family" and new "friends" for a well life, encourage them to remember those angels and saints are their family, too, always interceding for their wellbeing.

The price is high and the cost is great when it comes to healing from the secrets of abuse, but bringing truth to light is always healing and worth even the great suffering that frequently follows. In this process, survivors may feel alone, but they need never be alone. You can help them to see that.

Why a Spiritual Guide?

Let's say there's a whisper from God to which you agree, so you find yourself exploring a relationship with someone to help integrate your faith with your recovery program—what does that mean?

It's important to ask this question and understand its answer to avoid confusion later. Therapy and spiritual guidance are complementary but not interchangeable. They proceed in parallel, conscious of each other and supportive, but distinct. A therapist is well-suited to delve into the details of abuse, help order and understand them, help integrate them into a well, adult life. If you turn to people who are not equipped to help you, sometimes they withdraw because they are not qualified to help you and are overwhelmed. Recovery inevitably poses the question whether or not we are responsible for how we share details of the abuse, and with whom. While each of us make that decision differently based on circumstances and opportunities, none of us can escape the reality that we may traumatize others, even inadvertently. There are choices to be made in our hearts about boundaries we need to set—on ourselves.

One way to get the most from formal spiritual guidance is to find ways to make the exchange prayer-like when possible. One way to enrich a close friendship or more casual fellowship which fosters spiritual understanding is to leave the psychological impact of abuse for therapy, and to focus on whatever may help you grow and thrive as you recover. If you turn for therapy to people who are suited only to be spiritual friends or guides, you will likely emerge disappointed, maybe even feeling awkward. Both these feelings can kick up shame and harm your connection with your spiritual guide.

Conversely, a crisis of faith can be discussed in therapy, certainly, but spiritual guidance helps you tap into your relationship with God through the depth of the tradition of faith (and all it offers for you to work through the sense of abandonment and betrayal). Recovery, for me, was a quilt. Everyone was an important piece in the patchwork. A very close friend whom I eventually found was central. Support groups and reading were critical. Together, it took all of these to keep me wrapped in care while I grew well.

For many years I taught a graduate level course on Salesian spiritual direction to seminarians and interested lay men and women. I usually began that course by distinguishing spiritual guidance from counseling or therapy. Whereas spiritual guidance is growth-centered, counseling or therapy is often problem or issue-centered. When the problem or issue is resolved, counseling or therapy usually ends, whereas, since one's spiritual growth continues until death, spiritual guidance often continues throughout life.

Spiritual guidance always centers on one's relationship with God. It begins, first, by dealing with any obstacles to this relationship such as actual sin, grave or not, or any inclination to sin. It then moves to the cultivation of practices that foster and deepen one's relationship with God such as prayer, the sacraments, and the practice of virtue. When dealing with adult survivors of child abuse, eventually much time and attention will probably be given to obstacles that impede fostering and deepening of a relationship with God. For all people, these obstacles can be very difficult and daunting, and for survivors that is true as well. Yet, as suggested by the range and number of the topics of this book, there is a particular cast to those obstacles. Some of the most deeply rooted obstacles in a survivor may be, actually, wounds inflicted upon them while they were very young. Overcoming these involves psychological and emotional recovery as well as spiritual growth. The process requires, from the survivor and from you, a great deal of patience and understanding. There is much hard work ahead for this brave survivor. There is, too, much grace and sustenance from the Spirit to receive.

The evil of abuse has left a traumatized adult who now comes to you for spiritual guidance. The many-faceted face of that trauma, and the many-layered levels of those scars, need attention from a trained professional, and a spiritual guide, and perhaps others as well, but each according to his or her own professional competence. As spiritual guide, your competence lies in helping adult survivors remove obstacles to their relationship with God and, once removed, assisting them in the practices of their faith that deepen and foster that relationship.

As spiritual guide, you too will need a way to deepen your own faith as you struggle with the injustice and trauma to which this person has been subjected. Your own spiritual wellbeing will need tending to. See to it. Do not mistakenly make self-care a lesser priority. This will enable you to continue to be of help to adult survivors without becoming emotionally or spiritually exhausted in the process. To the degree you are drawn to offering formal or casual guidance to survivors of abuse or violence, you must be ready to build into your schedule time for rest, processing and prayer—to be fair to yourself, to others who depend on you, and to the survivors for whom you care.

LISTENING & DIALOGUE

Overview

A dialogue of affirmation forms a rich foundation for spiritual guidance for those who have endured the trauma of child sexual abuse by clergy or others in authority. It can fuel recovery as its gift of listening in the presence of the Holy Spirit and reflecting back the love and image of God already present in a wounded person struggling through suffering toward healing. This section covers a wide selection of topics that arise in the sometimes difficult therapeutic work of recovery, highlighting a language of love and a mindset of spiritual generosity in which spiritual guides listen, drawing a faith story out of a survivor and leading a survivor closer to God. Here on Veronica's veil appear both the image of human suffering and of God among us. This language and its mindset also help to ensure the dialogue does not re-traumatize a survivor or family member. They help open pathways to deepen faith for the challenges survivors are facing daily.

This section opens with essays about first encounters, with perspectives from a survivor having a successful diocesan program, a spiritual guide feeling trepidation about how service in this area is different, and a psychologist discussing things to consider with a survivor who is seeking to integrate faith with therapy. Remaining essays relate to common experiences and feelings survivors are processing in recovery and, so, are bringing with them as they approach the Church for healing and possibly reconciliation.

To help the work of grace in a survivor's faith journey toward healing, it is important to appreciate common issues and, also, to journey forward with prayerfulness on one's own. The essays in this section have been selected as a way to foster appreciation among guides but also to help survivors, all along the way, know others have walked a similar path, with faith, into a thriving life.

Listening & Dialogue: A Survivor's Perspective

On my couch with broken ankle elevated, I watched the television. Pope John Paul II was in his last days. News coverage was focused on a little window overlooking Saint Peter's Square in Rome. Surfing the Web on my laptop, I could find no services for his transitus in the diocese, but the website featured a Victim Assistance Office. That seemed new. I snorted.

A few days later, mostly out of boredom confined to the couch, I practiced a brusque New-York approach and called the number for the Victim Assistance Coordinator. My first words spoken were a terse, "So is this window dressing?" She chuckled, softly, and said I would have to decide for myself. Her name is Patricia Mudd, and since then she and I have become good friends.

Four things made this first encounter memorable and unshakable. First, it wasn't hard to talk to her. Pat's voice was extremely gentle, and her style was not forceful. It was very hard to reject anything about her, and, believe me, I was firing full cylinder, trying to find reasons to write this program off.

Second, Pat was prepared with information. She described a program with many options. There were prayer services and Masses and survivor circles and therapists and spiritual directors and priests who had been trained in this area. Most importantly, in the options I felt no constriction or sense there would be a "right" way or a cookie-cutter approach. This was my first sense of the program's credibility.

Third, I had to admit someone was actually thinking of my best interests. There was a commitment there, already. What's more, everything that followed bore out what she had said. People were good to their word. I was watching for a crack in the façade. I would find none.

Last, Pat was personally prepared. She was professionally trained. She was not judgmental. Neither did she react to my reactions. She was well versed in how triggers could rupture our precarious early connection. Above all, she sounded as patient as she turned out to be. Patience was very important, because many times I promised her I would be some-

where but failed to show, faltering halfway there, triggered and paralyzed. And, I was too ashamed to admit it to her in the early days. Yet, still she waited. She gave me the time I needed.

LISTENING & DIALOGUE: A SPIRITUAL GUIDE'S PERSPECTIVE

Several years ago I was invited to give a day of recollection to a small group of victims of abuse. I did not welcome that invitation. In fact, I dreaded it. A few months earlier a good priest friend had celebrated Mass for this same group. He had preached on what he presumed would be a shared Christian value: forgiveness. To put it mildly, what he said did not elicit the response that he had anticipated. This group of adult women and men who had survived sexual abuse as children were not at all ready to hear about the Christian call to forgive their abusers. All these years later, they were still enraged and angry at what as children they had been so cruelly subjected to. They were still very much dealing with the devastating and crippling effects of abuse. Nor did they feel that the Church had yet fully accepted its responsibility for the inadequate way in which it had for so long dealt with the issue of abuse, or had dealt with its clerical abusers and those who were victims. No, this group was not at all ready to forgive and in no uncertain terms they made that abundantly clear to my friend.

Hearing of their reaction to my friend, I was less

than enthusiastic about accepting the invitation to give them a day of recollection. I was quite nervous, in fact. I knew that I had better be prepared to address the issues that really mattered to these survivors, those that they were prepared to deal with and not with those, however lofty, that they were not. So I made it a point to meet with Mrs. Pat Mudd, Victim Assistance Coordinator, who was the director of this important, even trail-blazing, outreach program of the Arlington Diocese. She filled me in on the various aspects of the program and introduced me to a number of victims.

This was my first personal experience really hearing from survivors of abuse. I listened. Their stories were heart-wrenching, but what struck me more was their resilience and their profound faith. Sensing that I very much wanted to be well informed before the day of recollection, they were generous with ideas and support. They helped me prepare, extending welcome and friendship quickly. One of their main concerns was to make the day helpful to their many survivor friends, and we were able to forge a bond in my having the same concern. In some sense, I suppose, those exchanges marked the beginning of this book for me.

As I listened, especially as a priest, I acutely felt "guilty by association." I wanted to apologize for the incredible harm done to these deeply feeling and kind people. I found myself wondering whether my collar or how I dressed or what I said would be a trigger for some painful memory. But soon I realized that all they really wanted was someone who would listen and become better informed. Their reception of me turned into an invitation to enter as deeply as possible into the shame and hurt of their experiences, but also witness their great dignity and insights. From that perspective I was becoming better prepared to speak realistically to them of a spiritual journey. Some were just returning to the Church and its sacraments. Others were seeking a more regular, safe-feeling connection with the Church that had failed them so badly in the past. A few were converts. All wanted a deeper connection to Gospel values and teachings that many had heard preached as children, in some cases, from their abusers.

This was for me a holy watershed, as I hope similar listening and connections may be for you. My efforts to listen to this first group of survivors as individuals and in small groups, and to read their stories, prepared the groundwork for what turned out to be a sometimes emotional but happy day of recollection.

My talks on the day of recollection were just part of what the diocese offered to the survivors who gathered. After lunch, Bishop Paul S. Loverde, who provided the imprimatur for this book, and Father Mark S. Mealey, who wrote the foreword to this book, joined us in a small circle, and they simply listened, too. I learned later that this discussion was not unusual. It was easy to see how spontaneous and comfortable the survivors were with this bishop and priest. Bishop Loverde and Father Mealey had been the inspiration for this relatively unknown but very important diocesan outreach program. From the very beginning they had taken a personal, hands-on interest in its many aspects. They had been already doing what I was learning to do—be present and listen with love. The survivors were at ease with them.

At the end of the discussion, the bishop took a few moments to convey to these survivors that they were precious among his flock and that as their shepherd he was not going to distance himself from their pain. He apologized for the Church, emphasizing the grief he felt for their suffering, and he took special care to remind them that what happened to them as children was not their doing or their fault. His words had a strong impact on the group. It was so clearly from Bishop Loverde and Father Mealey's spiritual presence and respect that these survivors were drawing spiritual sustenance. Pope Francis would be pleased with a shepherd who gets close enough to his flock that he lives "with the smell of the sheep[10]"!

Since that first day of recollection, I have been invited to return to address this group. I have learned far more from them than they have from me. And I have grown to admire their courage and willingness to move, often one small step at a time, out of the darkness of their painful past and into a growing participation in the life of Church and its sacraments. Most of all, I have admired their openness to be assisted in this journey of spiritual recovery by priests who, for some victims, represent the very ones who had caused them so much suffering as children. In that openness, I see a form of forgiveness.

---

[10] From Pope Francis's homily, Chrism Mass, Holy Thursday, March 28, 2013.

Listening & Dialogue: A Psychologist's Perspective
Frank J. Moncher, PhD

As a therapist working with survivors of trauma, I often see that a time comes when a survivor needs to confront the abuser, directly or metaphorically, to continue the healing journey. For those who were victimized by clergy, this can include efforts to return to the Church of their youth. As a survivor progresses in therapy, it is expected that the increasing awareness and attention to the injustice perpetrated against their will will result in the emergence of feelings of depression, anxiety, grief, rage, and shame. One point needs to be made clear: these are normal reactions to the abnormal circumstances that were a part of their history.

As therapy progresses, survivors' former coping methods are challenged. Their various ways of escaping, hiding, or denying the abuse must be relinquished in order to move forward, but those methods, dysfunctional though they may have been, served the purpose of keeping the intense emotions at bay. Now as they explore the pain and begin to consider where their faith fits into their lives, they are making huge strides towards reclaiming that which was distorted and perhaps taken from them as child victims. This is not easy, and is accompanied by not a little fear, confusion, and distress. Yet they are coming more fully alive, and with the understanding guidance of a spiritual mentor, a door can start to open.

During this period of "heavy lifting" in therapy, the usual course is best described as sporadic. There are periods of courageous processing of distressing past events that are marked by growth and progress. These can segue into a distracted focus on the trials of daily living which are an inevitable part of life. Some of these crises are external and unavoidable (such as the death of a family member or trial of ill health), while others seem to be triggered by an interior need to return to the former equilibrium, no matter how painful. It is critical that any tendency to detach and isolate from supportive relationships be challenged, as it is those healthy relationships that will provide the landscape in which healing will resume, when each survivor is ready. Although returning to past dysfunction may seem illogical and cause frustration, it is nevertheless predictable and not typically cause for alarm, unless the person's pattern has in the past included self-harm. (These impulses, of course, must be dealt with promptly and professionally to prevent harm and despair. Coordination between therapist and spiritual guide with the survivor's approval can be helpful, so that they are hearing of their own true dignity and worth from multiple places). It is important to note that any seeming "backsliding" is not actually regression, but a necessary respite. Once feeling re-stabilized, it is encouraging for the survivor to be reminded that their prior progress is typically fairly quickly recouped, as the path already tread is an easier journey during the next pass through.

As during the initiation of treatment, the therapist must remain vigilant to the need for the survivor to have a safe place to explore their experiences. Even in an established therapy relationship where trustworthiness has been reasonably proven, a survivor's effort to resume the practice of their faith may encounter symbols and signs associated with the abuse and, then, old feelings of mistrust and fear are likely to be triggered. The survivor may recoil from the therapist and spiritual guide who had already gained this person's trust. The therapist or guide will need patience and understanding as the survivor sorts through what feelings are from the past, and what feelings belong to the present. At times like these, the relationship integrity and the caring of the therapist or guide might be challenged, in which case the openness to dialogue and respect for the survivor's needs must be re-emphasized, possibly many times.

A respectful patience, along with a clear communication of desire and willingness to remain attached to the survivor, is vital. The survivor's timeline, possibly unknown even to the survivor, must be respected. The therapist's role is one of containment of the emotions that the survivor experiences but perhaps cannot yet express. For therapist and guide alike, it is a matter of faithfully awaiting the survivor's expression of readiness to consider approaching the next challenges of the healing journey.

Shame

Abuse creates shame-based lives. Shame is a sense of being utterly inexcusable as a person. It is very similar to self-loathing, something many of us face daily. Our shame can lead to twisted ways of thinking and feeling about ourselves and others. The variations are as diverse as the many individuals we are.

Commonly, we spend time demeaning ourselves to others, and more time than that berating ourselves in that endless loop of negative thinking that can become obsessive at certain times. Others of us turn that negativity outwards, belittling others habitually. The criticism isn't measured; it's black and white, all or nothing. This negativity is almost cataclysmic.

Our shame is physical in many ways. For one thing, it's exhausting to hold up a façade and hide the imposter we believe we are. The closer to being known for who we are, the higher our anxiety level can surge. Some of us assume postures that make us appear smaller, as if we don't believe we deserve to take up the same space as everyone else. We wear many layers of loose clothing, to hide and to feel, literally, a sense of covering and security.

Shame colors our relationships. We select troubled friends whose neediness offsets our fear of more abandonment. For similar reasons we tolerate abuse or disrespect, or we sacrifice our own personal standards just to obtain someone else's approval. Criticism, which can be difficult for anyone to hear, can utterly devastate us, sending us back into hiding or chemical abuse or suicidal thoughts.

Shame is hell. Its role in a survivor's suffering cannot be understated. It is not to be confused with guilt that people (rightly) feel after they do something wrong. Generally, we assume the level of guilt is in proportion to the degree of error, and that it passes. Shame doesn't allow for any proportion. It doesn't permit balance, and it isn't passing. It is bondage, badly in need of deliverance.

―――

"Shame is hell." The survivor's description of the shape and appearance of that hell is a very poignant one. These words suggest a number of ways that shame stemming from abuse manifests itself in the survivor and their behavior. The self-loathing associated with shame, the efforts to become small or insignificant because of the feeling of unworthiness to "take up the same space as everyone else," the tendency to dress in layers of clothing to better hide from others—these and other such issues are probably best addressed with a therapist. Yet they are important to understand when creating a safe space in which a survivor may begin to explore a deepening relationship with God.

It is particularly helpful for the spiritual guide to be aware of the extent to which shame may negatively color the survivor's self-image. Shame may lead to efforts at self-concealment and/or a demeaning or belittling attitude towards themselves and others. Such manifestations may very well surface from time to time within the context of spiritual guidance. The guide who is prepared for these—and many other—

signs of shame will not be surprised if and when they surface. But does the spiritual guide have any tools with which to help the survivor lessen feelings of shame and their likely off-putting manifestations with others? Again, this brings us to the question of how to integrate faith with therapeutic recovery from abuse.

One possible tool is best expressed in these words of the Apostles' Creed: "He descended into hell." These words usually roll off our tongues without any impact at all. What do they mean anyway and what do they say to us about Jesus and Christian life? They often spoke powerfully to saints and mystics who found in them incredible spiritual solace. For them, they attest to the radical depths to which Jesus's self-emptying took him.[11] As fully human, the Son of God embraced everything in us and the human condition but sin. This embrace included every degree, kind, and level of human darkness and every experience of human pain and degradation. No dark place escapes his presence. Thus, Jesus did not know only on a theoretical level of the horrible feelings of shame that are the detritus still clinging to a survivor of abuse long after having been violated. Jesus descended into the very depths of their hell. He knew it from within, just as a survivor does. Others may not be able to know what a survivor knows or to feel the way a survivor feels, but Jesus does. As the sacrificial lamb he took on not only sin itself but all of its harmful and lasting effects.

---

[11] Philippians 2: 6-11

The spiritual guide can help the survivor come to an appreciation of the healing power that is available to them from the Lord's descent into their private hell. Jesus went there with them, suffered the abuse with them,[12] and suffers yet within them. He will never leave them until, together, they have climbed out of the depths of hell and into the bright light of the new heaven and the new earth. Now, this idea is very difficult for a person who experienced abuse as abandonment even by God and who emerged from abuse feeling unworthy of love in some or many respects. So, the work in spiritual guidance is very basic, very great, very slow, but very transformative with the rich gift of grace.

At the heart of this is the all-encompassing and all-powerful love of God. There is nothing about this survivor that God does not love. Indeed, His love for their having suffered is so great that He sent His only Son to die so that they would not suffer alone, in a world of such sinfulness that they would have been harmed as children. This radical love is something from which survivors in shame can hide, certain of their unworthiness. These are the rudimentary lessons we help them unlearn by reminding them always of the true nature of God's love.

One thing you can also do is renew within yourself in prayer after every meeting a commitment to this survivor's journey. You can then assure them that as their spiritual companion you too will stay with them

---

[12] "At that time Jesus cried out in a loud voice, '*Eloi, Eloi, lama sabachthani?*' which is translated, 'My God, my God, why have you forsaken me?'" (Mark 15:34)

on the journey until, over time, their shame is lessened and its legions of harmful legacy conquered. They will not be abandoned, and they are not someone shameful. Your promise to remain must be sacrosanct; it must be kept because of the abandonment it rebukes. With this survivor, your faithfulness is to be the human expression of the Lord's great promise of fidelity. The truth of this promise itself is healing, for it is the opposite of their childhood experience. It is the opposite of everything the abuser has taught them. Indeed, as you help a survivor's faith in God deepen through prayer, you are providing the antidote to shame, for God delights in this remarkable person. He knows they are not what happened to them!

ISOLATION

Shame has a way of isolating us. So does distrust. So do our secrets. Indeed, for some survivors, the price of peace itself is isolation. Yet, isolation is no synonym for solitude. Isolation is lonely. It prolongs the sense of being abandoned and lost.

Isolated, we also avoid the very natural process of setting (and respecting) boundaries with others. Having our own boundaries trampled as children, we grow up fairly clueless about having boundaries and about negotiating them in relationships. Here is one way we end up grappling with how the wounds foisted upon us can harm others.

God is a relationship among three Persons. God provides, also, our foundational relationship if we let

Him. Yet, it is a relationship He, quite opposite to the abuser, does not force upon us. He has said over and over again that He does not want a slave who has no choice whether or not to love Him. He seeks free people who freely choose Him. This unwillingness to force His love on anyone is why evil exists. Many, including our abusers, reject God and devolve into evil deeds.

The sacred relationship between Creator and creature promises to heal our relationships, new and old. Work in counseling provides a wealth of insights and practical tools for a lifetime. Encountering God is a way to enrich and stabilize all our relationships, whether new or old.

Most survivors describe recovery as affecting their relationships, which are richer, freer, and more open. They have healthful, flexible boundaries. In recovery, we stop being victims, and some of us will also need to stop making victims of others. Relationships are restored to wellness in the same measure that we are.

The turtle protects itself from danger by withdrawing head and legs into its hardened shell. Lacking a physical shell in which to protect themselves from their abusers, victims tended to isolate by withdrawing within themselves. Psychic and emotional isolation was a useful tool during the period of abuse. It distanced them somewhat from the pain and shame that was being imposed on them by the actions of another. But, as noted above, it also tended to prevent them from engaging in the usual give-and-take of relationships within family and society. Sadly, in too many instances this was wise self-protection, for many family and social settings, including some church communities, where abuse occurs are not safe for children either. So, while isolating was adaptive for the child, it leaves the adult needing to learn more or less how to live with others, including how to negotiate personal boundaries we ourselves may take quite for granted. This is not a character flaw or moral failing. This is simply a lack of opportunity—and, sadly, a lack of care.

To the extent that isolation kept the abuser at a distance emotionally, that was a good thing. But to the extent that it prevented a natural schooling in boundaries, it means that, at times, some survivors may have run roughshod over the boundaries of others, including your boundaries. Some may arrive quite wounded by adult relationships because they have let others run roughshod over them. People sometimes mistake the disorderly relationships of survivors for failures, when the fact that survivors are trying to relate to others, however poorly, is a sign of their hope and need for love. It is a sign that they are open to God. Even if their relationships are not working well, they are well disposed to drawing on God's presence to remake some relationships, to help them be strong enough to leave some relationships behind, and to guide them to new relationships for a new life in Him. Again, that survivors are not alone even in relationships, but are there with God, can be eye-opening and very difficult and yet sometimes hopeful to people for whom primary childhood relationships failed and for whom a trusted adult became suddenly a cruel abuser.

Depending on the stage of recovery, the survivor in spiritual guidance may still exhibit isolating tendencies and/or not be particularly skilled in negotiating boundaries, even with you. If the survivor is still isolating, a little or a lot, then you will want to be very careful to respect the isolation. Isolation is, after all, a boundary they are setting. You do not go beyond the boundaries people established for their own protection. This self-protection began to protect them as a child and may be continuing to protect what is child-like and vulnerable within them still. As survivors heal, they do find ways to open up more, but these ways vary and need to be part of the spiritual learning you both share. These boundaries are not necessarily about you at all. To be pushed away may not be about you personally, but rather about needing to feel more space—or to test if you will respect this boundary. There's no need to take offense, and, similarly, it's important not to take offense if a survivor steps on your boundaries. Let yourself be part of a network of people supporting this person as they practice the dynamics of living with people who respect and care for them.

One relationship that will not fail to enrich and remake a survivor's life is the survivor's relationship with God. The One God, as Trinity, is a Community of three Persons or, better, three subsistent relationships: Father, Son, and Holy Spirit. We are made to reflect the image of God who is Community. Thus, to be in relationship with God and with others is central to being human. This relationship is the most reliable and the most healing. It offers insights and help in being oneself, alone, and in being part of relationships, families, and communities. As an image of what is good and holy, it also helps survivors grapple with broken relationships for which they must come to terms. God as Community is at the core of work in spiritual guidance.

To deepen one's relationship with God there are many options. God is encountered in many ways, such as Scripture, sacrament, prayer, community (Church, others), and in nature. He is also found in the beauty of art and music and literature. These are often communal acts, or at least participation in something humanly collective. Try to discover the way in which the survivor you are guiding feels safest encountering God through others, and then help them find Him there. There is no text book for any of this. Much of it is trial and error. Then again, it's good to remind survivors that all life, and even our relationship with God, can be trial and error. There is no right or wrong way, there is God's love and guidance and call. He loves us even in the missteps as we seek Him.

In time, you will both find the way for survivors to enjoy a deeper relationship with God as Community. God is always found in relationship with others—in Himself as Community and in His dealings with people throughout salvation. Once a survivor finds more about God-in-relationships, they will discover others in relationships as well. That's why it is critical to begin your companionship with each survivor very clear in your own heart and very clear with the survivor as a meeting not of two but of three. With God central, there can be safety, and hope, and grace. From there, build into the future together.

Secrets

The truth of abuse is almost always hidden inside secrets. The abusers forced secrets upon us, through grooming, manipulation, or threats. Either ignorant or complicit, our families and other loved ones were wounded by secrets, too. Our church leaders, along with counselors like attorneys and psychologists, kept the secrets, enabling the abuse to continue. Any compassionate impulse to care for us when we were still upset children was sacrificed in favor of protecting these secrets.

One recovery adage says that we are only as sick as our secrets. Breaking the silence is a critical step. We begin by speaking our truth. We who were denied any voice as children must work to restore our voices as adults. Sometimes, to begin, we shout when we mean to whisper or whisper when we need to speak forthrightly. We who suffered in confusion often hardly know what to say at first. We are learning.

There can be a very high price for speaking truth. People who are not willing to step outside the tyranny of secrets accuse us, blame us, hate us, or reject us from their lives. We lose entire support systems. Other times, we watch our truth wound our loved ones as they grapple with the revelation and the loss of security and trust they had. In some cases, we even grapple with the possibility the abuse continues.

Confronting secrets is part of recovery, but so is developing patience. It takes time to learn how to create a safe place to face the truth buried in the secrets. It takes time to pick and choose whether and when to confront the secrets in our relationships, families, and homes. It takes time to mourn the loss of illusions.

―――

"What you hear whispered, proclaim from the housetops:"[13] This is the command Jesus gives to his Apostles. He wants them to shout out to the whole world the good news that he is communicating to them through the warm familiarity of friendship and discipleship.

In the context of the sad secret that is abuse, this command takes on a whole new meaning. When they were being abused, the young victims most likely did not even have the words with which to speak their secret. Perhaps the abuser's threats or their confusion or their shame kept them from speaking, even in whispers, to others. Those who mustered the courage to speak were often given a deaf ear, or told to keep quiet, or called a liar, and this caused them to retreat further within, in anger, confusion, and shame. No one wanted to hear, and many others could not bear to hear, what the wounded children needed to say.

Adult survivors are told that they are only as sick as their secrets. To be healed of the wounds and scars of abuse, they are encouraged to shout out their secrets and, in that way, to speak truth to power. Truth liberates and sets frees.

---

[13] Matthew 10:27

But how? In anger? In shame? With what words? To whom? In time and with patience, spiritual guidance can be the safe place in which they can tell their story. Maybe at first they will not be able to speak it directly to you, but they may be able to write it out, sharing it at first with a therapist, a close friend, another survivor, or simply with themselves—and, in time, with Jesus. First attempts to share are sometimes like putting puzzle pieces together. For many survivors, memories are reconstructed as if from chards of a broken whole. For others, much emotion emerges with the memories; these are feelings natural to feel during and after abuse, and they are part of the memories survivors are trying to put to rest.

The spiritual guide must avoid forcing the timing or the parameters of this process. In a gradual unfolding of their secrets, adult survivors need to be able to say what they must say and how they can now express it. Even now, they may not have the words to use. Maybe only in telling their story can they find those words. For others, telling the full memory or story is neither possible nor helpful. Some therapies seek to unearth all secrets before moving into a mode of active recovery, others do not. That's because different survivors need different approaches to heal. So, let the survivor lead. This is their path toward healing. Along the way, it is also their path to grow closer to God. Be a patient and compassionate listener.

Keep in mind that you are not listening to sins that need to be forgiven. You are not listening to what this person has done wrong as much as to their painful memories of abuse and all the wounded living that has followed. These are very painful stories that lacked a witness and often lacked love. They are stories of those who have been greatly sinned against and who now need to be healed by being heard with the ears of a compassionate heart—making real the presence of God. In this way, listening itself brings God closer to survivors, if we just stay out of the way!

Trust

Survivors have trust issues. Most obviously to everyone, we are among those who don't trust easily. And we withdraw trust quickly. And, in between, we test people regularly, in particular anyone whom we may associate with our abusers—like the Church. Distrust is not always unreasonable.

Defying the odds, we still seek to return and, along the way, we vigorously test Catholics opening the door for our return to the Church. I appreciate you may have had nothing to do with the betrayal of survivors, but there it is. The effects of abuse wane slowly. Meanwhile, every alarm bell sounds and every red alert is on high volume just to be in a church, or a rectory, or an office with a crucifix. We walk into settings very likely to trigger all the fear and agony of our childhood because we have no other place to go but to the faith of our childhood. It is, perhaps, the cruelest cut of all.

Least obvious, especially to survivors, is how recovery is about recovering trust in ourselves. We often feel the blame for the abuse for many different reasons, all of them wrong. We can be painfully aware of blind spots created by past trauma and how they have led us into new but similar dangers of abuse. We are building up from zero, after abuse has reduced our trust in a safe world to nothing.

―

"Little peddler, little pack" is how St. Francis de Sales once described his approach to the spiritual life. The wisdom in this saying suggests that in guiding a survivor of abuse, one's approach must be appropriate to the many challenging parameters stemming from abuse. This will be particularly the case when dealing with issues associated with trust.

I often describe spiritual guidance as the grace-filled progression from "good to better." More often than not, those who come for spiritual guidance have left behind serious sin and any lingering attachments or hankerings for it. They are at a different point, looking for something different, from the spiritual guide. Frequently, they have had stability in their personal and interior lives that permitted them to focus on how, through grace, to avoid even less serious sins and failings. These people attend Mass and participate in sacraments freely. For them the Church is not a place where pain and wounding has occurred. For them life has not been fraught with the pain of secrets and broken relationships and isolation. So the progression from "good to better" for survivors can be something different altogether.

Survivors may not yet be able to bear to walk inside a church, sometimes only managing to sit outside while aching to go inside. Others will be struggling with different triggers which make more traditional approaches in spiritual guidance painful, even harmful. Unlike Catholics comfortable in a faith that did not harm them, survivors may be longing for the faith but, with good reason, be anxious in proximity to things of our faith. This desire to return, somehow, despite the wounds, is a grace-filled beginning point. It marks how there is a big difference between how you begin and carry out spiritual guidance with the Catholic who never experienced the horrors of abuse and the Catholic who did.

Trust is a difference that is most noticeable from the start. Trust and mutuality are fundamental to spiritual direction. They constitute the usual environment for offering direction, and they are easily reached by most within a few meetings. The person tends to be at ease and spontaneous in sharing early in the work, and discussing the fruit of their prayer life is natural. In this context, people find it relatively easy to describe general directions life has taken since the previous meeting. Conversation is not a challenge. Exchanging inspirations, thoughts, and suggestions is not a struggle.

In the case of an adult survivor, however, trusting fully in anyone other than God may come slowly, if ever. Indeed, trust issues make accepting guidance itself a great act of courage. For survivors of abuse by clergy, that courage is quite stunning, yet surprisingly frequent.

Survivors seeking spiritual guidance (or therapy, for that matter) are taking a great step forward, feeling a high risk. Life has taught them the wisdom of not trusting, and certainly not to trust authority with their wellbeing. The spiritual friendship that characterizes much of Salesian spiritual guidance is, then, a huge risk for a survivor. This fact will be present often in your mind and heart as you offer survivors guidance, and it will be heartbreaking anew as you see a deeply good human being sometimes anxious with you because your relationship is vaguely similar to the one that turned into abuse years earlier. The very small first step into spiritual guidance is a huge leap on the survivor's part. It may take many visits just to let them arrive in your company and settle into this new altitude.

With the surprising trust, there is testing of others, even those who are trying to help them (especially if they remind them in some way of their abusers). So, you will be tested, in part to reaffirm you are not like the abuser or all the other people who promised care and failed to care in the past. But you will also be tested for the sense of dawning relief, even joy, that you are safe—that a safe person and a safe haven have been found sometimes after decades of a sort of spiritual homelessness. While being tested can be unpleasant, and being tested repeatedly can be annoying, it's good to see how a mix of relief, joy, and reassurance is the gift you are giving by being willing to be tested—and being willing to do what it takes to pass the test!

How do we pass the test? We are, simply put, professional. We show up on time, and we show up when we say we will. We keep our commitments meticulously, because others in the past failed to keep theirs. We don't make promises we cannot keep, because people in the past did just that. We are gentle, kind, accepting, and patient. We listen to the survivor. We hear them. And, we do not recoil, and we do not challenge, or in any way confirm the person's own likely hidden sense of shame and guilt. This is the space we offer to a survivor in spiritual guidance that permits something others in guidance already have—a stable and reliable relationship of love and spontaneity with God.

Understanding how trust plays a role from the first meeting also is your first step to contending with a key obstacle to survivors' relationships with God. Often survivors blame themselves for the abuse they suffered. For these and others reasons, survivors arrive for spiritual guidance with a certain poverty, "building up from zero." Before the work of becoming more like Jesus, it is important to spend time on how lovable this person is already, known and seen by Jesus. It is important to give this survivor, who was all-but invisible as a child victim to adults, a sense of the delight God saw in them in the past—and sees in them now. In doing so, you will find yourself with the gift of focusing on how much these wounded but tenacious people reflect the beauty of Jesus long before they may even know or believe. This is a sacred trust from the very start of spiritual guidance for survivors. It is one most do not even know enough to hope for, sad as that is.

Approaches with those who already enjoy a robust spiritual life will probably not work in the guidance of a survivor. That is not to say that survivors do not have very deep, even profoundly nuanced, faith or love for God. Many do. Many have a depth of faith that inspires those who have had far less painful lives.

You will find in their faith even more a sign of how God's grace works wonders in the lives of survivors. But, the survivors who walk into spiritual guidance seeking to begin a different walk with Jesus naturally find themselves working through the wounds from life inflicted to that point in time. It is simply where their focus is, and where it should be. Going from "good to better," they first must learn things as simple as how they are good and, also, how they who lived without hope or in shame as child victims can now hope.

From wherever they may start, and for perhaps a long time, survivors may only be able to take small, faltering steps in the next phase of their spiritual life. They deserve patience. It is a great encouragement to each survivor to know that God only asks each of us to do what we can do, no more. He simply asks us to do that with as much love as we can muster. For God, it is not the "size" of the act but its quality that counts, and its quality stems from the love with which it is done. This is a very important and healing concept for a survivor who might have spent part of their life trying to "act big" when they were feeling very small, overwhelmed, and scared. They can rest now, as their relationship with God starts letting Him do more of the heavy lifting.

There is a saying in Salesian spirituality: "Great deeds may not always come our way, but at all times we can do little deeds with perfection, that is, with great love." For this reason, St. Francis de Sales places great emphasis on what he calls the "little virtues," the simple little acts of kindness, care, compassion, and love that we can practice with one another many times each day in the nooks and crannies of ordinary life. For survivors, it is to self that offering these little acts of kindness and compassion may be most difficult, even impossible. Often survivors are very caring and perceptive; the wisdom and compassion they learned in suffering is something they very well know how to offer those around them. That is not the same as what they offer themselves. A healthy and appropriate love of self is often wounded in abuse. As some blame themselves for being abused, they no longer trust themselves to protect themselves. It can be hard to believe, because it is so obvious to us that children are innocent of this crime, yet it is the starting point for many who seek spiritual guidance. So, it is there where we start with them.

So, part of spiritual guidance is encouraging the survivor to begin practicing these little acts of trust and love personally. The concept can be quite uncomfortable for them. Simple acts of self-care we take for granted, even eating well or brushing one's teeth, can be a great feat for one who lived without parenting. Reminding survivors that God's love is personal, and that He wants them to be cared for, is quite possibly the radical work of spiritual guidance here. We help them experience how He loves them; this fundamental reality may take a long time to establish. It may, indeed, be the only work you do. With time, survivors may come to see and believe that God has made them in His own image. Their shame and self-loathing will lose strength as their belief in this truth becomes more certain. Do not underestimate how brave and difficult it will be for some survivors to surrender to this transformation. Survivors more than most benefit from accepting that they are God's very own handiwork. Our work is to keep finding ways to say that He never makes junk. Here is the beginning to build up from zero.

Abandoned

Almost every survivor needs to work through very difficult feelings toward their mother and their father for the failure to protect them. Some parents were unaware, having been groomed as expertly by the abuser as the victim was. Other parents were willfully ignorant or complicit. The possibilities run a full and very troubling gamut. The same is true for other adults, such as aunts, uncles, teachers, or coaches, who might have known to intervene. Sorting through the snarl of adult victims and enablers is a first step in grappling with how abandoned child victims have been.

The memory of being abandoned is palpable. So, when we finally trust someone, we cling without even knowing we do. Or, we cling and know we cannot yet open our grasp to let go. Along the way we just never had a chance to learn that only in broken relationships do extremes like abandonment and clinging appear. The finer balance between needing and letting go is something we can only develop as we recover from trauma.

My faith survived, in significant part, because something in me believed that God would suffice where people would always fall short. This conviction managed to survive the perversion of faith my abusers used for access to me, yet I still felt abandoned by God. Resolving this contradiction took years and was very much part of my own recovery.

In one of his writings, St. Francis de Sales describes a father and his young daughter walking in a beautiful garden on a warm and sunny spring day. The father holds his daughter's hand as she skips happily along, stopping from time to time to pick a flower or to grasp at a passing butterfly. Never during their stroll does she let go of her father's hand, nor does he hers. Their clasped hands represent the careful and protective vigilance of the father for his daughter's safety. His quiet presence permits her to delight in the simple joys and wonders of a child at play.

That beautiful scene came to mind as I read the above description. It is just one example of the feelings of abandonment experienced by survivors of abuse. For some reason or other, those adults who ought never to have let go of their child's hands did so. Those they had counted on for protection and security were not there when they needed them most. In truth, child victims were abandoned.

At times, when survivors finally gain the courage to trust again, they may tend to overcompensate for the still acute feelings of their childhood abandonment. This tendency may be a passing phase or a personal habit. For one example, they may cling, becoming at times overly dependent. We would not expect the child in the above story to feel the need to always hold onto her father's hand. Indeed, part of the maturation process is to let go of his hand and to try one's own wings. From a sense of security holding the father's hand, the child in the end is secure enough to leave the parental nest altogether. It's not hard to see how losing this sense of security too young can make independence hard later in life. Recovery for survivors is in some ways about a transition during which some survivors have a great need to depend on someone. Here, a mix of trusted friends, therapist and spiritual guide can provide a safety net.

Alternatively, some survivors have managed to grapple with the abuse and their childhood circumstance by being exceptionally independent. They won't cling, and they won't need you—or perhaps let themselves need you. These survivors have learned the lesson of abandonment differently, and their recovery will involve unlearning that independence. For these people, you will find yourself needing to be constant and reliable so they can test the waters of depending on someone, while they learn with you that to depend on God is failsafe.

It is important to remember, thinking of the little girl holding her father's hand, that at the moment of violation the natural development in a young life is interrupted. Some children stop maturing. Others grow old and mature far too fast. What is needed by the adult survivor in your care is a path forward from that dark turning point. What they need is a safe and supportive environment in which to resume growing. They may have matured and be highly functioning adults on the outside; we are talking about the pain and turmoil they endure privately that must be resolved—in therapy and in spiritual terms as well. Therapy and spiritual guidance play different roles but can work in concert to support that growth, even celebrate it as a parent might. In this way, spiritual guidance has moments of great shared delight.

As part of the safety net that helps a survivor grow beyond the wounds of abuse, you need to encourage acts of independence that are not also acts of isolation. Only by listening can you understand what the challenge is for each person. Each little victory is a step forward to be celebrated, because for many who have survived abuse the joy ended when the abuse occurred. At one time in life, growth led to exposure—and abuse. At this time in life, growth can lead to spiritual joy. In time, perhaps some survivors will venture farther than they even imagined, like the little child in the story, now free to let go and run after their own passing butterflies.

The story of the father and child raises the thorny issue of what may be ambivalent feelings regarding God in the adult survivor. Feelings of being abandoned by God will recur for many survivors. Many of them have had to grapple long and hard with the painful question of God's apparent absence during the abuse: even *He* failed to protect them. This process of depending on, and then letting go of, a spiritual guide in small steps is one way many survivors experience God as the only reliable constant in their lives. Their faith is maturing. Because God is their one sure and certain anchor, the spiritual guide can help them to rely on Him more consistently and, in doing so, to cling less to others who are fallible.

It bears repeating that the spiritual guidance for an adult survivor is often about helping an "inner child" grow into the adult that he or she could not become because of the lasting impact of the abuse. One painful reality survivors grapple with is that, after the abuse, they are changed as children—and as adults. They will never know who they might have been had they not been abused; this is a death they must grieve in therapy and in faith. In therapy and in spiritual guidance, some ritual of grief, of letting go, of laying to rest that which is gone is very healing.

Yet, with that, there is something more. With God's grace and close care, survivors are able to find the adult they can now be, and that person I know from firsthand experience is someone whole and remarkable. As we help grace build on their nature, we must be ever aware that nature itself at times must first be healed and made whole in order for grace to build more surely upon it. There is grieving to be done. There are things like having been abandoned that one simply must accept and feel and then let go. Only then can grace work with this wonderful person to help perfect their nature and reveal God's image to the world in them.

Rage

Outrage is a right moral response to evil, and it has a place in recovery, but the rage of survivors is not limited to outrage. One of the most powerful emotions we experience is rage. It may have started during the abuse and never stopped. It may have lain dormant inside a frozen grief to be unleashed suddenly out of nowhere. It may be the core of our depression or self-harming behavior.

Anger has many faces. It can be a hair-trigger temper, or fits of rage, or chronic impatience, or a critical personality. In that sense, anger is reassuring, because it keeps the risk of further abuse at bay. It can have some self-protective power in the way we, as adults, now do for ourselves what adults failed to do for us as children. The other side of that coin is that rage isolates us.

Anger can be creative too. It heightens our awareness, in contrast to the numb state into which many of us sank after being abused. Its power propels us through the difficult changes and separations needed for recovery. It can even energize our flagging will to live.

So, anger is a gift as well as a liability. Either way, it requires choices. Just because we have been harmed by others, does not mean we have no other choice but to harm others with our anger. We get to choose whether anger will be a feeling, which ebbs and flows, or a lasting identity.

Anger requires its own time to burn out like a great fire, but it also requires our choice not to give it more fuel if we want to cultivate lives free from the destructive impact of abusers in our past.

By temperament St. Francis de Sales was naturally hot-tempered and fiery. But at some point he made a profound commitment to "live Jesus" and to minister to others in imitation of the one who once described himself as "meek and humble of heart."[14] St. Francis chose to change, much like survivors have chosen to recover from abuse. Much work follows that choice.

St. Francis worked hard and long at cultivating the preeminent virtues of Jesus, succeeding so well that today he is commonly known as the "gentleman saint." Among the most comforting words of Francis are these: "The saints once were what we are now." It took their full, free, and generous cooperation with grace for saints to leave behind home and family, status and sin, to follow the gentle, compassionate, and forgiving Jesus. It will take grace for survivors to follow their path to change, too. With grace the sometimes violent rage and justifiable anger of survivors can subside or be lifted from them. The spiritual guide walks that path and comes to know this anger. Over time, survivors can find ways to channel their anger in productive, even creative, ways such as exercise or artistry, community service or personal transformation. Taking steps to follow Jesus daily helps fortify survivors in their efforts to change.

How does "following Jesus daily" actually happen in practice? St. Francis de Sales was the eldest of many children. He saw that his siblings learned how to speak by imitating the sounds, words, and speech pattern of their parents and others. Later as spiritual guide, he suggested that a similar practice would help

---

[14] Matthew 11:29

those he guided to learn how to imitate and live Jesus, gentle and humble of heart. Thus, he urged them to listen to how Jesus spoke and to observe how he acted by prayerfully meditating upon his words and actions in Scripture and by imitating them in a concrete way in their own lives. In time, grace will gradually transform them into another Christ, that is, into someone whose words and actions increasingly echo those of Jesus: "The life I live now is not my own; Christ is living in me."[15] This transformation through imitation is the work of grace accomplished through prayer and practice.

A victim of abuse is often filled with both anger and rage. As suggested above, these are both a consequence of past abuse as well as a protective shield against future abuse. What happened once could happen again. Thus, survivors can be on their guard even with those who want to help them heal.

What is the spiritual guide's role, knowing that a survivor may be filled with anger while still desiring a closer relationship with Jesus? Begin by letting them be who they are at the moment. That is, let them be angry. "Don't be angry" is not the advice they need to hear. They may need just the opposite, that is, they may need to know that they can be angry and freely express their rage with you—and with God. Although their anger may be expressed in a way that suggests that you are "guilty by association," do not take it personally or react negatively. Once they know that you

---

[15] Galatians 2:20, as translated in the NAB, "... yet I live, no longer I, but Christ lives in me."

can handle their expressions of anger without distancing yourself from them and without expressing shock or dismay, the result may be a small opening for mutual trust and a comfort level that, with time, will hopefully develop and deepen. In the presence of unconditional and loving acceptance, a gentle and welcoming presence and an uncritical spirit, even rage and anger can begin to subside.

Always begin with where the survivor is. This is as true of a survivor who is angry as it is true of a survivor in any frame of mind. Provide them with a safe place to be exactly who they are. Then, gently, step by step, as you both come to know who this person is, you can also help discern virtues they may want to practice as part of a more healthful life. You and the survivor can trust that the Holy Spirit will help guide this process. Like St. Paul, we can take comfort even in our weaknesses for God's "power is made perfect in weakness" and grace, which is always sufficient, heals.[16]

Is there a saint whose story is particularly special to you, a story that can serve as a cornerstone in your ministry with victims of abuse? Sharing something about yourself can also foster comfort in survivors. You may want to spend some time in prayerful reflection on the biographies of saints in order to discover experiences in their lives that can relate to those of survivors. Did they, for instance, have to struggle long

---

[16] 2 Cor. 12:9, as found in the NAB: "Three times I begged the Lord about this, that it might leave me, but he said to me, 'My grace is sufficient for you, for power is made perfect in weakness.' I will rather boast most gladly of my weaknesses, in order that the power of Christ may dwell with me."

and hard to achieve balance and perspective after a traumatic youth? Were there evil people in their lives whose actions greatly harmed or even destroyed for a time their connections with God or Church?

Who is your saint? How can the story of that saint help you in your ministry with survivors of abuse? How can sharing the story of your saint with a survivor help reveal something of yourself, creating a safe-knowing, as you are helping them feel safely known and loved by God?

Depression

Unprotected from an abuser, abandoned by adults who should be our protectors, sacrificed by powerful leaders in the name of expedience, really, who wouldn't be depressed? There is something quite sane about depression.

We survivors emerge with some portion—small or large—of the many characteristics of depression. There is the chronic sadness and weeping, the churning anger, the impatience, the hopelessness, the disinterest in everything life offers, the cognitive dissonance, the insomnia and nightmares, and the sheer exhaustion from doing nothing at all.

We also can have manic energy at times—the sleeplessness, the exhilarating drive, the busyness, and that furious force of personal will—only to crash into darkness again.

Depression and other mood disorders can be treated with counseling, meditation, exercise, dietary and lifestyle changes, and also with medications. But all the sorrow isn't biochemical. After stabilizing with help from qualified professionals, we still need consciously and methodically to find ways to short circuit unproductive habits in thought.

Working with how we process our experiences, we are returning to the crayon box to select additional colors beyond charcoal and black. Many of us begin by dismissing the suggestion we pretend there are colors in the darkness. With time we realize it's a matter of opening ourselves to light, so we can see colors that were already there.

Depression can be passing or chronic but needs the care of qualified health care professionals. This good care, when it is respectful of the survivor's faith life, will help a spiritual guide serve a survivor's quest to regain or deepen connections with God, self, and others. Also, knowing a survivor is in good care frees the spiritual guide to practice the virtue of compassion which, at its root, means to suffer along with. That is, as long as someone with depression is getting the right medical care, you will be supporting their healing journey, not enabling them to resist care.

Survivors, indeed all people, who are sad or depressed sometimes need gentle companionship most of all. You may not know what to say or do, but you can listen to their stories or pray with them or just be silent together. Depression can baffle those who suffer from it, so not asking for explanations can be very helpful. This is possible only if you are sure appropriate medical care is tending to this state of pain.

According to St. Francis de Sales, next to sin itself the worst possible spiritual malady that can befall us is what he describes as spiritual sadness. It is very important to stress that, unlike sin, spiritual sadness is something that befalls us. It happens to us, in a way that abuse or other trauma does. In that sense, spiritual sadness is like being a victim. It is not something for which we are guilty. Some survivors are depressed in differing ways, but all survivors suffer from spiritual sadness. I would be hard put to find a better description of what St. Francis means by spiritual sadness than what is written above about depression. It is a heavy and almost physical weight that holds us down and keeps us back. Its opposite is spiritual joy. While psychotherapy must treat depression, spiritual guidance can offer ways a survivor might deal with its heavy sadness, especially relying on insights from St. Francis.

Naturally when we encounter someone weighed down by spiritual sadness we wish to impart spiritual joy. A survivor is seeking that relief, too. Yet, part of the role of the spiritual guide is to help clarify what is realistic. It may be that this person must feel the sadness rather than numb it with alcohol, drugs, or other self-abuse; once felt, the sadness can subside—or be let go of. But, also, it's worth exploring what relief there may be from spiritual sadness. Understanding that is an important way for faith to mature, for our connection to God to deepen. That is because Christian joy is not some giddy feeling of passing happiness or fleeting exuberance. It is the deep down conviction that God is love and that I am loved by God, even by name. Joy is the icing on the cake of my faith in who Jesus is and in what he has done for me. Thus, joy is not so much a feeling as it is a faith conviction. It can, therefore, co-exist with the sharpest pain and deepest sorrow, physical, relational, or spiritual. It can even co-exist with depression.

Christian joy is a dimension of the supernatural gift of love that, according to St. Paul, is poured into the heart of every believer through the gift of the Holy Spirit.[17] For St. Francis de Sales, the Holy Spirit and all of His spiritual gifts reside in the "high point" of our spirit, that place deep within us which is beyond every variable of feeling, emotion, or circumstance. It is possible, then, to be depressed and sad on every human level while still filled with spiritual joy. Faith alone can lay hold of this truth, but with faith the Holy Spirit can be very much at work in a survivor who is depressed. The idea that faith is not feeling is particularly important at times like these.

Another possible Salesian help with depression is the spiritual tool *couper court*, which in French means "to cut short." *Couper court* is useful in many circumstances. Survivors may be quite open to the idea, for depression is often treated in part with cognitive tools for managing depressed thoughts. *Couper court* is a similar, indeed a faith-based approach, which is taught by you but used by the survivor. Whenever, for instance, a survivor is experiencing depressive feelings

---

[17] Romans 5:5

or thoughts, they can practice cutting those feeling short by distracting thoughts in some creative way. If home alone at the time, the survivor may want to go outside to be distracted by nature or by people passing by. If the survivor is in bed, they may want to force themselves up just to take some action, such as playing music or walking the dog. Creativity is needed here, along with trial and error.

It's wise for you to pause, now and then, to remember that working with the Spirit is a creative act. Survivors often have very lively senses of creativity, which they used to endure trauma and its aftermath. Now, their creativity can be tapped to find new ways to think and live. Creativity can be put to service of God's will in their lives. Creativity can be a fount of spiritual joy even during dark days or dark periods. Your role is to encourage each survivor to discover what works individually. While creative and hopeful, this work can be very scary or daunting.

Depression may also make prayer seem hopeless. Prayer even when it is dry and sterile can bring with it a peace that the world does not know how to give. This peace is from God. Even if the survivor feels hopeless in prayer or in life does not mean God offers no hope. God is constant and creative; survivors in these dark times can rely on Him for what they do not have themselves. Try to remind survivors to pray in the desert and, with or without hope, to wait to be "surprised by joy."

NUMB

Mostly, I was numb. Day to day I had a lot of feelings, and some made no sense insofar as they did not match the circumstances. For example, I could be having a perfectly happy day, but my heart could be aching to the point of breaking. I could be in a setting my brain told me was perfectly safe, but my anxiety level could be through the roof.

Survivors whom I have known and loved used drugs, drinking, promiscuous sex, and other self-harming behaviors to stay numb. Our ability to connect feeling to event had been cross-circuited to defend from feeling what we had felt when the abuse occurred. How else could we, as children, handle feeling that matched the overpowering and life-destroying experience of abuse as a child?

What remained, in young adulthood, was grief which some wise people told me was frozen grief. It felt heavy, like an interior glacier. It had to break up before my feelings and intuitions and judgments could flow easily. Ever see an ice floe on a northern river starting to break up after a harsh winter? The ice screams before there are visible fissures, and then the noise and mess of the cracking ice floes begins.

Early recovery can be a lot like that. Frozen grief breaks open and lets spring return. There is a re-encounter with our youth on the other side, but it can be a very difficult and messy process in the meanwhile. It is good to have seasoned support people around.

Children victims of abuse are powerless to physically repel their abusers. Often all they can do to protect themselves is to distance themselves from the experience itself as well as from its painful and confusing memories. One way they do this by a sort of numbing inner encasement. When, as adults, this numbing technique is no longer able to keep the pain at bay, some adult survivors turn to such things as drugs, alcohol, promiscuity, isolating social behavior and unhealthy people. These remedies may work to maintain the numbing approach to some extent and for a while. But ultimately, this self-destructive behavior must be seen for what it is: a powerless antidote for a pain so deep that, although masked for a while, cannot be healed when numb.

Faced with the limited help numbing can offer, survivors, if they are lucky, come to the realization that they are powerlessness to heal the hurt they feel by measures that only tend to further demean or diminish their spirits. Then, as in AA programs, they finally turn to a "higher power." For survivors who may come to you for spiritual guidance, you likely represent in some way that Higher Power and as well as their hoped-for access to His assistance.

Don't be uncomfortable because their high expectations of you do not match your perceived or real limitations. Recall that God likes to work with the weak and the wobbly. This is true of the survivors, and it is true of you. Sometimes all they need to hear from you are such sound and consoling thoughts as the ones that follow. Try to help them see what you see: they are not their feelings, however strong, crazy or pressing their feelings may feel at the time. Indeed, feelings, whether they feel good or bad, are morally neutral anyway.

Your role is to reinforce what they will also be finding in programs that help them reject these unhealthy numbing agents. It is a sufficient feat to look only at one day's challenges and to trust that the Lord's help will be with them every step of the way. In keeping the challenge focused, they will hopefully turn step by step away from the unhealthy choices they have made, and reach more and more for the Lord and his healing grace. The more they rely on God, the more their feelings will correspond to their true state before God; that is they will begin to see themselves as they truly are: God's dear and beloved children, siblings of his Son and tabernacles of his Spirit —his handiwork and his heirs.

None of this self-awareness will come easily or quickly, especially to people who have managed to turn take the need to feel numb further into chemical dependencies or other self-destructive behaviors. There will be immediate needs to manage compulsions and intense feelings that erupt when the numbing agents are removed. Yet, you can be present without enabling. You can come to understand, by listening, their program for recovery. This includes understanding how people may and do, while in recovery and guidance, turn on occasion to unhealthy but familiar fixes, some more dangerous than others. Sometimes, there is backsliding, especially when old memories or feelings are triggered. At those times, gently encourage them, with God's grace, to take all the right steps to resume their recovery program, or their therapy, and try again.

Success in the spiritual life lies in our willingness to keep struggling for it. It's important to remind survivors, again and again, of the merciful Father in the parable of the prodigal son. The Father welcomes them with joy, no matter how far away they may have distanced themselves from him or how often they may have turned to things and persons less than him. This is an important message, most easily heard if you deliver it in an unhurried manner, crafting your guidance always to match their pace.

Self-Wounding & Suicidal Thoughts

Seldom did anyone assure any one of us that the abuse had ended. Very, very few of us ever were sure that it was over. At any moment, the other shoe could drop. Even if the abuser moved away, we knew too well how relentless the abuser was. Distance was no assurance that that danger was over. There would be no sense of security again.

After abuse ends, pain doesn't end. For all of us, there is a psychic pain, an emotional pain, which we had to manage most commonly alone and with the skills of a child. A few of us eventually told someone. Many of us just removed it from our sight, sealing it up away from our daily lives. And we moved on.

But the truth seeps out. One way it does is that we pick up where the abuser left off, inflicting wounds on ourselves. We may repeatedly choose harmful people to trust. We may use drugs to numb feelings that won't stay locked away; it's possible to tolerate the physical damage because the threshold for what we can bear has been so terribly compromised by experiencing abuse.

Some of us self-mutilate, picking up where the abuser left off. Or, we may be tempted to suicide, aching for fast relief and willing to finish the abuser's work, which murdered childhood and even our whole, full personhood.

The wounds of Christ are quite different. There is no comparison. His wounds were a conscious choice made in free will. Our wounds are what His wounds are meant to save us from. What the two have in common is innocence hated by evil.

The wrong choice in people, a turn to drugs, self-mutilation, thoughts or actual attempts at suicide—these are among the ways that survivors of abuse engage at times in self-wounding. For the spiritual guide, the question is how to work with someone struggling against the very dangerous impulse for very real self-harm.

Usually by the time survivors seek spiritual guidance, they are already dealing with active self-wounding thoughts or activities with qualified professionals. If they are not, however, getting help for this problem must be a priority. Spiritual progress during a crisis and danger is not sound or safe.

You need good references, just in case. A good spiritual guide will have a list of trusted people and numbers prepared. One of those numbers should be the diocesan Victims Assistance Coordinator, who will be accustomed to respecting the confidentiality of your work as a spiritual guide but who can also offer recommendations. If the survivor will not call, if the family will not call, you should consider the Victim Assistance Coordinator as a resource for you. Our diocese has a long and varied list of therapists whom other survivors have found helpful. Yours may as well, or your local Catholic Charities may have suggestions. You certainly want contact information for suicide hotlines and information numbers for addiction programs. What is very important is that neither you nor the person seeking your care mistakes spiritual guidance for qualified therapy. Without experts to confront manifestations of self-wounding activity, spiritual guidance might inadvertently enable the abuse. As a spiritual guide, you understand that your gifts lie elsewhere.

Yet, spiritual assistance for survivors who have actively self-wounded but are now in therapy may be especially helpful. Self-harm is linked to self-loathing in many cases. If you are prepared to be gentle and low-key enough with the message, there is much to offer one who still does not yet have an appreciation of their goodness, beauty, and worth in God's eyes. To the abuser the child was an object, something to be used. Abuse is de-humanizing. It may be for some survivors that, as a safety measure, self-wounding behavior mars beauty or appeal in some way, thus making them less desirable to any potential new abuser. Or, it permits others to release a depth of agony or to be distracted from the same. For too many it becomes a kind of habit or compulsion with no conscious reason left. In this and other troubling ways, survivors seek to complete the destruction that their abusers began.

The Salesian adage, "Be who you are and be that well," is completed with the words, "so as to give glory to the Master Craftsman whose handiwork you are." If you can remind, gently, repeatedly, a survivor that they are indeed the very handiwork of God Himself (and that God never makes junk), you will be a voice of the Spirit in their lives, perhaps for the first time. In faith, survivors find a new lens through which to evaluate themselves, even as they sometimes are discovering in therapy that they must reject their low view of themselves. Where do they turn, but to God? When they do, they begin to see themselves as God sees them. Here is an irrefutable confirmation of their preciousness, a sense of which is too often lost in the humiliation of abuse.

In God, survivors come to value themselves as He does. They can leave the distorted self-lens behind. It can be replaced by another, a truer and better one—God's perfect 20/20 vision of his precious child. Created in the divine image, incorporated into the wounded but glorified body of Christ, and God's own handiwork: survivors can take these truths of the faith very personally, with prayer and time, not as argument but as revelation. Here is the truer and better lens. Each child victim was an object to his or her abuser, but each child victim and adult survivor has always been, and will always be, precious and irreplaceable to God.

Losses

So much has been lost from the trauma of child sexual abuse. We have lost a sense of security, of trust, of spontaneous play, of parents and family. We have lost our childhood and, technically, our virginity. We have often lost our faith tradition—even our connection with God. In turn, we have been lost by all the people who failed us. Feeling that failure acutely, sometimes universally, we assume in our abject loneliness that we have also been lost by God.

There is a treasure in a field. There is someone smart enough to do whatever it takes to claim the field and unbury the treasure. The treasure we unbury in recovery is our very self, born as God created us, free to choose goodness and life. There are survivors who, without knowing, are lost treasure, too, that God waits for others to find and welcome home.

―

"I once was lost, but now am found." That familiar line from the beautiful hymn "Amazing Grace" expresses the whole theology of salvation in the simple language of being lost and of being found. Because of our sin, we have become lost and, as lost, we are now powerless. We cannot find our way back to God without the help of God Himself. The Gospel is simply the good news that we who once were lost have now been found because of the grace and saving deed of Jesus.

How does the language of being lost and of being found speak to the situation of the abused? The abused is in no way the sinner in the matter of abuse; they are the victim of sin. Still, because of the sin of another against their innocence, survivors can be lost spiritually and emotionally. They can feel powerless. Practically speaking they really are powerless when they are mired in the pain and shame of an abuser's perfidy against them. They need the grace of Jesus, not to be free from sin but to be free from the unfreedom to which another's sin has bound them as children victims and, now, still, as adult survivors.

Lost and powerless, survivors come to spiritual guidance as a buried treasure. This treasure may be as deeply buried as their memories or emotions. It will not be a simple matter to unearth the treasure and bring it from the darkness of earth into the bright and healing light of recovery.

How does one begin to help in this process? Truth is freeing. Therefore the simple acknowledgment that one is lost, or parts of one are buried, is often the essential first step toward being found and unearthed. But that first step is often accompanied by the paralyzing feeling of powerlessness. That is, knowing that one is lost without yet being given the gift of being found can be anxiety-producing or deeply sad. The realization that one is a treasure buried beneath the heavy weight of abuse is often a source of grief before it is a source of joy. For all of us, however, that combination of truth and powerlessness wins grace for us. So, for the sufferer of abuse, a similar combination can win great graces.

To help the survivor recognize need for the grace of Jesus is a first step toward receiving it. Again, this is not the saving grace that frees the sinner. We are focused now on the healing grace that helps a victim to find what another has caused them to lose. This is the elevating grace that helps them to recover once again the deeply buried treasure that they have been all along, the treasure that needs only to be brought up from the earth for its beauty and dignity to be seen and celebrated and, once again, to be begin to be fully actualized.

All this is a first step, but an essential first step: being found by being unbound, and being unearthed through grace and raised up to the bright light of God's love. With grace, survivors are found, and we are often early witnesses to the full wonder of this beautiful person being unearthed.

Grief

Abuse involves death. Our childhood dies, for one thing. Pieces of our personality die. Dreams die. What might have been ... is gone. Our family, on some level, dies too. So much is lost. There is much we are left to grieve.

Then there is a muffled keening, a resistance to grieving at the threshold where the denial, anger, bargaining, and acceptance wait to be felt, endured, and laid to rest.

Grief will not be rushed. It has its own timing. Grief is not a step anyone can skip after something precious has been lost. It may be delayed because people force a child to repress the truth or because a child's psyche simply does not have the capacity to process trauma alone.

Grief is like a menacing hawk overhead. It casts a shadow fully over everything around at first pass, but slowly its circles grow wider and higher, its shadow gets smaller and passes less and less frequently. It may seem to have gone entirely, but at times a fleeting shadow can be glimpsed at the margins of what we see. Because we have known grief, we know what the shadow is, and we know it will pass.

Our lost childhood must be grieved. Our losses must be grieved. What might have been must be grieved. The shadow of grief must seem overwhelming before it can become a familiar, fleeting sorrow on the periphery of our recovered lives.

―――

The survivor of abuse mourns for what once was but is now forever gone and for what might have been but now will never be. The abuse harmed its victim's body, stole their innocence, and crippled their spirit. How could such a loss not be mourned? It remains the dark horizon against which the adult survivor now struggles to begin anew.

As suggested above, the hawk's dark shadow may diminish over time but it never completely disappears. Indeed, there are times when it suddenly shows up again, as dark and menacing as ever, triggered by some chance reminder or unconscious memory.

The first step in grief's healing is the mourning for what has died or, in the victim's case, for what has been stolen. The spiritual guide must be willing to give the survivor the opportunity, the space, and the time to grieve their loss. It cannot be rushed or hurried. Grieving has its own timing. It is, also, the beginning of recovery, and it remains a part of their recovery for a long time.

Whenever a loved one dies, there are many tears, even in those who believe in resurrection and new life. Grieving a death is as natural as celebrating a birth. Indeed, the lack of grief at a death or the lack of joy at a birth usually suggests something amiss in one's psychological or emotional development.

Maybe the adult victim has never been given the opportunity to grieve for their loss or to shed tears over what might have been—and for what now can never be. Perhaps they never permitted themselves to grieve fearing that it might be perceived as a weakness; for many survivors, to be weak is to invite further abuse. And, grieving for some is giving up control; it makes life seem out of control, and it's hard for survivors to believe that, once out of control, life can ever be restored.

Still, grief delayed must at some point be experienced, even when it occurs many years later. It may very well be that the survivor is able to work through their grief only in the safe and accepting place of spiritual guidance. The same spiritual tools that you may use to assist anybody grieving the loss of a loved one will be helpful: a ready ear, compassionate view, a consoling word, and the willingness just to sit and be with the one who mourns—the indispensable gift of a caring presence. Don't worry about what to say. At those times let heart speak to heart.

DEFENSIVENESS

When I brought a stray dog home after signing his adoption papers, he would quickly fall into a seizure whenever I raised my hand or stepped toward him too fast. This dog had been abused. The most ordinary action could catapult him into convulsions. Over several years, I worked patiently to de-sensitize him until he became quite a merry little pup. To do so, I learned to avoid any action that could trigger his terror, and I practiced a careful consistency in all I did.

When a soldier returns from battle, he or she often starts when a car backfires or a helicopter passes overhead. Triggers exist for children of trauma, too. For survivors of clergy abuse, triggers can be what Catholics hold most holy, such as a crucifix, or the smell of incense, or a Roman collar.

We survivors restore our relationship with the Catholic faith through a process of desensitizing ourselves to triggers that repel us from the experience of Catholicism—or of Christ Himself. It can be very slow work.

Like all recovery work, we need to create safety first. And, then, we begin to test the waters. Sometimes we need to rely on spiritual companionship to visit a church, or attend Mass, or say the rosary.

Whatever the triggers may be, the first step is to know how to recognize what triggers us about our faith and about God—and to gently let God help us evolve beyond these obstacles and closer to Him.

There are some things likely to trigger negative reactions or bring to the surface bad memories in adult survivors. Understanding that this experience is inevitable is helpful for the spiritual guide. But to know of triggers in the abstract is not the same as to know what will actually trigger the survivor you are guiding—or how they behave when a trigger releases emotions from the past. The awareness of triggers helps you to be on the lookout for sudden changes or unusual reactions. When they occur, it is important to depersonalize them and to slow the pace enough to ask and to tend to the feelings the survivor is having, even if that is praying quietly until feelings have subsided.

What do you do when this happens? Try not to react in a manner that signals dismay or concern. This could cause the survivor to shut down completely. Your reactions will sometimes be read from a point of shame, particularly when a survivor is vulnerable or shaken by triggers. Rather, calmly suggest that something seems different all of a sudden. Do they want to talk about it? Do they think something might have been a trigger? Would they like to take a break or simply be quiet for a moment?

To the extent that they are willing to talk about the trigger or the memory it has reawakened, you may gain valuable insights into what may make this moment an opportunity to bring God into the pain. Perhaps, too, there is a scripture reading or prayer or practice that might be helpful for this trigger. These are uncharted waters, and there is no clear guidebook as to how to proceed. You follow the survivor. Only they can lead, but you both walk together behind the

Lord at times like these. You may see only His back, but He knows where you need to go and how to get you there. Are you able simply to let the Spirit lead, following a close step behind, convinced that He is always the real Guide anyway?

A practice that I find helpful when I am not sure how to handle what I am hearing or what is taking place is to say a quick, fervent, and silent prayer to God for help. Sharing this idea with the survivor at the right time can be helpful too. God never fails to come to our aid. Sometimes, these momentary upsets can be His gentle reminder that He is the Lord. When emotions or memories are triggered, even survivors can be surprised, especially if they are early in their recovery. Often they will sense a shift but not understand it. They, too, can learn to say a quick, fervent prayer to God for help. This is an exercise in trust. Having Him at the center of this struggle for healing is essential. After all, He is the best Friend of all.

Perversion

Child sexual abusers are, what most people call, perverts. Their compulsion to feed a perversion in their own complex of desires turned me, and others, into nothing more than a fix. Many of us agree that the harm—and the perversions—were not limited to the physical abuse. Indeed, many of us experienced the wrappings of the abuse to be a greater agony. Those wrappings were perversions.

Abusers perverted the role of trusted adult into that of a determined predator. They turned caring into molesting. They perverted the Roman collar or other trappings of sacred or secular authority into tools for access to us children. And, that was just the beginning.

Abusers turned concepts of holiness into dangerous perversions. We, who were taught obedience to God, learned from abusers "surrender" meant annihilation, physically or emotionally. We who were humble children were taught humiliation. And, we were the ones who suffered the disastrous effects of predators manipulating forgiveness into the travesty of enabling.

Recovery is a process of unlearning the predator's perverted view of us and the world. We work to sort through the false from the true lessons of childhood. We work to set aside lessons we took for granted and consciously to seek what is good and whole. Recovery can be a lot like a living, growing faith.

This process of discovery reveals all the perversions. They are not limited to the degradation of our bodies. We, who were taught to be powerless, find the power to believe we are more than a fix. We can go further, with courage, to discover we are each a child of God, treasured by God.

"Recovery is a process of unlearning …." Up to the time children were sexually abused, they had a very different view of life than was theirs after their abuse. Like all children, they had once simply accepted life as it was represented to them by parents, teachers, priests, and relatives. In many cases, caring adults surrounding them before abuse may have tried their best to protect them from the harsher sides of life. Where families were broken or troubled, still children had a sense of equilibrium, some sense of boundary, and certainly no idea of what could have prepared them for the trauma of abuse. Children had a sense of the wondrous and magical. The perversion of abuse did not just tamper on the edges of a carefree and simple view of life; it totally shattered whatever sense of wellbeing a child had. It suddenly and harshly tore apart any idea of normal, breaking young and vulnerable hearts just as it harmed their little bodies. Abuse took away the joy of childhood and much of life that followed. Many survivors refer to abuse as having killed their childhood or their personalities, even their very selves.

Abused children had to quickly learn how to protect what little was left in them. The actions of one adult made them distrustful of most adults. They were cast adrift, on their own. One person in authority caused them to be wary of all authority. There was no power to stand up against the abuser. One representative of God and Church caused them to doubt the goodness and truth of both. Once carefree, open, and vulnerable, they quickly adapted to this dangerous world, learning to become wary, to hide from affectionate overtures which might lead to abuse, and to shut down emotionally as a way to survive the too-great pain. Growth on all levels was arrested.

"Recovery is a process of unlearning …." Abuse is a wound that harms all levels of each person, yet each person's wounds vary, as does how survivors adapt to the trauma. Backgrounds vary, personalities vary, and abuse varies. All these factors, along with many others, lead to the simple fact that each survivor is uniquely wounded and has unique needs. Their healing journey will be highly personal. For this reason, a mixture of help must offer a range of ways that each person can use to slowly make progress in healing through unlearning. Through training, experience, and compassion, the therapist, for example, will help survivors look at memories and behaviors in such a way as to free their present from past harm, sorting out the wrong lessons from a better way of being. But, how this is done varies greatly from survivor to survivor. Some survivors need to delve into the detail of the past; others describe needing to do so only to a certain point.

Similarly, the spiritual guide helps them become open to God's empowering grace and to become the persons they were always meant to be—with a clear sense that this person is unique in God's eyes. The impact of the ravages of abuse is unique, too. What survivors learn, even about their abuse, will lead them back always to a distinct and unique connection with God. It's your job to help focus on that wondrous truth, which even the trauma of abuse cannot break. With the Holy Spirit at work between you, you can point out the courage, creativity, and resilience in the wounded child who carried on despite such enormous burdens! You can offer the image of this person, in God's eyes, as a reflection to hearten them, for they have likely seen only the reflection of abuse in themselves. Thus, the work to help survivors unlearn is sometimes about helping them see themselves through God's eyes.

Another contribution the spiritual guide can offer to this "unlearning" process is the Salesian approach to "detachment." In the pursuit of a deeper and more loving relationship with God, which is the goal of spiritual guidance, the one being guided is assisted in giving up any sin, imperfection, character defect, circumstance, or relationship that prevents or hinders growth in one's principal relationship with God. For survivors, some things from which they may detach are faulty judgments of themselves as "bad" or self-destructive behaviors.

Detachment is a life-long process, because our relationship with God can always grow and deepen. The process of detachment has a flip side in the practices of virtue, prayer, and the sacramental life of the Church. For St. Francis, as we detach from whatever distances us from God, we attach to these holy and grace-filled options that draw us closer to Him. As we become more and more attached to God, that is, as we fall ever more deeply in love with Him, then our process of detaching is less a strain and more a gain (to use a term for a different kind of exercise). Indeed, we don't so much let go of some things as they drop away from us, one by one.

So, the way St. Francis de Sales helped those under his spiritual care to fall in love with God was by encouraging them not to focus on detachment as much as giving priority to those spiritual practices that foster loving union with Him. This approach can be very supportive for survivors in therapy trying to change, to let go of the painful past, and to move past unhealthy defenses into a fuller and happier life. For this, St. Francis's focus on teaching those we guide how to pray, especially how to meditate, is very important. Reliance on the sacraments, especially the Eucharist, which St. Francis calls "the sun of all spiritual exercises," is a way to fulfillment in all of life. Both prayer and the sacraments are actual experiences of loving union with God. Their grace is transforming. They change people from within and gradually remake people into another Christ.

Yet, the spiritual guide must be very sensitive to the pain in a survivor's background. For example, the setting for Eucharist and even the experience of prayer can be affected by abuse. Some of the most safe and holy experiences for others may have been perverted by abusers to harm the child. Therefore, as spiritual guide, you need to understand what is safe—and, more importantly at first, what is not safe—before you begin to teach a survivor ways to enrich life with prayer. You need to understand if there are triggers to overcome before exploring ways for the Eucharist and other sacraments to be more central to a life in the process of healing. As you listen, the survivor is already letting go by sharing. As you encourage, you are already helping survivors let God speak directly to their hearts. Through the power of his grace He will gradually transform them from within into another Christ. One after the other, the hard and harsh lessons from abuse in their past will begin to be replaced with new lessons that are true. In this process, God's grace is a gentle power that works within human freedom without in any way diminishing it.

Don't be discouraged if the very things you suggest to help become attached to God are triggers for pain. Of course we grieve with the survivor in our care for the lasting impact of abuse. If something is associated with a survivor's abuse, they will naturally recoil from the idea, for now, maybe for a lifetime. It may be you need to set some things aside for now, or forever. But if the survivor expresses a wish to try, you can also explore whether a friend might accompany the survivor to the Eucharist. Or, alone, a survivor can use a step-by-step way to grow less sensitized to a sacrament in which they really want to partake. Letting go of the memories associated with trauma is a really hard thing to do, but starting with a deepening connection to God provides an attachment that can make detaching from pain possible.

Delayed Responses

We survivors are like deep wells. You can drop a penny and not hear the water for a long time.

We react slowly for many different reasons. One reason is that many of us became estranged from our own feelings when the abuse happened. The way we survived was to shut down. By cutting ourselves off from the feelings, we almost erased what was happening. It was a clever defense. The problem is that we end up, later in life, not knowing how we feel.

Some of us were mortally confused when the abuser told us that what we experienced as horror was caring or love. The world around us had become dangerous and confusing, so many of us took five, or ten, or twenty steps deep inside. All that remained was a mask to interact with the world.

Living that deeply within, we are well-poised for the interior life of prayer, but we are not always ready if we are chronically shut down. Even on our best days, it can be quite a while before what is happening around us sinks in. Often, we must withdraw and reestablish our private safety before we can process even good and welcomed things.

As we recover, we do become freer. As our lives grow safer, we are not as measured. As our lives grow more open, we are not as hidden or restrained by the façade we needed to function. As our sense of self expands beyond that of victim, we are able to share much more, much more spontaneously.

Given the likelihood of delayed responses in survivors of abuse, the character of the conversational exchange with them will necessarily take on a different rhythm. It is important to accept this rhythm. It can become a very prayerful experience for you both.

The "deep well" image above is a good one. As the spiritual guide, you might ask a question or make a suggestion and then wait some time for a response. It will likely take a longer time than is usual for survivors just to take in what you say. There may be a pause to weigh its significance, formulate a response, search for otherwise unknown feelings, and then answer. As suggested above, often they feel the need to withdraw and reestablish their sense of private safety before they can even process what you've said. This is true for good and welcomed ideas as it is for any error you may make. Don't take their need for space personally. Instead, welcoming delayed reactions is one way you can offer compassion to survivors.

Your awareness of the value of the deep well and the need to withdraw for safety will help you appreciate pauses or delays in conversations generally. It will also help you practice a quiet, unhurried, and prayerful presence at all times, but especially while waiting for their response. Their word will come from a place that is deep within them and will likely have been spoken at the cost of considerable effort and energy. What survivors share from this depth in themselves can be quite remarkable. Be sure to listen with respect and gratitude.

Here is just one way you might help them feel more comfortable in their need at times to retire deep within in order to hear, assess, and respond. Their descent into the depths is in many ways comparable to the caves of the desert fathers and mothers. They went to those caves to be alone with the Alone, to be nourished upon God's Word, to struggle with demons and to be comforted by angels. They left those caves only at God's inspiration to speak an uplifting word to others. We have greatly benefited from the wisdom learned in those caves and then spoken to the world. Helping survivors see that the same can be true for them fosters not just a self-acceptance, but also a sense of self in light of God's will. Here, as spiritual guide, you will be similarly blessed for helping survivors, like the desert fathers and mothers, to see this habit they have as a withdrawal to spend time with the Alone and, together with Him, to struggle with their demons and their angels, to be comforted and, from there, to speak of their faith experiences to us.

Trust, mutuality, spontaneity, and comfort in disclosing one's inner self to another—none of this is likely to be easy for a survivor. The first few sessions might have as goal just trying to observe the depth of the well of this person, and how long it takes for the penny to hit the water. You may also face important growth as a spiritual guide. Can you be comfortable in waiting for God's timing, no matter how long it may take? Can you learn to measure success not so much by dramatic results, but by offering and maintaining a gentle, loving presence in which you respect the freedom and timing of the other just as much as God does?

WORRY

We worry. We worry a lot. Worry for some is another version of our constant vigilance—or illusion that we are on high alert, watchful to fight or flee any sign of the next instance of abuse. Worry has energy, which some of us mistake for power. Having known the depths of powerlessness, worry's illusion is comforting.

Worry is about fear, too. From the moment I was abused, I lived in a state of constant fear. Everything I knew before was destroyed in a moment. As I grappled with that reality, I turned to ways to figure out how to avoid or how to escape ... and so my fear moved into reasoning, moved into worry that only fed my anxiety. Yet, it proved useful, when I was a child.

Worry is a tough habit to kick. It was useful. Even now, it keeps us in our brains and distanced from our hearts. It picks up on real troubles, so there's the illusion it is accurate. One moment, we are reasoning out a solution to a problem and the next we are tumbling into a rabbit hole of anxiety. At its best, worry is reasoning without an off switch.

The problem is that we survivors have known really good reasons to worry, at a time when no one else was likely to have known enough to worry about our welfare. Part of recovery is moving out of worry into a place of faith. Another part of recovery is finding new ways to tend to our welfare that do not feed our anxieties.

―

"Worry is a tough habit to quit." To break a bad habit, one is encouraged to practice its opposite virtue. The opposite virtue of worry is trust. "God alone suffices," as St. Teresa of Avila wrote in prayer. As we know, trust is difficult for survivors of abuse.

Once survivors begin to trust God, that is, once they are able to satisfactorily resolve why God seemed "absent" during the abuse, then they have Someone in whom they can begin to trust, if partially or fitfully. Survivors may test God like they test us. Trust God to give them the joy of relief and assurance you, too, strive in human terms to offer. In this process, as spiritual guide, you will help survivors to make little acts of trust in God from which to learn. This offers Him opportunities to reveal His love and assurance to them. He can help them with venturing further, tiny test by tiny test, to "test" the trustworthiness of you, and others, and God, gradually, ever so slowly, dropping that worrying guard. This process may never be completed, but the progress toward deepening trust and less worry still changes lives.

As for worry itself, the following prayer of St. Francis de Sales has proved helpful to countless people over the course of more than four centuries. It may be helpful here as well:

> Do not worry about what might happen tomorrow: the same loving Father who takes care of you today will take care of you tomorrow and every day. Either He will shield you from suffering or He will give you unfailing strength to bear it. Be at peace, then, and put aside all anxious thoughts and imaginations.

This prayer may spark sadness or anger in a survivor. They will remember all too well how God did not shield them from abuse. As their grief or anger shows toward this or anything you discuss, remember to begin where they are—not where they may be, or you hope they may be. You may wish for their peace, indeed they do too, but honor the starting point, even with prayer, any prayer.

And remember how much harder it is to give up worrying and other defenses. It can feel like accepting risk for being abandoned again to such utter harm.

Your role, as spiritual guide, is not to debate these issues. Any intellect can agree with all the sound reasons that the abuse is over and cannot happen again. Your role is to grow yourself so you can speak heart to heart. Find, for this one person, some short prayer on hand, like the one above, with which to begin each session. A prayer that helps them open to the love of God without losing a sense of security—and without triggering pain.

I often invite, when possible, the person in spiritual guidance to pray aloud and in their own words. There are many reasons for this. Prayer reminds both of us that we have come together within the sacred space of a shared faith. Their prayer permits me a privileged access into their interior space where they meet God and speak heart to heart. Being permitted to "overhear" prayer often gives me a heads up as to the issues that they will likely bring out during our meeting. For what is on this person's heart is frequently the same subject matter for both prayer and spiritual guidance. Yet, for survivors, this may feel like an intrusion. You must use care as you find ways to help them reveal their hearts without causing anxiety.

Why do I bring this up? Each topic in this book has been suggested by Teresa, an actual survivor of abuse. Her reflections on these topics provide rare access into the unique perspectives and the many issues that both stem from the trauma of abuse and that have had a negative impact upon her adult life. For her to move through the successive stages of healing and recovery, that is, to go from victim to survivor to thriving adult, these issues must be successfully dealt with in some manner. Teresa's frank, clear, and often searing perspectives provide a welcomed assist. Spiritual guides begin to see how therapy intertwines with one's faith life, and for those who are not Catholic but are treating Catholic patients there is insight into the same, but from a different vantage point. What we all hear as we listen to this survivor's words is how abuse has taken her into what, for most of us, is unfamiliar terrain. That she is willing to describe the negative effects of her experiences provides a roadmap we can use to guide others out of the hell of abuse. Again, it is in our listening to those who have traveled the road we have not that we learn how best to help them deepen their relationship with God.

It might prove very helpful, especially in the early sessions of spiritual guidance, for you to invite the survivor in guidance to suggest the topic that they would like to deal with at that particular meeting. Such an approach gives you, the guide, a clear and sharper focus, one that is more likely to speak directly to this person's spiritual needs at this time. Another good way to let the survivor determine the beginning of spiritual guidance is to ask them to share their story to this point; you will find, as I have, they recount stories rich with faith that has often remained unheard and unknown until now.

Control

Being abused destroys any sense of security we had. What remains instead is a firsthand experience of how chaos and danger reign. This experience dominated formative years, whether we were very young or in our teens when we were abused. Chaos overrode our right to ascent as well as our ability to understand. More instinct than conclusion, our awareness was riveted on the power of predators.

This explains why small changes can feel like huge disruptions, which introduce vulnerabilities, which invite danger, and so we are terror-stricken by what seems unpredictable, even flexible. People say we have "control issues," but the term hardly scratches the surface of how much talent and energy of so many of us became entirely consumed in the single-minded enterprise of saving ourselves from predators and abuse. Efforts to control are really part of our efforts to restore a feeling of safety to memories that cannot be changed. As we feel safer in God's care, the need to control softens—and sometimes disappears.

The list of controlling characteristics is long and varied. Some of us are bossy, some are manipulative, some are confrontational, some are motivational, and some simply outrun everyone else. Underlying every one of us is the unthinking impulse to guard against all vulnerability and anything else that might open the door to abuse. The problem is that by guarding against pain, we shut out joy. By bolstering against vulnerability, we lock out others—and God.

The survivor's need to be in control makes them naturally resistant to the guidance of another, however gentle and low-keyed the approach. Their decision to enter spiritual guidance is, then, already a brave decision that probably comes at the end of a long and painful journey in which they first attempted to find all that they needed to survive within the security, the predictability, and, ultimately, the limitations of their own resources. To permit another to enter the "safe house" that they have spent many years constructing is an act of faith, not so much in the spiritual guide but in God in whose name the guidance is offered.

St. Francis de Sales relies completely on the care and guidance of divine Providence. In that same spirit, I am assured that the person before me has been sent by God, and I pray that they will eventually have a similar assurance about me. Belief in Providence makes all the difference. It is God, not chance, that has brought us together. His grace has matched my particular gifts with their particular needs.

Having this trust in God is critical. Survivors need a sense of control over their environment to feel safe, and sometimes, especially in moments of anxiety, they can seem quite controlling. It's good not to resist this, but rather offer more control. Perhaps you can let them choose between two rooms in which to meet, or choose among chairs, or make choices about what drink you might offer them. These courtesies are, of course, simple, but they help pace interactions to keep them from moving too fast for a survivor to feel safe. They also make sure the survivor feels they are in control of what is going on around them. These habits have been very helpful in our diocesan work.

In this and many other ways of consulting with survivors to help them feel heard in depth and even in details, we meet with faith and rely on the assistance of grace. We know that success—no matter how it is measured—will be God's handiwork, not mine, not theirs. This conviction is freeing. It lifts a heavy burden from my shoulders while giving them a great and comforting assurance. Whenever we meet, even when a day or a certain period of time feels out of control for the survivor, there are always three present: the guide, the one being guided, and the true Guide. He will help them be safe, as they relinquish control not to us but to Him.

In this way, faith in God's providence and presence will, in time, lessen the survivor's need to control and increase their ability to trust. With that, an important foundation for progress in spiritual growth has been laid.

Habits & Obsessions

Keeping busy is a good way to avoid other things, for anyone. The bigger the elephant in the room, the busier we need to pedal to keep the admission at bay. Survivors lived with an elephant in the middle of their world when they were enduring abuse. Many have endured the silence that covers the crime ever since. The abuse was the secret everyone danced around to avoid. A single hint that the truth could emerge simply shifted into a higher gear whatever avoidance defenses were already furiously keeping the secret under wraps. Raised in this high-stakes energy, with a bleeding psychic wound to avoid ... we can be very busy with the tools we were handed to use as a way to ignore our own truths.

And, later, as we grow, our lives can be cluttered with situational crises or crazy-making people. Habits and activities can become our single-minded focus. Many of these situations, people, habits, and activities are not detrimental in themselves. It is our focus on them that leads to imbalance. Our lives are out of balance as we ignore a whole swath of feelings and truths.

Early in my own recovery, I found it unforgettably fascinating that I was struggling with habits that were the main force of resistance to my own healing, whereas the habit of the religious people I encountered in New York City were a sign of surrender, identity, and peace.

The world is too much with us; late and soon,
Getting and spending, we lay waste our powers;
Little we see in Nature that is ours;
We have given our hearts away, a sordid boon!

These first lines from the poet William Wordsworth come to mind as I read what is written above. In the poem, Wordsworth laments the fact that the busyness of the world prevents us from seeing and enjoying nature's beauty around us. One can only imagine how he might assess today's world with its frantic pace and cacophony of noises. Yet, in this noisy and distracted world, survivors are seeking a safe place to be heard and understood. They are seeking a deeper bond with God.

We may all learn from many saints and mystics who used to practice a quieting and an inner calming so as to be better prepared to hear God's voice in prayer. This permitted them to enjoy His presence in daily life. Isn't this what we are helping survivors to do? The scriptural incident frequently cited in support of this quieting is the story of God's appearance to Elijah on the mountain. The Lord did not appear to the prophet, as one might have expected, in the mighty wind or in the powerful earthquake or in the roaring fire but in "a still small voice … in the sound of sheer silence."[18] Survivors, especially at certain points in their recovery, are feeling metaphorically the earth quaking under their feet, and are feeling almost overcome by winds and burning pain and memories, but in these we are helping them discern God's voice, speaking to them, always of love.

One of the common themes in most spiritual guidance is helping people to slow down and achieve a calming silence in a sacred space. In sacred space encountering with the Holy can occur sometimes more easily. Much effort is expended on planning strategies and forming habits to acquire that sacred space. Finding sacred space is difficult enough for most people. Yet, finding it is exponentially more difficult for survivors of abuse. They learned early on that by keeping busy, very busy, they could, for a while at least, hold "the elephant at bay." Keeping busy lessened the ache; keeping very busy helped them to forget, for a time at least, the pain

---

[18] 1 Kings 19:12, from *New Revised Standard Version Bible: Catholic Edition.* Copyright © 1989, 1993 the Division of Christian Education of the National Council of the Churches of Christ in the United States of America. Used by permission. All rights reserved. This same verse, as translated in NAB, reads "a light silent sound."

altogether. Keeping busy was a hedge against how unsafe "sacred space" can feel for survivors of abuse. And, sacred space for those abused by clergy has become unsafe space.

You must understand you are helping survivors who most likely understand, intellectually, the value of mentally and physically and psychically slowing down. What you both face is their childhood lesson that slowing down could also mean becoming available for harm. Or, as adults, slowing down invites painful ache and disturbing memories to surface. Elijah's experience of finding God in "the still small voice" is at best counter-intuitive for most of us. It may have no meaning, or be frightening, for a survivor of abuse. It may be quite impossible, and it may be harmful for you to push for any kind of slowing down until other issues are managed.

Yet, survivors do want to slow down. When they are ready, or when it is the right time for just an "imaginative exercise" that requires no change at all, you might share the image of the "cloistered heart." It's the approach of a Salesian group of lay people whose lives are still very busy. They are totally immersed in the many different marketplaces of the modern world, places from which they cannot physically remove themselves. What they do is keep their hearts cloistered. That is, they commit to keeping their hearts quieted, stilled, and hidden, even in midst of the busiest of days, surrounded by the peoples, noises, and distractions of their many worlds of family, work, and play. This takes a certain mindfulness and an ability to pray with confidence in very brief instances. Yet, it is within the quiet stillness of their own hearts, despite the noise all around, that they meet God and converse with Him. For survivors who have often created rich, interior, and hidden lives, away from dysfunctional settings, the idea of the cloistered heart may be familiar. This may already have prepared them for this next step along their faith journey.

In small and incremental steps, the spiritual guide can help the survivor construct rooms for own their cloistered heart. At the same time a survivor is tearing down walls by which they have kept people out of their lives, they may find having a private, safe space set away with God especially important. Rooms can be imagined places for prayer, for laughter with God, for remembering safely. There, at least, they can find a place safe enough to work through, in the presence of God, the memories and pain of the past. Surrounded by God's protective grace, survivors can face any obstacle that arises in their recovery from abuse.

Boundaries

Abuse is a violation. It destroys the integrity of our personal space, often before we have even gained a sense of what that space is. As a result, confusion about setting boundaries, which are needed in a healthful adult life, is a challenge. With some good effect, we move away from the toxic setting, or we stop visiting, or we visit very infrequently. We don't return calls, or we cut off all contact. As we recover, however, the real boundaries need to be set from the inside, regardless of how we ultimately must deal with the panoply of characters in our abuse stories.

Those stories are about how we were denied a sense of privacy. Despite all the secrets that hide the truth from the outside world, our own sense of personal boundaries was trampled. It is a sense that can be very hard to reestablish. It can be difficult to discover now what we were too young to know very well when it was stolen from us.

Setting boundaries is not second nature for many survivors. Without a clear sense of limits, it's hard to know who we are, and what we need for wellbeing. With that blind spot, it's hard to know when someone is supporting or undermining us. The responsibility for creating safe places is vexing.

———

During abuse, a victim's personal space is severely violated, destroying not only whatever early boundaries they may have managed to establish in early life but also almost guaranteeing that issues of adult boundaries will persist for years to come. Boundaries once broached in so violent a manner are, paradoxically, either now drawn very tightly in or are given a very wide breadth. Thus, one either almost completely shuts out the world or, at times, has no defined boundaries as an adult, resulting in the inadvertent habit of riding roughshod over the personal boundaries of others. Most commonly, survivors will have both these struggles in different areas of life and to different degrees. What matters is that, for some, this inability to balance openness with safety is part of their recovery process. This is the antidote to being terribly isolated or overly exposed to hurt.

The idea of boundaries has been discussed several places in this book, because boundaries were what the abuser first violated and because boundaries are in some way—and that way varies greatly among survivors—a key in the recovery process. So, they will also be front and center in spiritual work.

As spiritual guide, you ought to avoid two things regarding boundaries. First, do not be put off if your own boundaries are at times suddenly broached by a victim who has not yet had the opportunity to master this art. Do not personalize this error, but also do not encourage or reward the error either. Your ability to maintain professional boundaries is a way to maintain safety in the setting and also to offer one role model for how to express and maintain boundaries.

Second, take care not to breech in any way the boundaries of a survivor. Some survivors will be very protective of their own space. Keep in mind those boundaries were once cruelly trampled upon. Other survivors may seem unaware of their own boundaries, emotionally or in any other way. Part of recovery is rediscovering boundaries, and your ability to anticipate at least basic boundaries of respect and professionalism help this person learn—and feel affirmed as new boundaries are developed.

No matter how meticulous you may be in setting the tone of respect and sensitivity, you may find yourself surprised from time to time when suddenly a protective wall is thrown up where, just moments ago, there was a friendly fence or even a welcoming overture in a discussion. What likely has happened is that something has triggered memories and made this brave person before you feel unsafe. Again, don't personalize their response, but do examine your own behavior. Your relationship may have even advanced enough to ask simply what may have made them react. Our best teachers are, in the end, the survivors telling their truth.

A last thought on boundaries is that, in the course of spiritual guidance, examples may surface of incidents in which survivors over-step the boundaries of others. These can be teachable moments, giving you the opportunity to help them see that they have over-stepped and to suggest ways that, given similar situations in the future, they might act in a manner that will honor those boundaries. Very often survivors who are growing in this area simply need a safe place to observe and learn from their errors, yet they can be overcome by the shame that comes from abuse but asserts every mistake they make is cataclysmic. It either proves along with the abuse the worst about them, or it shakes up a fragile sense of safety which they doubted they deserved anyway. So, an error can paralyze some who have endured abuse. Simply affirming their inherent goodness and the mercy of a God who understands they are learning permits these survivors to rely on God to change without feeling fundamentally damaged. Obviously, this sort of exchange presupposes a comfortable trust level between the two of you. That takes time, but it is worth the effort to contribute to this person's recovery from the ravages of abuse. Pray that happens, with time and God's help.

Relationships

Recovery sorts through memories, and it also sorts identity out of the cringe of abuse. We are not our pain. We are not what happened to us. It can take a long time to connect that truth with how we feel about ourselves.

Recovery also asks us, all along the way, to look at our relationships. Which ones support our true self? Which ones have we outgrown? Which ones cause wounds all over again? This is particularly difficult work, especially because we seek, like anyone, love and approval from our relationships.

Along the way we face how all relationships—past, present, and future—fall short. There are people in our past to forgive for these shortfalls, and people in our present to accept for their flaws. Life becomes a patchwork of people who are suited to help us in some ways, but no one is able to suit us in all ways.

When someone falls short, the disappointment can trigger all the shortfalls of our past. That is true for anyone who is learning how to accept people on their own terms. For survivors, that can reawaken many deep feelings, like the terror of abandonment and the grief of an unsafe child.

Yet, how to believe God will not fail us, when the abuse lingers as a tempting example of how He didn't care enough to save us in the first place?

Human beings are social beings. We are created that way. Therefore, in many ways we are our relationships. Indeed, Christian faith tells us that, from the very beginning, we are created in the image and likeness of One God who is nevertheless a community of three Persons. Thus, to be in relationships, first with our triune God, and then with others is what, ultimately, makes us *who* we are. And the quality of those relationships affects *how* we are as individuals, for better or for worse. Relationships with others that give God a place help us in our path.

Sometimes, however, relationships are perverted by people who are bad, even evil. This is certainly the case in the abuse of children. As children, the victims have no control, indeed no concept, in creating the relationships they find themselves in. When a sexually abusive relationship takes place before the child has had the opportunity to become the person they were meant to be, future relationships are likely to be seriously short-circuited. This is not to say survivors do not have strong marriages or otherwise deep friendships at all. Some do, some do not. However, all face the need to overcome the lasting impact of relationships perverted by abusers and broken by those who failed to protect the child.

As is brought out above, a survivor's relational life may be damaged and fractured in different ways. Some survivors carry their pain into new relationships which end up wounded because of their own brokenness. Often survivors seek relationships that are unhealthy or potentially dangerous. They can even resemble the abusive or abandonment relationships of the child victim. While even healthy people disappoint each other through human weakness, for survivors in healthy relationships these can trigger memories of abandonment or insecurity. For survivors, this natural shortfall can feel devastating. For all survivors with their many different relationships—some even with the people from their childhood who failed them—it's important to remember there will be a range of wellbeing. Some will be dependable and good, others may be quite troubling or dangerous. Helping the survivor know how to sort out the melee is their relationship with God, who reveals in Himself what kind of relationships He wants for his loved one.

To start, spiritual guidance is built upon relationships of mutuality, respect, and trust. Given the often-fractured relational background of a survivor, it will take much time, patience, and practice to establish a solid and comfortable footing in those areas. Survivors often expect hurt or disappointment in relationships. They may look for even minor mistakes as proof, and they may not even divulge their conclusion you have proven them right. So, for your part, only patient fidelity to a spiritual relationship with them will, over time, reassure them and provide added support to the groundwork this person needs as they courageously build new and healthy relationships with others. Be patient. No matter how hard it may be to wait for glimmers of trust, it is far more difficult and more courageous for them.

Given His apparent absence during the abuse, each survivor's principal relationship with God will need healing, too. This is a good starting point. It is the very important personal side of the theodicy issue: why did He let evil happen to me, abandon me, if He is all-powerful, if He is all-loving? This is work to which the guide and the survivor are likely to return to again and again. Be prepared with insights, practices, biblical readings, and prayers that direct that issue in a positive and satisfying direction. Yet, the dialogue in spiritual guidance for a survivor isn't a debate. If you find yourself moving away from a heart-to-heart bond you should take care: one or both of you may be avoiding the pain of the questions about God or the memories of such horror. This is why listening comes before offering insights, suggestions, and even prayers. Scripture and its inspiring stories come after this survivor's story. The many answers man has devised for the theodicy question are always, ultimately, tested not in the mind but in the heart, where God resides.

Even as a survivor finds some peace with God, they are likely to have a recurring sense of abandonment. It may not return in full force, but it often returns as a question or doubt. Does God really love me? Is it possible He left me to suffer when I needed Him most? Here, faith is formed in a sense at the crucifixion. In Jesus, Innocence suffered a violent death by crucifixion. Before that, Jesus was rejected, betrayed, and denied, even by his disciples and friends. So many aspects of the crucifixion relate directly to what survivors suffered as children and later as adults. Is the crucifixion of his only Son somehow God's answer to the theodicy question? Surely redemption was possible without such suffering and pain?

In a sense, as a companion to someone grappling with this and other questions after having been abused as a child, you are witness to their crucifixion. A willingness to be present to a survivor means this does not happen entirely alone, and that experience bears witness to God's presence to the survivor at every moment of their lives—from childhood through now. For this, you are not called upon to explain or answer the theodicy question as much as to be a channel for God's presence as the survivor finds their own resolution. In time, survivors can learn the answer to that question in the same way that every believer has to come to resolve it in life: within a direct, loving relationship with God Himself. In this relationship, the heart grasps what the mind cannot.

Broken Bonds

Abuse breaks relationships. This begins when it ruptures a child's relationship with the abuser dramatically, because the abuser has been exaggerating the sense of safety and trust as part of the grooming process—only to turn vulnerability to his own advantage.

Abuse isolates victims from their caregivers. It creates estrangements through family systems just because very big secrets come between us. Abuse breaks bonds.

The estrangement is very real for victims, especially when they are still in the dangerous settings. But that sense of having nowhere safe to escape lasts for many of us all our lives. Knowing how to build safe spaces becomes part of recovery.

Our relationships with other people of faith are precarious as we explore a possible return to the faith of our childhood. While we intellectually may know people's missteps may inadvertently fail us, we are unable to switch off the high-alert warnings. For many of us, to return is to accept navigating between our anxiety over the past and our desire for homecoming.

―

"… To return is to accept navigating between our anxiety over the past and our desire for homecoming." It is important for the spiritual guide to know that for the survivor, the desire for you to be helpful is situated in that uncharted space between their anxiety over the past and their desire for homecoming. This is the bridge you are helping them to cross. It is a bridge neither of you really know, for it is different in every person.

What every survivor does know is that they do not want the past and they do desire homecoming. You have been invited into this quandary, so you are at the crossroads together. In the eyes of the survivor you may have a foot in both their past and in their future. This is particularly disorienting if the abuse was perpetrated by clergy and you are a priest. If, by vocation, you represent their abusive past, then survivors are likely to be anxious and wary of you, perhaps keeping you at bay. Can a helpful relationship be forged with such obstacles? Yes, because God is with you. For a survivor you are also likely to represent an important bridge to where they long to be, home again in faith and Church. Thus, at best, their attitude toward you may be ambivalent or vacillating. Survivors may not know from meeting to meeting how they feel about you. They may leave one meeting showing signs of trust, to return trusting less; you can assume that, while away, they were grappling with fear and doubt over trusting more. This is natural. It will be unsettling for both of you, but as long as you understand what it is, it does not need to be an impasse to an evolving bond.

Can you be comfortable living "in-between" in this way? It will be very helpful if you can. It will provide the "permission" for survivors to be who they are—and to feel whatever they may feel—at any given moment. They will be free to let go of the public face many cultivate to appear "normal" or to fit in. Survivors in recovery want very much to leave behind the fear, anxiety, and wariness of the past and finally return to a sense of safe home, including for many a return to God and for some the Church. All of this desire is a grace, and it is all on God's timing.

The pace for survivors is naturally slow, wisely so, as they take care to unlearn how unsafe all the world can be. So, no survivor knows when or how they will lose bonds with the past harm and forge connections with a whole future. Still, because of these profound desires for freedom and home, they will make their way, through fits and starts. Your constancy through that, with a reflection of God, will in itself be a great grace. It will assure them that your fidelity to spiritual guidance does not depend on anything except your will to do so—and your trust in God to help you. With time, prayer, patience, and fidelity they will find their own way across that bridge.

Hurt

Hurt people hurt people. It's more easily said than written, and, sadly, more easily done than said.

Shame-based as we are, the idea of hurting others can catapult us backward into self-loathing. Or, to avoid that vortex, we may have shut off the connection between others' suffering and our own hearts. Somewhere between these two extremes there is self-forgiveness.

No matter where we may fall on the empathy scale, it's very difficult to sort through ways in which our own wounded state has hurt others. In our limitations, we face our failure to be the caring, loving, and supportive people we want to be—and want to know. The problem lies in how the person whom we want to be is sometimes a false ideal.

We have made errors and misjudgments and missteps that have hurt others. We are sure to do so again in our lives. That is how humans are. It is not how we are because we are damaged by abuse. One step of recovery is how to embrace our own imperfections as natural. They are an integral part of us. Even our wounds are part of the wonder of who we are. Our imperfections are the opening for God to do good work.

We survivors often mistakenly believe that a restored life is a perfect life. That is not the case. A restored life looks imperfect, and it has a big dose of self-acceptance. Only when we accept our imperfections can we forgive ourselves, and that's when we really come to believe that others who love us will accept and forgive us too.

St. Francis de Sales encourages us to love our abjections. Abjections are those things in us that are broken or weak; they are our limitations, imperfections, and short-comings. They are who we are but who we dearly wish we were not. Yet, we must remind survivors to love the very abjections that often drive them into therapy.

Why would the saint urge us to love such things? For him, humility is truth, and truth is the simple and honest acknowledgement that "this is who I am." Am I, for instance, an introvert, always uncomfortable, reserved and shy in a crowd, but wish I were otherwise? Given the apt gesture or the right word for the situation, I can emerge, but not without help. For the saint, these are our abjections, the things about us that, given the chance, we would change. Certainly, survivors want to change some things about themselves, such as those traits that are rooted in having been abused and that restrain their adult joy. But, first, there must be love.

When abjections are humbly acknowledged and embraced as "what is," they can become "the footstool of God's mercy." This is a helpful spirit for therapy, and it opens survivors to prayer and graces to help their recovery. In humility and with a willingness to be helped, we can acknowledge that the truth that any good we do or are—well, that's all God's work in us. To God be the glory!

Humility as love of our abjections helps us keep in mind that we have only so much power over who we are. Survivors often, in their determination to heal, push themselves quite hard. Their efforts can be Herculean. Yet, with humility they are freed to let God do the heavy lifting. Humility leads to thanksgiving for what grace does in us and to praise of the One whose gift it is. It is our humble recognition of the alchemy of grace: grace changes darkness into light! Grace for survivors, rejecting the darkness of abuse and seeking to welcome more and more light into their adult lives, is important. This is why there is, for survivors, much hope in the words above: "Our imperfections are the opening for God to do good work."

Your role is to help the survivor embrace the person that they are, warts and all, and to accept their abjections and imperfections, not as something they want but as something that is. You are not enabling the alcoholic's drinking, nor self-abuse, nor failure to follow doctors' orders in cases of mental illness. What you are doing is giving the foundation for the self-regard, and for a bond with God that makes overcoming all these other things possible.

Grappling with one's sinfulness is difficult for survivors whose greatest struggle can be coming to grips with how innocent they are of the defining sin in their lives—the sin of abuse against them. Thus, the concept of sin, and its paradoxical hope of being redeemed and saved from sin, is unusually complicated for survivors. Spiritual guides need to understand that the idea of sinfulness itself can be a trigger for someone who has been demeaned and wounded in abuse. Finding a way to distinguish between the sins of others from one's own sinfulness takes time. It is part of the work of loving one's abjections in humility. It is important to draw lines between what is one's self and what is someone else's sin in one's life. This sorting process is a way toward freedom from abuse and part of the survivor's path to salvation.

This does not mean that survivors do not work, with you, to root out any sin in their lives. In spiritual guidance, one goal is to be the best person that one can be within natural limitations. After all, "Be who you are and be that well" is a hallmark of Salesian spirituality. Yet, these spiritual discussions are sure to be, from time to time, fraught with the sorrow and grief of the past. They will provide ample opportunity for reflecting on what sin is at all. Part of that is your helping survivors correct what might be an idealized understanding of perfection, an unrealistic expectation of self that survivors can have simply because, as children, they were left in isolation to figure that and many other things out all by themselves. In that way, survivors often have unrealistically high standards for themselves, for which they have judged themselves very harshly for failing to achieve. Indeed, for some, this is further proof of why they "deserved" the abuse.

Similarly, some survivors need to understand what is not their sin, that is, the abuse was in no way their sin. This cannot be said enough: "It was not your fault." Here, as survivors name what are their true abjections, we see the beginning of true self-compassion. God works with our weaknesses and with our sins. Survivors are entitled to this loving relationship. Your role is, in part, to help them understand how God seems (to all of our surprise!) to prefer to work with "earthen vessels." We are not called to be perfect, and we are accepted fully no matter how broken or unworthy we feel. As survivors begin to believe in God's acceptance and love, their struggle to love and accept themselves becomes much easier.

THE CARICATURE

People call us "victims." It's a word loaded with connotations. We were, indeed, victims. Most of us have used the term to refer to ourselves. Yet, victims are too often portrayed like the abuser saw us—one-dimensional, compromised, hobbled, or broken forever. We are seen, at most, as having a qualified degree of hope.

It's important to realize that, before anyone takes any step at recovery, a victim is a survivor, too. They came through the crucible. That is, the crucible is behind us. Bruised, battered, lost, confused, broken, or furious, victims are on the other side of the worst. They have survived.

Many victims begin to call themselves "survivors" at the point when they make the first decision to heal. It can be a costly decision. Unfortunately, recovery is not accidental or spontaneous, any more than grace can do its best without our cooperation. Once that decision is made, recovery can progress, usually in fits and starts—and with many detours. Some survivors do face a watershed they say is beyond the survival attitude; in our sacred circle, those people call themselves "thrivers."

For most of us, a healed life requires a very specialized set of skills we develop during recovery. We are engaged in a process of relearning our birthright of dignity, and we are finding ways our broken hearts can be "handled with care." This sense of being precious in God's eyes is very different from the world's idea of victims who are caricatures of despair and demented isolation. Our imagination in recovery can be unlimited if animated by grace through faith.

―

From victim to survivor to thriver: the progressive states of healing suggested by the descriptions, "survivor" and "thriver," are precious signs of hope! Self-chosen designations by those once abused, they represent a courageous rejection of descriptions chosen for them by others. In that sense, the victims who now refer to themselves as survivors have already taken a brave first step toward a journey that is likely to be a long, difficult, and uneven one.

Still it is a journey that promises to lead to a healthier self-acceptance and increasing self-actualization both humanly and spiritually. Along the journey, survivors will become more whole. They will become more and more the persons God always wanted them to be before the face and hand of evil intervened in their young lives. The shocking trauma of abuse often arrests development in one or more areas—human, social, and spiritual. But survivors have now chosen to move beyond the passive state of victimhood in which they were acted upon against their will. Doing so, they are rejecting the brutal and demeaning manner in which someone else treated them. However sporadically or awkwardly at first, they are taking charge of their persons and their lives. Their past may have been in the perverted hands of another, but their present and future will be of their own making. Into this hard work, we help them find and draw sustenance from God's grace!

The decision to move forward and the knowledge of how to move forward are not the same thing. Thus, the moment a victim chooses to be a survivor they also open themselves up to need help. That can be confusing, even scary. How do they know whom to trust—or how to accept help?

This is where friends, counselors, therapists, and spiritual guides come in. The challenge for the spiritual guide is to assist survivors in their spiritual journey as they face the past, remake the present, and move into a very different future. This is often how the process of recovering from abuse is described. It can turn a survivor's life upside down before order is restored, and a spiritual guide is there as a guy line but also a companion.

St. Francis de Sales compares the spiritual guide to the angel who guided Tobias on his journey into a strange and unfamiliar land. A helpful tool for the guide in assisting the survivor on this journey is the Salesian principle, "Be who you are and be that well." Just what does it mean to have become a *survivor* of abuse? What kinds of things or ways of thinking does a survivor have to let go of? What do survivors have to learn to do or to be to foster wellbeing? What virtues will each survivor need to practice to take the next step toward thriving?

No person is a carbon copy of any other person, and no survivor is a carbon copy of any other survivor. As spiritual guide you need to accept *who* the person is before you and *as* they are now. You begin with their unique gifts as well as with their fears and doubts. There may be human, social,1 or spiritual shortcomings that can be the sad legacy of an arrested development caused by the trauma of abuse. Every Christian is called to become what, through grace, St. Paul was able to become as he joyfully exclaimed, "I live now, not I. Christ lives in me!"[19] What is the next thing the survivor needs to do or to accept or to believe or to hope to become a little bit more like Jesus? What step, however small, can they now take to help them to imitate or to live Jesus in their present life as St. Paul once did in his? Indeed, how are they reflecting Jesus now without even being able to recognize Him because of the shame and self-loathing inflicted upon them by abuse?

The survivor is likely to want to get to the journey's end in one quick and decisive step. Understandably, they will be eager to leave far behind all the baggage of a painful past. This is where the guide needs to assure them that not only does the longest journey begin with its first step, but that God already welcomes them in hope at the journey's end. His grace can take a survivor forward just one step at a time, closer to Him now, and forward to Him in a loving eternity.

Each survivor's social, human, and spiritual development can resume from where it stopped. In a sense, each survivor grows up from the wounded child whom they were. It just takes time. Patience and perseverance are important virtues here, as they are in any life. How can you help a survivor combine their strong desire for healing with the slow slog that it will

---

[19] Galatians 2:20, as found in the NAB: "... yet I live, no longer I, but Christ lives in me."

take to achieve it? Don't hesitate to repeat yourself, assuring them that you are willing to accompany them along that path for as long as it takes. Their desire for healing joined with your fidelity gets both of you half way there.

INSOMNIA

Blink. Blink. Darkness. Insomnia can be a way of life, especially during the nadir of therapy when the past returns with its maelstrom of emotions to eclipse the sane present. Breathing techniques can help, sometimes. Warm milk, reading, stretching exercises, all the tricks can work, sometimes. Rigorous exercise, overwork, socializing, drinking, drugs, all the things that exhaust a person, can send us to bed, to sleep, only to wake up to the depression or anxiety we expertly avoided all day long. It seems as if, sometimes, we are meant to sit wide awake and tortured in the company of ghouls.

Insomnia taught me something about prayer that daylight never did. Prayer isn't, as many tried to tell me, one more trick in the arsenal for countering insomnia. It is, instead, a way to use insomnia as an opening for God. If I prayed even "free form" prayers I just filled the dark with rattling words that fed my anxiety. If I sat with God, however, and kept as quiet as the night, I could sense His Presence in the darkness.

Now, I still dislike the inconvenience of insomnia, but I more easily embrace it as a chance to sit with

God, and even sometimes feel like its arrival is God's way of tapping me on the shoulder to keep company for a while.

―――

Insomnia is common among adult victims of abuse. It is something that they share with many others who suffer from post-traumatic stress. Once you, as their spiritual guide, are assured that they are dealing with this issue medically and with the help of their therapist, as needed, you can begin to help them deal spiritually with the hours of darkness and sleeplessness.

What different people associate with darkness and sleeplessness can be very different, so, again, listening for what matters to each survivor is the best starting point for finding ways, together, to infuse even their wakeful nights with grace and God's presence. For example, some people associate darkness with fear and are frightened when they suddenly awake during the night. They imagine all sorts of dangers lurking in the darkness. Adult survivors often find their usual defenses against painful memories are not there for them when they can't sleep or are suddenly awakened during the night. They may find themselves especially vulnerable then. A helpful spiritual practice at those times is a very brief but ardent prayer that is said softly and repeated frequently. One of my favorites is the Jesus prayer: "Jesus Christ, Son of God, Savior, have mercy on me a sinner." It is a calming and comforting prayer. To me, it speaks of the power of Jesus over every form of evil, darkness and danger.

Another brief but fervent prayer is a favorite of St. Francis de Sales: "Jesus, be to me a Jesus." Recall that the name of Jesus means Savior. Simply repeating the name of Jesus, mantra-like, in a soft, unhurried manner soothes the spirit, quiets the imagination and brings about a deep inner rest.

Here, too, is where the loneliness of a sleepless night may be softened with an awareness of the angels and saints. A growing devotion to their guardian angel, with the deepening awareness that their angel never sleeps, adds awareness that they are not alone.

While many other meditations and prayers for sleepless nights of anxiety or grief exist, bear in mind that they all may be, in some way, double-edged swords, at least initially. Where was Jesus as my Savior then? Where was my guardian angel? From the start of your work with a survivor of abuse you must be aware that every suggestion you make, however spiritual, may trigger thoughts and feelings quite opposite to those you had hoped for or anticipated. This can be good, for each of these steps may be, if gentle, a step closer to God as you work through the impact of abuse on the countless holy gifts in our faith given to us by God. And, importantly, you must be open to growing ever more accustomed to the unique approach that spiritual guidance must take when the one being guided is an adult survivor of child abuse.

Mantras

During intervals when walking into a church was far too painful, I found myself engaged in different ways to bring praise to Christ into my life. Listening to Gregorian chanting was, like most praise turns out to be, a deeply soothing practicing.

People think chanting is mindless, and in a sense it is. It quiets thought and feelings, and leaves us open to God's presence. But what is mindless is not meaningless.

Sometimes I explain chanting to non-believing friends as a macro for the computer. We have already thought through the sequence and its meaning, even its purpose, and after that we simply need to repeat some sound or image, like a stroke of the keyboard, to evoke all the rich grace that waits to overflow the bulwark any time we say "yes."

Certain mantras of my recovery are like that. My therapist, early in my recovery, taught me how to short circuit flashbacks and triggers by repeating privately and gently, "This time is not that time." I rely on that chant even now, moving through TSA checkpoints where I can feel violated, or when I unexpectedly encounter a graphic image or story of child abuse from which I usually shield myself.

Another powerful mantra is the Serenity Prayer, which reminds me of my own limits and potential. It became a reality check and, eventually, a discipline. If I was not able to change something, I knew I had to accept it or move beyond it.

Late in my recovery process, I began to cultivate my ability to praise. It seemed I had been asking and pleading and apologizing and even yelling all my life. I had been a victim and a survivor but not really a praiser. So, I started to chant the Divine Mercy "Holy God, Mighty God, Holy Immortal God, Have mercy on us and on the whole world." This chant stretched my faith, and is making me a more open vessel for grace beyond the grace for survival.

If not necessarily by name, the practice of mantras has been part of the spiritual life from time immemorial. Ever since Jesus gave his disciples the command to pray always, holy men and women have tried to understand just how such a command is carried out in the hustle and bustle, the nooks and crannies, of everyday life. Since Jesus doesn't ask the impossible of us, they rightly reasoned, we must be able to pray always.

This is how St. Francis de Sales suggests that we can fulfill the Lord's command to pray always. For him, prayer is essentially a conversation with God that occurs within the larger context of a continual loving relationship and true friendship with him. Once we have decided to accept God's invitation to friendship, that relationship becomes the ever-present horizon or backdrop for literally everything else in our lives. In that sense, the state of grace is already the state of prayer in its most general sense; it is that special state of continual, habitual presence of one friend to another.

But no loving relationship or special friendship ought to be placed on automatic pilot and especially not our relationship with God. Friendships need to be tended to and nourished frequently, for communication is essential to friendship.

For St. Francis de Sales, this is accomplished in a number of ways. When once asked how long he went without thinking about God, his answer was about every fifteen minutes. This is why he suggests that we send up a little word or quick thought of praise or love to the Lord every quarter hour or so throughout the day and even if we happen to awaken during the night. This need not take any time at all. It is really just a little reminder that our Friend is present. We simply acknowledge his presence, greet him, and tell him we love him. This can be done even in the midst of the busiest day. At one point he writes: "at hundreds of times during the day let us join our life to God's love." How? By brief little prayers or, if you like, by short mantras, and by the practices of lifting up our hearts to God and of going into spiritual retirement, that is, for example, by briefly imagining ourselves cradled safe and happy in the arms of the Lord.

Understood in this way, mantras are simply ways to always be connected to our Friend, in good times and in bad, at both happy and sad moments, while at peace and even when in crisis: always. Thus, the command to "Pray always" and the promise that "I am with you always" go hand in hand.

TURNING POINTS

Overview

Recovering from the trauma of child sexual abuse—or any abuse—can be a long process, but it is characterized by uneventful, even peaceful periods and also by quite dramatic turning points. Turning points are personal watersheds, distinct "eureka" moments, points in time after which there is no return to what life was like before.

Turning points may be surprising but they are seldom sudden. They are, instead, built on many little known and less sensational triumphs week after week, day after day, even hour after hour. While most of recovery is an endurance course that can be grueling and even boring, these moments can help survivors gain confidence in a sense of success and help energize the process overall.

Understanding the purpose (and limitations) of turning points in the ongoing experience of recovery and survival, this section opens with survivor, spiritual guide, and psychologist each reflecting on watershed moments, what they feel like, what helps them flourish, and how not to rush them to happen. The collection of remaining essays is focused and small, featuring occasions at which turning points most often appear.

Yet, the essays in this section also provide insights into how turning points may be dramatic and obvious, or something a survivor may not notice for days, weeks, or months after it has passed—after they have already moved into a new way of being or thinking. This section helps a spiritual guide offer prayerful support for the full continuity of effort—and failure—that can lead to these wonderfully surprising moments. It also helps to remind survivors and their families that the most discouraging, confusing, and even arid periods are nonetheless leading to pinnacles of relief and joy.

Turning Points: A Survivor's Perspective

I have spent my life trying to outrun the fire burning wildly on my back. Then, one day, I couldn't run any farther. I had come to the end of myself.

It is a place where all my struggles have surrendered in sheer exhaustion. It is a place where the incessant internal loop berating me for all my failures, and all my half-failures, runs out. It is where the status of my achievements and the promises of my personal improvement techniques have no influence. My tireless efforts to control all the variables have led to nothing. I am tired here at this terminal spot.

Here is where therapy, with its personal insights and useful cognitive tools and behavioral changes, has nothing more to give. Here, my voracious reading and meticulous journals amassed during decades of recovery have no wisdom or relief. At this abject end of myself, there is no drug, no drink, no other numbing element, no crazy-making friend or overestimated foe that can spare me anymore.

I have thought my way to the end of reason. I have wished my way to the extreme of disappointment. I have cried an ocean of tears and chased false promises in earnest. I have imagined great things to which I escaped, for a while, and have forced many solutions, fixed many broken people, edited many revelations about myself which I never delivered. It all led here, where I am spent at the end of myself.

At the end of myself there is still much to do, like surrender, love, hope, forgive. If I dare to be brutally honest, I still really do wish for dreams to come true, wonder if truth might prevail, suspect that I can slip the vice grip of shame.

Here, I understand why many, possibly most, survivors resume their compulsion of choice to escape this place and never return. I can see why this limit can feel like death, and why some survivors I know have arrived at a place like this and taken their own lives. To spin on my heel and return to everything I was doing before is possible, but being here finally changes everything.

If I can only believe that for just this once that Christ is with me, I will have the grace to see in this end a new life. All of the defenses and illusions of victimhood can drop from me here, like the shell of a seed that dies to be born. This moment will pass. I cannot stop its fleeting nature. I can choose to make it my beacon for moving forward. I can stand here at the end of myself and choose a life where God can begin.

TURNING POINTS: A SPIRITUAL GUIDE'S PERSPECTIVE

Desire and choice: these two most important ingredients come at the beginning of all spiritual growth. Both of them pervade the moving description common in many addiction and recovery programs: "sick and tired of being sick and tired." Survivors can struggle alone for years in different ways, only to end up utterly spent and at the end of their own powers. At that point they face a difficult choice: Will they go back? Give up? Or go on?

Often, at this point in their lives, survivors desire a way forward, but they know it must be one that will no longer depend solely on their own efforts. These are tenacious people. They have tried many different ways to leave the effects of the abuse behind, and to varying degrees they have succeeded with energy, creativity, and perseverance. But often they find they have not gotten to that place of peace for which they long. They are seeking a safe, secure, and life-giving sanctuary. They are seeking a deepening in their relationship with God, and the scars of abuse sometimes stand in the way.

Although a different context, they make the same cry St. Paul once made: "What a wretched man I am! Who can free me from this body under the power of death?" Paul answers his own question with the only possible answer for him: "All praise to God, through Jesus Christ our Lord!" (Romans 7:24-25). In spiritual guidance, we are helping people move from cry to praise as does St. Paul when, in the poverty of his own powerlessness, he has hit bottom. He now reaches out to another for help, but not just any other. He reaches out to Jesus.

Turning points are points of decision, and they are marked by a sense of urgent need. There seem to be three possible options for survivors who have reached a turning point. They can once more try on their own. They can give up the struggle altogether. Or, like St. Paul, they can choose to reach out to Jesus. For many, especially those abused by clergy, that is a choice fraught with pain. It is colored, again, by the theodicy issue: He once abandoned them to abuse. How can He help them now? And, yet, survivors still reach out for spiritual care, and that makes us an interim step toward our Savior. Their desire for a way forward is real, pressing, and urgent. Like Paul, they are drawn to the One who really can take them forward. As the spiritual guide, you are helping people make the choice they already are drawn to make. They are drawn to the way toward healing, toward Jesus: "I am the way!"[20]

---

[20] John 14:6

Your role is to accompany them as they realize Jesus is their most loving companion forward. In this way, you will make the journey as three, together and in the company of the Lord.

―

Turning Points: A Psychologist's Perspective
Frank J. Moncher, PhD

As therapy progresses, along with times of great optimism, natural fatigue can be expected. The survivor may weary of the intense emotional work they are doing, and eventually they face a critical choice point—to risk moving boldly forward through uncharted waters beyond which lay the promise of healing and freedom, or to return to former ways of being, which while painful, have a strange familiar comfort. As before, this is the business of the survivor, who needs to exercise control and volition, so the therapist's role is one of support and clarification. And no clarification is more important than revisiting the starting place: "You are believed, and it was not your fault."

In the backdrop all the while is the shadow of forgiveness … a difficult topic to be sure. Psychologically, forgiveness is not merely a one-time decision, but rather a process that begins when the choice point begins, and then the process continues throughout the journey until its closure. Forgiveness is an essential aspect of the fulfillment of the journey, yet is a byproduct of healing, not an expedient solution unto itself. At the end of the day, to reach this point requires a true integration of one's history into one's personhood, and as in previous stages or phases, patience is essential for both the survivor, who desires freedom from the past, and for the therapist, who desires healing for this person. But the process takes time. No one can know the pain endured during the abuse, nor presume to suggest how quickly that pain will subside enough to present the time when forgiveness might be offered in order to move further toward healing.

Along with forgiveness, another common and key aspect of turning the corner is how to ensure support is in place. Because there has likely been a disruption in the survivor's ability to trust their own feelings in the past, both before and after a choice is made to heal they will need regular clarification about their instinctual reactions to others: confirmation and affirmation of those reactions which are on target, and gentle processing and redirection of those reactions which may contain residue from the past. As the sage spiritual guide notes, "We are not our feelings," nor can we ignore them. A healthy detachment is the goal, where a survivor neither denies their emotions nor allows them to run roughshod over their lives and push them towards unhealthy ways. It is inevitable when the survivor reaches each turning point for emotions to churn, even for confusion and doubt to set in. Part of recovery is identifying and relying on a network of support, of which the therapist and the spiritual guide are part. Survivors who learn to mobilize their networks in time of need have passed an important turning point in feeling like victims. The journey becomes far less disorienting for having company. No one should make this journey alone. Survivors have already suffered alone far too much in youth.

So therapy also takes on a new character or focus: this time outward, but in a perhaps surprising manner. As much as a survivor reaches out to obtain support as they do the difficult work of processing the trauma in therapy, they also will become a gift of hope to those around them. Of this they are not often aware. Heretofore, the survivor has necessarily and appropriately focused on their own selves, their needs, their perceptions; now, as they move towards greater freedom and healing, they will risk "forgetting oneself" and trust that in doing so they will be blessed to be more of who they were created to be. This is daunting business, and very much must happen synergistically with spiritual guidance and growth. At its core, the truth about the person being revealed is that which recognizes the profound beauty and need for connectedness, the way in which we all discover who we truly are by making a sincere gift of self to others. The survivor, for good reason, is suspicious and cautious about such attachments and vulnerabilities, yet we know psychologically for them to flourish they must come to terms with these issues to move forward. Of course, speaking and sharing, breaking the silence and secrets with family and friends must be pursued judiciously, for their own sake as well as the sake of the others who may be at varying stages of readiness to hear about the horrors of the past.

And still, it is the truth which will set each survivor free, and which must be spoken, in justice and charity.

With a renewed sense of hope and clarity about the past, some progress in the journey of forgiving, the ability to differentiate past feelings from current feelings, and a healthy set of attachments to particular others who are significant in life, the survivor may come to an end of therapy. For others, a trusted therapist can be akin to their family practice physician, whom they see for annual "check-ups" or periodic "sick visits" when a booster is needed to regain equilibrium. I would like to close with something often felt but seldom said: the trust you place in your therapist is substantial, and we are impressed by your courage, grateful for what you teach us about the ultimate victory of good over evil, and honored by your entrusting us to hear your story.

Deciding to Heal

The decision to heal is seldom conveniently timed. The decision to heal is messy to begin, messier to pursue, and even after restoring a more healthful and orderly life we remain content with the messiness of our nature.

Healing won't just happen, any more than any life-threatening condition will benefit from treatment unless we start at a physician's office and go through all the appointments. We decide to go through with the process every day, and in the process find ourselves deciding between persevering and giving up many times a day.

We don't just decide to heal. We decide how we heal, and more importantly we decide who we want to be after our process of recovery delivers us somewhere we do not even know about yet. That is, we may be recovering from something terrible in the past, but we are deciding more importantly who we want to be in the future.

There are a few tough confrontations we have with ourselves as we begin to heal. One is that we, who have been hurt deeply, may have hurt others—even as a result of our wound. We may have not trusted, or may have lashed out in pain we did not cause. We may have rejected or doubted love. We may have misjudged in an effort to protect ourselves as no one else did. Or, we may have been too busy surviving the aftermath of the abuse to grapple with our own unique personal shortcomings. As we move into our recovery, somewhere down the line, after we learn we are not guilty of the abuse done to us but may have done wrongs along the way, we will need to make our own list of amends to others.

Also, we face a very difficult question about who we will become. Will we become a symptom, or will we keep moving beyond what we think and feel as wounded people and open ourselves to the full person God intended us to be? Will we feel anger and integrate it into a fuller life, or will we become an angry person—that is, become our anger? The same goes for grief, hatred, distrust, shame, and even for being a victim. A bottom line decision in recovery may sound strange, but it is true: how big can we become?

To help us, we have a God bigger than any problem we face, a God waiting—no matter how we let ourselves grow to absorb the full shock of the abuse—to enrich our very identities with the gifts of His Spirit. It is, again, our choice whether to accept His healing graces, but our responsibility not to push ourselves to accept changes or stretch our faith any faster than is gentle, safe, and gradual. Decisiveness is not, in grace, a different version of self-hurt. It is about self-care, and self-care is often about choosing to let God care in ways we cannot care for ourselves.

Salesian spirituality is realistic, practicable, and do-able. For that reason, St. Francis de Sales defines success in the spiritual life as our willingness to continue to work at it. Success lies in the struggle itself. This is a very helpful approach to all who seek spiritual guidance, but perhaps especially so to a survivor who has made the decision to heal. Everybody can continue to work at it, no matter how easy or difficult the process may be, and no matter how many more setbacks there may be compared to a sense of success. The willingness to pick ourselves up, dust ourselves off and begin anew is, in God's eyes, already to be successful in the pursuit of holiness. This can be shocking news to many people, including survivors, because God's love and mercy is surprising in its relentlessness and affirmation.

Yes, indeed, for every step forward there may well be two backwards. There will likely be fits and starts, progress and lack of progress. Discouragement is always at hand, as is the fear of failure. For survivors who may be struggling, too, with anxiety or depression, it is easy to have a wavering confidence. Still, the decision to heal is already a response to grace. It's important to repeat this truth. That decision is the most important first step in being healed. It is a decision to reject the familiar but unwelcome terrain of victimhood, to reject one's anger or fear or shame as a final identity, and to reject being defined only as victim either by oneself or by others. In the end, the decision to heal is a decision to become what God Himself wants us to become and, with His grace, what we can become.

All this may seem overwhelming to the one who has decided to heal but who must now undertake the difficult steps that lead to healing. This path is a very long one which takes time. Early in the path survivors grapple with their innocent role in the abuse. They build, with grace, some firmer footing in their lives based on God's love for them no matter what they have done or are. Yet, later along the path, another important step involves seeking forgiveness. This may happen long before they are able to forgive anyone who has harmed them. They may seek forgiveness from God, or from someone whom they have hurt during a difficult and pain-stricken life. These are all steps toward healing which occur naturally, in gentle timing. As noted above, "We have a God bigger than any problem we face," and we have His special gift to us of the Holy Spirit.

St. Francis de Sales has a simple but profound understanding of the gift of the Holy Spirit in sustaining survivors in the work needed for recovery. In the one gift of the Holy Spirit, God has given us every other spiritual gift as well.[21] The Holy Spirit pours into our hearts and is expressed in us differently at different times, sometimes as humility or as gentleness or as kindness or as service, and so forth, depending on the circumstances of any given moment or by the unique needs of the person we encounter. This is true for survivors and for us, their spiritual guides. The Holy Spirit is present among us. The gift of the Holy Spirit is there, too, to help survivors choose the right word and the right timing in which to ask forgiveness, and in which to receive forgiveness.

The Holy Spirit also helps survivors understand how each one can come to his or her own place of forgiveness toward the abuse—forgiveness of those who abandoned the child victims, who protected the abusers, and who abused. This forgiveness will look very different in each survivor's life. Some survivors describe feeling a huge weight lifted off their shoulders when they completely forgive, others describe turning their desire for revenge over to God without actually uttering forgiveness as we might define it. Again, the Spirit is among us, in all of us, working in each person, and for survivors who have chosen healing the Spirit is helping them lay down the burden of having been abused, including finding when and how

---

[21] Romans 5:5

to forgive the many, many wrongs that need to be forgiven in God's time.

The issues of forgiveness that play a profound role—for some, after a long, long time—in healing are very difficult. They are complicated by how forgiveness was a tool for enabling abusers in families and communities and, sadly, in our Church. The Spirit will help each survivor find a way to reject enabling or accepting the abuse while finding a way to let it all go. With the Spirit's help, and not on our time table or even in a way we might expect, the Spirit will help each survivor understand how and when forgiveness is needed to proceed further in recovery. As spiritual guides, we help survivors believe in the presence of the Holy Spirit within them. This runs quite contrary to personal shame and social or public judgment survivors must endure. It also does not erase or negate what wrong has happened. Yet, it is His power that can assist survivors in the important but difficult work of forgiveness.

With that understanding, the adult survivor can be assured that they have the grace, the spiritual power, to do what they need to do as they work their way with Jesus from a decision to a life that has gained new levels of wellbeing. As with all people, for survivors this healing includes many things, but few so difficult and central as forgiveness. The spiritual guide is there as companion, encouraging survivors to go forward at the pace and with the approach that works for them as they move, step by step, from decision to healing with the Holy Spirit as their light and true guide.

BREAKING SILENCE

The first silence we break as survivors is in our own hearts. We permit ourselves to speak what has been held in silence of one type or another. Some survivors told someone when they were young, but even if the adult reported the abuse the event can fade into an unspoken history. Some survivors have told absolutely no one at all. It's all silence we carry into our own beings, into our lives. The silence has another name: Secret.

Some of us face dire penalties for speaking the truth in our families or communities or churches where the abuse occurred. Even if we were abused decades earlier, our witness to our abuse can enrage people for many different reasons. We can become victims all over again.

Many survivors dread sharing their truth with family members or friends. We expect others to reflect back what we are feeling—shame, self-hatred, grief, or anger. What we often find is compassion and respect, if not among all the people we tell, certainly among the ones whom we can trust.

One of the most important options we have when breaking the silence is choosing the Who and When and Where. Like consciously choosing our support network for recovery, we can decide whom to tell first, when we tell them, and where and how to share our truth. In other words, by making these conscious choices, we are taking the opposite approach to being victims. Then, we had no control over what happened, but now we can control enough factors in how we speak truth that we help ensure the best outcome for us and for the people we tell—with the least damage.

―

Abused children tend to keep the horror of their abuse to themselves. Many were told by their abusers not to tell anyone, perhaps even threatened them if they did: "This is our little secret, isn't it?" Many could find no words for what they endured or were too ashamed to speak the unspeakable. Who would believe them anyway, a mere child, and he so important and impressive a person?

For children victims, silence was not the comfort of solitude but the secret of shame. Over time, it became an increasingly heavy burden, a powerful weight, always there, holding them down or back or keeping them hidden within themselves. As a way of hiding the horror even from themselves, some began to wonder, then deny, that it ever actually happened at all. "How could it have happened? It must not have happened!" Reality, too difficult to face, sometimes got lost even to memory. Or, it was numbed with alcohol, drugs, or other dangerous behaviors—anything to distract from the pain buried somewhere deep inside.

Healing, recovery, begins when, at long last, survivors find the courage or the words or the grace to confront the horrible reality of their abuse. They force themselves to remember it: "Yes, it did happen." Then, at some point, they are ready to break their silence, reveal their secret, perhaps first only to themselves, and in time to one trusted person and then to another.

But for some survivors, the "flood gates opened" experience often follows. They want to tell everybody everything all the time! It is so freeing, so liberating, to finally be able to break their heavy silence and, at last, to tell their story. Or, for some, it is as if they are telling every person, looking for the one person who has the secret to relieve the pain. What they seek is God's healing Word, but it may take time to realize that, or be open to Him. Meanwhile, some simply want to shout out their secret from the roof tops.

If they are in spiritual guidance at this juncture, the guide will help them to discern to whom to tell their story, when, where, and how. Not everybody is qualified to handle this truth, and the result can be quite hurtful to the survivor sharing it. Sharing with the wrong person at the wrong time often re-wounds a survivor. Over-sharing just increases the extent of the re-wounding. Inadvertently, a few survivors even can "vicariously" wound others by offering so much detail to people who are in vulnerable states themselves, and unable to process another person's trauma.

Some, especially those who failed to notice the abuse or listen to the survivor as a child, may resist hearing this news at all. They may be unable to face their role—or hope for mercy from God. They may remain staunch enablers of the abuser. Others may be fragile from sharing the same family or abuse background; they may be able only to deal with another survivor's truth as a gradual unfolding. As trusted companion, the spiritual guide can help discern how to move forward in a way that most helps the survivor both in letting go of the past and in becoming the person God created them to be.

Breaking the silence is healthful but difficult. How to proceed can be a complicated matter, ideally planned and well-considered, but sometimes spontaneous and messy. Being an affirming part of a system of support for the survivor as they tell the truth is important. As with all steps in recovery, this person must proceed with thoughtful preparation but also with the very real chance of making errors on the way to greater successes. We remain constant companions, encouraging, helping God's grace guide the steps forward.

Redefining Safety

The most important—and often most challenging—step is to ensure personal safety for recovery. Exploring and re-exploring habits for a safe life are worth more than one discussion. Ensuring personal safety happens over time. It may mean moving out of denial about psychologically or physically dangerous relationships, or moving into a recovery program for substance-abuse or self-harming behaviors, or beginning therapy. It may mean just coming clean with a spouse or children after decades of burying what was suffered in childhood.

There are additional steps to take toward safety. They can be simultaneous but will not really take full root until the primary, basic safety of self is achieved. That first step exercises sometimes our first-ever step in assuming responsibility for our own wellbeing for which we may have no successful model in a childhood wounded by abuse.

Creating a safe space in our home can be a safe step to faith, because we can create an altar. As a child my mother had a May altar, and she kept statues around the house. As my recovery progressed, I cleared off a table in a quiet room where I collected tokens I associated with my recovery. Eventually I added a statue and rosary, and the gesture of gathering mementos gave the place a sacred quiet. It became calming and easier for me to pray there. It became a safe place.

Over the years I eventually created a prayer room, with a few treasured books and my Bible, with my rosary, some statues and many beautiful items that, for me, express my love for God. I welcome Him into my prayer room as the constantly open door into my entire home and full life. There is a prayer jar there, where friends and family know they can drop a note I will never read but pray over in my daily visit to this quieting, safe place. For me, my prayer room represents the destination of my recovery—a healing never done but in constant intimacy with my loving, accepting, and inspiring Creator.

The child's sense of safety and security was utterly shattered by abuse. Never knowing when or where the abuse might resume, there was no place to hide and no time when one felt really safe. Life changed forever.

An adult survivor will find it very helpful to create a place into which, any time they desire, they can feel safe and secure while spending time with the One with whom they are always protected, loved, and safe.

Part of spiritual guidance is to encourage the creation of a little corner of a room or, if possible, a little room itself where one can go to pray or read or just be alone with the Alone for a little while, even in the midst of the hustle and bustle of a large, loud, and rambunctious family. That space can be very simply furnished with perhaps a candle, a crucifix, and the Bible. Or it can be filled to the brim with all those things that center us or comfort us or remind us of what is good and true and beautiful. One's holy space is an expression of individual creativity, which is something survivors have exercised in abundance in finding ways to survive their ordeal.

A benefit is, also, is that this is an exercise in self-care. Indeed, the survivor exercises personal responsibility in providing for a safe environment by setting up a sacred place. It may be a small step but it is a very important one. For survivors, safety is sacred, and what is sacred must be safe. Yet, for those abused within the Church, sacred spaces may have been very unsafe. This exercise also helps restore a sense of sanctuary. From the spiritual strength gained in this sacred space, survivors deepen their reliance on God so that, in time, they can rely on Him more to broaden that safe place to include more and more places and more and more people. With God's love to help survivors remember their own value, they will be able to choose good places and good people, increasingly replacing what might be unhealthy places and people.

And a sacred space can be there, waiting, for them to return from this changing world and relax with the Lord, catching a breath and renewing strength. Safety is necessary for recovery; a sacred space is very helpful for spiritual growth. So this exercise for survivors helps recovery and spiritual growth.

Communing with God is not limited to sacred spaces. One cannot, of course, always be physically in that safe and quiet place. But, throughout our spiritual guidance, the imagination can serve God's work, too. When we are in unquiet places, our imaginations can take us to a safe place whenever we want, even in the midst of the busiest day or the largest crowd. St. Francis de Sales used to retire from time to time for a few moments during the day to the open side of the Lord, resting just beneath His Sacred Heart. He was renewed there in both body and spirit.

Jesus made an invitation to such a place when he invited his disciples to "come by yourselves to an out-of-the-way place and rest a little."[22] He knew the importance of quieting down, of centering, and of just relaxing with the Lord. There, one is refreshed, renewed, comforted, and readied for whatever follows. Many good things happen when one is alone with God in a safe and sacred space. Our role as spiritual guides is to help survivors find many different ways to cultivate such sacred spaces in their lives.

---

[22] Mark 6:31

Believing Self

Self-hatred is fueled by a failure to believe our own stories. It is also fueled when we believe the wrong interpretation of the story of how we were victims, because we often blame ourselves. Having endured abuse in isolation and confusion, it can be very hard finally to make sense out of the truth we lived.

My first therapist was the first person I ever heard tell me, "It wasn't your fault." The idea was so shocking, and the feeling that she had some creepy insight into my innermost thoughts was unnerving. Over time, I started to repeat the idea to myself. It made logical sense. Sometimes I even believed it, for a moment.

Without telling anyone other than my therapist for decades, I had no one else to believe me except myself. And I doubted myself. The braver I grew, the more I was able to maintain a steady focus on memories I had long avoided. The more I looked, the more I felt pain I had ignored. I was sewing the feelings back into the images, and it was living hell. What made everything harder was that I often stopped and wished I was imagining things, or was even crazy; it would be easier than believing I had endured such horror.

Life sends experiences to help us believe ourselves. Like everyone, I met people whose personal problems led them to challenge daily truths or opinions I had as an adult; as I learned to remain true to myself, the lesson sunk deeper into my psyche and helped me respect the truth of my past. I also spent over five years going from specialist to specialist who, seeing my childhood history of abuse and my current therapy, dismissed the amassing symptoms as "all in my head." Something in me refused to trade their truth about me for mine, and I continued through almost two dozen specialists, only finally to discover the prior physicians were correct. It was all in my head. I had a brain tumor.

I survived the benign tumor and the surgery required to remove it. I also gained a steadfast certainty in how no one, no matter how much authority they had, could ever override my own sense of truth—as a child dismissed by bishops, as an adult dismissed by doctors. No one should have such a wound of doubt gashed into their childhood or should need such a life-and-death drama to restore self-belief, but I consider the latter a gift needed to heal the former.

The wonder of recovery is not always going to be limited to the journaling and therapy of talk about the past experience and present relationships. It is going to take self-discovery into every living experience and transform them. God is at work in us. With grace, we can become aware of His healing presence.

For the Christian, the paradox of self-discovery often lies in the forgetfulness of self: "Whoever would save his life will lose it, but whoever loses his life for my sake will find it."[23] In this passage Jesus is speaking, of course, of losing one's bodily life through actual death for his sake. But, expanded more

---

[23] Matthew 16:25

fully, it can speak as well to one's whole reality, including one's self-image, one's self-belief. Scripture invites us to "put on the mind of Christ."[24] To the extent that we lose our self for his sake, we do just that because our present self-image or self-belief is gradually replaced by the truer image that Jesus has of us.

The survivor of abuse will find it impossible to untangle all the myriad of emotions and feelings that overwhelmed them during the period of abuse and especially during the discreet acts of abuse. Did they somehow invite the abuse? Did they, on some level, like the attention, or were they in some way pleased with the abuser's affection? What does it mean if they loved the abuser? As abusers seek particularly after the isolated even neglected child, it is often the case that a child felt very conflicted emotions, drawn to the only attention or care in their life but repulsed and confused by abuse. Our hearts are torn to consider a child isolated in such a quandary, but now we meet them as adult survivors.

Questions continue for survivors. If only they had been more courageous, could they have spoken sooner or been able to repel him from abusing them or their siblings or friends? For a survivor, such questions and examples of second guessing are legion. Imagining them as just a child, we wonder how they could possibly expect such things from themselves, yet survivors carry sometimes a terrible burden of guilt for what was done to them. It is why many share

---

[24] Philippians 2:5, or as translated in the NAB: "Have among yourselves the same attitude that is also yours in Christ Jesus."

that the first place they reveal having been abused is in confession, trying to wipe the sin of their failure to stop abuse sooner.

I call this "pretzel-thinking." Just as there is absolutely no way to untangle a hardened pretzel without breaking it, so it is impossible to untangle the cacophony of thoughts, emotions, and feelings associated with the violence of abuse. Certainly, survivors need to sort through them to some degree, as a way to loosen the power of the web over their adult lives. Yet, human understanding alone is not enough to break the power of self-recrimination. In a sense, this personal indictment serves a greater wound, that is, the shame of being abused. Survivors who are still shame-driven will view themselves as guilty. Their pretzel-thinking supports their view of themselves as essentially bad, for, as some see it, if they weren't so bad wouldn't God have spared them?

Breaking this self-condemnation is difficult, but not impossible when a survivor shifts away from unhealthy ways of seeing themselves to realistic views of how Jesus sees them. How Jesus sees them is all that matters. He knows that they were children, and innocent, and victims, no matter how their own adult thinking may now try to suggest otherwise. Compared to God's overriding view, survivors can come to see their own thinking for what it is, that is, a temptation to keep them rooted in the past, stuck in the mud of faulty understandings created by abusers and enablers, forced to be uncertain about one's own preciousness to God, and even paralyzed with self-hate.

An exercise for spiritual direction is finding safe ways to lose themselves in Christ and experience being found by the Good Shepherd. Imagining scenes with which we are familiar in faith can help, like being carried as a babe in his arms safely without fear of abuse, or wrapped around his shoulders like the lost sheep. Here, or in other personal images relating to Jesus, survivors find who they were always meant to be. They may bask in the smile on his face as he carries them from the danger of being lost to the joy of being found and safely near the Lord himself—"I once was lost but now am found." For people who were lost since childhood in some sense, what an amazing grace!

Being Believed

Not having been believed is one of the most damaging experiences for an adult who was an abused child. It creates doubt in us that lasts a lifetime by warping the mirror of others in whose esteem we were basing our own self images.

Over the decades of a restless recovery process, I encountered many wise people who were well qualified to tell me that I did not cause the abuse and that I did not control the abuser. I believed what they said was true—for other victims but not for me. Most of those people were central to my steps in recovery, and they were guides in my seeking a cure. Many fell short because they thought the cure would be of my own making. Most of them believed I would fashion it through a process of self-help.

What people seldom acknowledge is that the self-help programs at the heart of the recovery culture is not really about getting help from one's self, but rather from a power greater than one's self. Only the really committed people in 12-Step programs evolve to that deep level of recovery.

The good work in these programs is done precisely because God is stripped of all possible religion-based triggers. I grew to think of God as understood in 12-Step programs as a wholly different view of Jesus stripped of his clothing. It permitted me to keep my eyes fixed on Jesus, without cognitive dissonance that I felt thinking about the Church. His crucifixion would not be robed in power or a high priest's robes. Even he made sure I could focus on was what his dying and Resurrection really meant in my life—without the trappings of religion that were fraught with fright for me. Everything could be built up again from there.

There was the first priest whom I ever told I had been abused. Like many survivors, I confessed it as my sin. (I had done that before. Many survivors do.) Fortunately, the Franciscan refused to absolve what was not my sin. The encounter left an impression, as did his reaction to our talk in his office later that day. The first thing he said was that I was not at fault; I was innocent.

There was something credible in a priest saying another priest was wrong. As a child, I grappled with how predators I knew had been empowered by Christ to decide what is held bound in sin on earth and loosed of sin in heaven. Without the predators being censored by other priests or bishops, I assumed they retained that power. A dozen years later I resumed my attempt to reconcile with the Church, and I met another priest, an Oblate of St. Francis de Sales, who believed me. His first words were that it was not my fault. He didn't ask me to hide my story, but to find ways to tell it for my own sake and the sake of others. He didn't just believe my story, he valued it.

Then, when the bishop in the diocese where I live met with me, it was as if the hierarchy was speaking when he told me it was not my fault, that I was innocent. The lingering spell cast on a child's trusting view of priests was finally broken. It really was like the unmistakable voice of the shepherd finding what remained lost in me. Healing could flood into places no other voice could reach.

To be abused is an unspeakably horrible experience. Not to be believed when they are finally able to tell the story of their abuse is the sad but all too frequent experience of adult survivors, and even of some child victims. Apparently, there is something in the rest of us that just can't bear to hear their stories. I guess we don't want to believe that any of us could ever be capable of such heinous acts against our own children. That may be understandable, but where does our resistance to even listen to—let alone believe—their stories leave survivors? And where does it leave other potential victims, except vulnerable to abusers who continue in secrecy?

All survivors need three things from us: they need to be able to tell their story; they need to be believed; and they need to be assured that none of what happened to them is their fault. There are other needs, of course, but these are fundamental for anyone who seeks to provide a safe spiritual relationship to support a survivor through the work of recovering from abuse.

And, more so, survivors need a fourth thing: they need to find God. They need to be reminded and to rediscover that God never lost them, God never left them. When the abuser has been a representative of the Church, they also need, in time, to find some way to resolve the wound from the Church, however they may do so. In the usual course, the Church preaches and we come to faith. When the Church herself, in the person of the abuser, violates the child it also destroys the Church's credibility as the child's safe way back to God. Yet, many survivors of abuse within the Church continue in their Catholic faith, but not without wounds. Others reject that faith quite understandably. In that sense, abuse seeks to destroy faith itself. Our goal is to help the survivor's relationship with God deepen and, in a safe way for them, to help them work out how they may continue in a relationship with the Church. For some, this work involves finding a safe way to remain Catholic, for some it means making peace with the Church but finding no way to feel safe inside her walls again.

That is why, as in the account above, programs such as AA are held in such high esteem. Their "higher power" is deliberately stripped of any particular ecclesial or confessional garb. That stripping clears a path for the survivor to find a return to God that does not lead through the Church. The good news is this: once many survivors have found a way back to God without the triggers of specifics to harm or frighten, they are able to receive the grace, the guidance, to find a way back to the Church which, in the abuser, totally failed them as children. This is one of so many miracles in the lives of survivors.

"God wants all to be saved and come to know the truth."[25] The survivor of abuse wants that as well. Telling truth about the otherwise hidden past is at the core of work in therapy and 12 Step programs. The path in such programs or therapies relies on the idea of a "nondenominational" God. While not through the Church, this outreach to God may, in time, lead survivors back to the Church. It definitely leads many back to God, and consider how brave even that partial step is. For survivors of abuse, any authority figure relates to the authority of the abuser. Most must resolve the sense of authority as flawed and even abusive to move forward. Many must find a way to forgive authority figures in their lives for having abandoned them as children to harm.

For those abused by clergy or other authorities in the Church, for those survivors hurt in some way by the Catholic reactions to victims, there was still something that kept them practicing Catholics. They may have had a deeply rooted faith, or may have remained Catholic to preserve family ties. Some were nomi-

---

[25] 1 Timothy 2:4, or as translated in the NAB: "… wills everyone to be saved and to come to knowledge of the truth."

nally Catholic, others active. Some were careful to avoid interactions with Catholics but attended Mass. The variations are many. What's important here is that survivors all grappled with ways to be related to God with or without the authority of the Church, even as they struggled with disappointment in authority in God and in the Church and others. For a survivor seeking a deeper level of reconciliation with the Church, there is great personal risk. There is even added risk in seeking God; the status quo, which may involve many old defense mechanisms, is going to change. That survivors try at all is a sure sign of the Spirit moving in their hearts.

In this way, for most survivors the path back to feeling comfortable with God and in the Church is likely to be a long and difficult slog, with many fits and starts, with all sorts of foreseen and unforeseen triggers. Yet, more straightforward paths to God have been lost to many survivors because of all the lies and betrayal at the heart of abuse. This is part of the tragedy of abuse and its lingering effects. Survivors, tenacious as they are, find other ways home because they are drawn home to God. They are called, in a way, to be even more creative finding less-trod paths, but the Creator can help them. Their goal must not be to achieve perfection or speed, but to practice gentleness and patience. Are we prepared to patiently accompany them as they create entirely new ways, albeit slowly and perhaps unevenly toward home? Jesus will never leave these brave people. Will we?

Asking for Help

Asking for help is harder than anyone thinks, and most survivors consider it even harder. For us, it can be impossible. Sometimes, even still, it is impossible for good reasons, such as a toxic relationship where the tradeoff for love is denial that the abuse happened or accepting damaging treatment.

A wise first step in asking for help is thinking about it before you feel like you need help. Making a phone list is a great way to circumvent sitting in a room needing to talk to someone but having no idea who to ask. Talking to a few close people about having them on call is smart before the call needs to be made. What is the best way to ask them for help—an email to set a time? A call at certain times of the day?

But there are other obstacles to asking for help. We find ourselves needing to reduce how self-reliant we are. We became self-reliant—which is a good trait if it is in balance with interdependence on others—because we had to. Out of balance, however, self-reliance spells isolation and confusion. Others of us became overly reliant on one person or a few people. Out of balance, this might mean that we have been unable to leave a safe environment from childhood to become adults, or we are stuck in a toxic relationship.

Then there's the problem of the human nature of anyone who wants to help us. Everyone is limited. No one can live our full life for us or make our final decisions or grapple with their outcomes. Asking for help sometimes is a double-edged sword, putting us in touch with people enough to discover that even the most wonderful people have only so much to give.

And, then there's prayer, futile as it may have felt in the past, fraught with as much baggage from our broken childhood as it may be. Prayer is an opening to the only source of infinite and unerring love and guidance there will be, grounding us as we develop our interdependence on others to create an adult and mature life.

"Lord, teach us to pray."[26] The disciples knew that prayer is access to God. They wanted for themselves the same loving relationship that Jesus enjoyed with the Father. They saw that his relationship grounded Jesus and kept him faithful to his mission no matter what. Jesus spent whole nights in prayer, in intimate loving communion with the Father. The next day he went out among the people to share with them the fruit of those encounters with God: healings, advocacy, forgiveness, friendship, the Good News. The disciples wanted that same spiritual routine and a share in that same saving mission.

Abuse—especially if it was perpetrated by someone who, for the child, represented God in some way—seriously undermined trust in prayer. Some survivors have a pronounced relational rupture with God; others have something less but nonetheless may need to learn to trust again. For anyone who feels abandoned by God, there can be a change of heart that

---

[26] Luke 11:1, or as translated in the NAB: "Lord, teach us to pray just as John taught his disciples."

leads to learning how to pray all over again or maybe praying spontaneously for the first time. Here, spiritual guides can be very helpful as prayer becomes a safe place to ask for help again.

Prayer, as a heart-to-heart conversation with God, is one of the central spiritual activities for anyone in spiritual guidance. Prayer is an end in itself, for it is already an experience of loving union and communion with God. Great things happen through prayer. The one who prays is gradually transformed, re-made from within. Survivors' "fiat disposition," that is, their openness to God's will for them, prepares them to welcome whatever God asks them to do or to accept, as it did with Mary. In time there will be but one will, one heart, between them, as it was with Jesus: "… that they may be one, as we are one."[27]

St. Francis de Sales encouraged mental prayer in which one meditates on some incident in the life of Jesus so as to "put on the mind of Christ"[28] and to resolve to imitate him that very day in some very concrete and tangible way. In time and in this way, survivors begin to be as Jesus was and to act as he did; they begin, in the language of de Sales, to live Jesus.

With a survivor who wants to learn to pray, a good beginning is to read with that person a scriptural passage that depicts an incident in the life of Jesus. Read it slowly and pause prayerfully after reading it. Then speak your own reflections on the incident, unhurriedly,

---

[27] John 17:22
[28] Philippians 2:5, or as found in the NAB: "Have among yourselves the same attitude that is also yours in Christ Jesus."

softly; carry on your own conversation with God that speaks to what you are learning from that gospel passage. Let survivors overhear you praying. In spiritual guidance, the ability to reveal yourself appropriately, without overstepping boundaries, is both comforting and insightful. It is a powerful sharing, and it can be a powerful turning point. Francis says you only really learn to love by loving. You also only really learn to pray by praying. Against the example of the abuser who perverted love and caring authority, your self-revelation of love and prayer may be very helpful.

Many people are able to move into a more prayerful relationship with God in this way. They do not really have to ask God for help as He knows their heart, their desires and their needs better than they know them themselves. This is an antidote to the loneliness of being a survivor. It is also the beginning of a deepening sense that it is okay simply to want to be with Him, to spend some time with Him. The sacred spaces we clear gain special purpose. Healing and growth, on every level, both human and spiritual, move forward with new graces, all from drawing closer to the living God, for the creature is always re-created anew in the presence of the Creator.

GATHERING SUPPORT

Our support systems matter. It is very important that we, early on, make a conscious effort to identify who is safe. That includes accepting what they can offer us and what they cannot offer us.

There are people who have no place in our support network because they are dangerous emotionally, psychologically, or spiritually—even physically. This first level of elimination can be the most difficult to see and accept, and the most painful to make. It is very much like the radical surgery to remove a tumor that precedes all the other treatment.

For immediate support, there are people who are trained or fluent in our recovery, such as therapists, more experienced survivors in group programs, and trained spiritual guides. These people often begin as beacons for our early recovery and transition into particularly knowing companions along the entire way.

There is housecleaning that will be done. It will be messy. Survivors have a high tolerance for crazy-making people, and self-absorbed takers, and enablers of wrong-doing. Abuse has desensitized us to how "healthful" feels, so we founder without discrimination. Recovery will help us unlearn the lessons that desensitized us. It will rewire the gears, but relationships will be disrupted to the degree they rely on the old, wounded self. Some people will adjust, others will not. Some will stay in our lives. Some will go from our lives. We will grieve the loss of people and the loss of an old self.

The people who remain, whether family or friends, all have something unique and special to offer us. They become distinct pieces in the quilt we sew together for our process. Yet, our recovery requires our decision to remain alert to our support network, in honest contact with it.

We will grieve even the best support network. Everyone there will fall short at some point. No one in our adult support network can ever replace the parent who can be everything to a child, who can fill a child's life. We must grieve the loss of that parent whose total wonderfulness was forever broken when the predator destroyed our childhood.

When recovery leaves us sad or weary, we have an established network of receptive people on whom we can lean. But that is partly our own work, accepting how everyone will be human, imperfect, even inept if loving. When only the perfect parent will do, when we need someone who will not fail us or have their own needs to manage, we have God, a loving Father waiting for us to turn to Him. We have Jesus, our Savior waiting to lift us up out of the darkness. We have the Spirit to carry us to a new way of living that is free of the scourges we were too young to bear.

In his ministry of spiritual guidance, St. Francis de Sales placed the emphasis on interiority, that is, on the heart of the one under his guidance. He believed that as the heart is so will be all one's exterior activities and relationships. And he wanted Jesus to be the heart of our heart so that, in time, Jesus himself might be seen once again walking upon the earth—in us. The biblical support for this inner transformation into another Christ is Galatians 2:20: "and the life I live now is not my own; Christ is living in me." Francis would add something like: "and Jesus is acting through me." All of this is captured in the phrase that stands as a summary of his Jesus-centered spirituality: "Live Jesus."

I find a contemporary expression of this approach in the practice of many young people today. Many of them wear a rubber bracelet inscribed with the initials, "WWJD:" "What would Jesus do?" Gradually transformed, through the grace of prayer and sacraments, into another Christ, the Christian continually asks the question, "What would Jesus do?", and tries to answer that question by acting as Jesus would act in this particular set of circumstances or with this particular person or group of people.

How can this approach help survivors deal with the sad fact that all people, even good and supportive people, at times disappoint them and fail to live up to their expectations? They must deal with the painful fact that support systems—parents, teachers, Church—in the past failed to protect them from abuse. And, they must deal with the troubling reality that, for many survivors, part or all of some families reject and even disown survivors for revealing the truth of the abuse. As is noted above, "Everyone there will fall short at some point." These fallings short vary in degree and across time.

The example of the mixed relationship between Jesus and Peter gives us a hint at how to deal with good people when they disappoint and fail us. Although Peter was the first to acknowledge Jesus as the Messiah, he was initially strongly resistant to the place that suffering and Cross would play in the Lord's mission. At Jesus's invitation Peter bravely jumped out of the boat and began to walk on water but, seeing the waves, began to sink and drown. Within hours of boldly asserting at the Last Supper that he would follow Jesus anywhere, Peter denied even knowing him, not once but three times. Yet, after each of these disappointments Jesus forgave this brave and good man, warts and all, and welcomed him back into his friendship, even making him the rock upon which his church is built. Jesus was able to see the heart of the man and his good intentions and at the same time to forgive him when, through human weakness, his actions at times failed to measure up to his intentions. Was this Jesus's way of teaching us to look beyond the failures and disappointing behavior of others and to see only their good intention while accepting them warts and all?

Affirming Boundaries

Wellbeing is all about boundaries. Child sexual abuse is all about the destruction of boundaries. Healing from the latter is about restoring the former. Recovery is about recovering boundaries.

Naming boundaries is very hard. For people raised in relatively safe environments, boundaries are so second-natured that it's hard to consciously name them. For survivors, the internal canvas is a blank. It's not just a matter of where boundaries are or what they are; it's a matter of where they come from in the first place. Where do we find them in ourselves?

Knowing boundaries was hard for me. Then I realized another value to my feelings. For example, when I felt my anger surge unexpectedly, I started to take a step back and survey the situation. What was the trigger for my anger? Usually, I noticed someone or something was crossing my boundary and making me uncomfortable. Once I saw the problem, I could deal with it more directly. My anger had become an early warning system. It was being channeled to help me thrive.

Setting boundaries will be messy, because learning a new skill is always messy. It's better to make a messy start than to go nowhere. Practicing on people we trust is a great way to learn how to assert boundaries—and how not to.

―――

In his *Introduction to the Devout Life*, St. Francis de Sales describes a bird that builds its nest on the water in such a way that, whether there are calm or rough seas, the nest never topples over or takes on water and its opening is always pointed at the air and sky above. Somehow that image comes to mind as my work with survivors returns again and again to the importance of boundaries in everyday social interactions, but especially for survivors whose boundaries were completely shattered by abuse. We need to build such a nest around us so that, while open to the air and sky of daily social interactions, we are nevertheless protected from the threatening waters of overstepped boundaries.

The survivor's first instinct is often the right one: to wall oneself within oneself, keeping safe at least the center of one's center. Over time that wall can become quite hardened. From fear or shame, some survivors find it difficult to leave this hiding place. But relational isolation is arid and even dangerous.

Survivors do venture out of that center, while seeking some way for others to be kept at a comfortable, manageable distance. Here the hard work of recovery begins. How to have boundaries without having walls?

Knowing what boundaries are may be second nature to most of us, but it is a real challenge for people who have been violated by something as traumatic as abuse. Observing feelings helps people understand themselves, so the rush to judge, even confess, feelings like anger is not always the most helpful way to respond to the very strong and sometimes seemingly negative feelings survivors must process. It's one thing to understand that a feeling interferes with our relationship with God, but it's another to work with it to understand how to let God work through even our most difficult feelings to heal us.

Help the one you are guiding to observe their feelings in the light of God's care. The same can be said of their needs, which people often assume have no place in a holy life. There is an important difference between denying oneself and ignoring one's needs. Understanding this difference is often a part of spiritual growth. For survivors, coming to this understanding is more difficult because, as many will tell you, abuse harms and even annihilates the self. Some survivors are seeking a self to deny. Others are completely unaware of needs before they can meet them. For these people on this quest it is important to help them find their own clues about their own needs, boundaries, and identity.

Affirming these things helps survivors become confident affirming them to others in sometimes far less receptive settings, including difficult family or social settings where the effects of the abuse may linger well beyond the point when the survivor chooses to heal. Some support systems are waiting for the survivor to share their needs, boundaries, and self. Others were the very systems that created the confusion and supported the abuse in the first place. Spiritual guidance helps each survivor rely on a deepening relationship with God to help stand firm in who they are, regardless of how they are received in settings outside your office or meeting place.

Relating to Family

Our families have been wounded by what happened to us. It is not uncommon for other siblings, or cousins or friends, to have suffered the same fate. Some families provided easy prey for predators because they were in crisis over other things, like financial strain, emotional disorganization, divorce, substance abuse, or mental illness. Other families were what might be called model families, and still were prowled by predators. All families in which a child has been abused have been wounded by the secret. Many family members, especially siblings, who were not abused, show similar emotional and psychological wounds from a secondary victimization as if they absorbed the unspoken truth. Later, when a victim shares their past, finally breaking the dark secret, families begin to heal—but only after a secondary wound is inflicted.

Some families are not supportive. Victims are as often rejected by their families as they are embraced. There is a great price to pay for speaking the truth, and there is no assurance people are ready to hear it and have their experience of family relationships upended, even if it is true. This means victims can struggle with a second wounding, when their recovery makes them the pariah of part or all of a family. It also means victims face profound moral dilemmas, for example, knowing the predator remains free to prey on a new generation of the family.

Some families—in whole or in part—are supportive. Their support for the victim is fertile ground for a beginning sense of survival and hope for recovery. Wounded as well, the most supportive ones exercise a seldom-noticed courage and tenacity, like a lame person pushing a beloved friend in a wheelchair toward Lourdes. They will suffer also the loss of a sense of family, possibly the rejection of family, and certainly grief and a sense of guilt. Their faith will be challenged. They may need professional assistance, and spiritual assistance. Sometimes their personal stories of abuse may finally surface. Always their bonds with the survivor can deepen and their other relationships can become enriched.

Regardless of how receptive to a survivor's story family members may be, their response reflects the range of reactions in every survivor—from disbelief and self-hatred to grief and confusion. In recovery literature and everywhere else, some of the most forgotten victims of abuse are all the family members and friends who suffer with the survivor. Oddly, but wonderfully, one of the most effective ways for these secondary victims to recover is walking with the survivor on that personal Via Dolorosa.

―

Spiritual guidance is almost always one on one. Yet, neither the guide nor the person in guidance is a solitary or isolated being. They have relationships with many people and especially with family members. Indeed, they are part of the human family, which is a living organism, and members of the Christian family, which is the Body of Christ. In Jesus, we are all interconnected.

Every action either betters the whole or harms the whole. As suggested above, the abuse of one family member negatively affects in some way everybody else in the family. Healing is therefore necessary for all, parents, siblings and, depending on circumstances, perhaps even extended family as well.

There are venues for family therapy. There are even support groups for family members who are dealing with the negative effects of abuse in the family. But the spiritual guide's principal responsibility is to the survivor. What guidance helps a survivor in relation to family where members are wounded, but also where sometimes members were abusers or enablers or even now participants in a damaging family dynamic?

In the New Testament, especially in the Acts of the Apostles, there are examples of whole families coming to the faith through the example of one member of the family. When, for example, the Roman centurion Cornelius came to faith, the Holy Spirit fell upon all those who were with him and all were baptized by Peter.[29] The survivor's progress in spiritual healing will naturally have a healing effect on family members as well, but it is important to be sure the survivor in your care doesn't feel responsible for others before being responsible for themselves. This impulse to care for others in the family, or to engage in arguments with the family, at times can be a way to avoid facing the more pressing issues in one's self.

Yet, as a survivor deepens in a commitment to recovering from abuse and as their relationship with God deepens, things do change. These are not always changes for the better, but they may mark progress in families out of denial and into the healing truth. Sorting through all this is difficult for the survivor and for you at times. For example, a pressing question is whether other children remain at risk of abuse by a family member who is protected by the denial of others. In these instances, the survivor needs the counsel of qualified professionals, and you should turn to the guidance of the diocesan assistance program. There's a reason family members prefer to deny these dangerous situations, because facing them is much harder. Be sure to rely on trained professionals.

Many, indeed most, survivors do not have to confront these immediate dangers any longer. All seek to progress from a wish for healing and a decision to heal toward healing itself. With the Holy Spirit welcomed into the process, there is much to hope for.

---

[29] Acts 10:44-48

Perhaps for many, spiritual guidance can help them be open to the grace that "runs ahead" and prepares their hearts for the sometimes hard work of confronting what was wrong—and loving what is good. This may touch upon parents, for example, facing the harsh reality that they were taken in by the abuser as well, failing to protect their child. It may involve, for siblings, their failure to believe their brother or sister's story when she was finally able to tell it—or their own need to confront abuse from the same person in childhood. Many siblings carry an unreasonable burden of guilt, blaming themselves for failing to protect their sibling, forgetting that they were just children, too.

All this, even as everyone may move toward healing, is disruptive and painful. Yet, grace has a ripple effect. Its power for good can spread out from the one-on-one encounter between guide and guided to all those affected or wounded or harmed in some way by the abuse. The relationship of spiritual guidance will have, therefore, through the power of grace, a positive effect for those open to the Spirit in any way.

Fostering Intimacy

The physicality in child sexual abuse is often mistaken by outsiders for sexual intimacy, when it is not. It is a child being overpowered by an adult, physically and mentally, and used. It is a dehumanizing event.

Survivors who did not resist often mistake their actions as consent. Survivors who resisted but were still overpowered often mistake their actions as sur-

render. Here is where the mortal confusions about what is free choice, and what is true surrender versus annihilation, are rooted. Both interfere with future intimacies, including physical ones.

There are many helpful steps in therapy for exploring how a survivor approaches intimacy as a healthful part of an adult life. We arrive in therapy having come to a certain point in our physical relationships. Some of us have become promiscuous to feel much and know no one. In too-simplistic terms, we became overly sexualized by having no way to integrate a far-too-early sexual experience into our total selves. By contrast, others withdrew, or staggered from one broken relationship to another, or avoided our own sexuality simply as a way to feel nothing that might trigger confusion and fear. Mostly, many survivors have managed healthful relationships, but even some of these have remained walled-off despite physical intimacy.

An overly sexualized culture complicates matters. People, not just women, are bombarded with reasons to dislike their bodies, and are shamed by media for aging, for weight, for disabilities, or for other perceived imperfections. It is a culture of shame despite its exhibitionism. Survivors can be triggered easily in this era of profligate promiscuity and vulgarity, shutting down before they are empowered to shut it off. It isn't easy for anyone seeking godly, modest sexual norms in this environment. It requires a foundational decision, which was denied each survivor at the point when abuse began.

It takes self-esteem to claim back the right to decide for ourselves. Even the most grounded person will face challenges and will surmount them only if their self-esteem is rooted in an awareness of God's image of us—and not the image offered by the world or understated by ourselves. Survivors of abuse have already been dehumanized in physical intimacy. Especially for any survivor whose abuser was a God-like authority (clergy or parent) it can be very hard to turn to God to rediscover our self-esteem in Him. Yet, all other sources of self-esteem are fleeting and only partly restore intimacy of any type, including physically.

Restoring intimacy follows on restoring self-esteem. It is about exploring how surrender physically is not annihilation. This is particularly important physically. Intellectually we know that we were not born to be harmed, but it takes time to let our bodies, which have memories of their own, experience that. How? The more recovery reveals to us who we are, the more we can understand what feels safe—and what does not feel safe. We can begin to believe, as a central part of our own story, what boundaries we need for physical intimacy to be spontaneous, joyful, and safe, as God intended our relationships it to be.

The biblical book that probably best describes the God-given beauty of human love, intimacy, and sexuality is the Song of Songs. It is a favorite of both St. Francis de Sales and Pope Emeritus Benedict XVI (see, especially, the latter's powerful encyclical, *Deus caritas est*). Through the lens of this sacred book, salvation history is best understood as a love story between God and each human person. In this image alone, the evil of abuse by adults of children stands in terribly stark contrast.

Yet there is more in this short book of the Bible than a contrast to the perversion of abusers. Before becoming sacred scripture, the Song of Songs most likely existed as several love songs sung at Jewish weddings. The story is a simple but moving one. Two lovers get separated in the chaos of a crowded marketplace. Both run throughout the city in a frantic search for their beloved, asking everyone they encounter if they have seen their beloved, describing what they look like in loving detail. Finally they catch site of one another, run toward each other, embrace, kiss, and cry out: "I have found you at last and I will never again let you go!"[30]

Their story represents salvation history, for it represents God and each person—that is, God and each survivor. In the beginning, God and the human family became tragically separated (original sin). The story of salvation history is the account of each trying to find the other. The Incarnation is the moment they finally find one another. There, they meet, embrace, kiss, and promise never again to let the other go. Inspired by this book, St. Francis de Sales tellingly describes the Incarnation as "God's kiss to creation." The fact this survivor is sitting with you even exploring the possibility of spiritual direction is a sign that they, too, are running

---
[30] Song of Songs 3:3-4, as translated in the NAB: "... when I found him whom my soul loves. I held him and would not let him go."

through the marketplace, seeking the God who is tirelessly seeking them. Your role is to facilitate that reunion on a daily basis.

This short Scripture is also a way of assisting the adult survivor of sexual abuse to come to an appreciation of human love and sexuality. Each survivor finds a way to the distinction between the de-humanizing use of sexuality to exploit and even harm them as children and the humanity-affirming role of sexuality in human love and union. For all, this resolution is complex. For many it has taken root before recovery work in therapy may even begin. For a few it results in promiscuity or other compulsions. As a way to deepen their relationship with God here, where a survivor has coped with this false use of their bodies, you might suggest meditating on this short scripture. Ask what God might be telling this survivor about how they can involve God in healing this abuse of their bodies and the very physical memories that can linger.

Everything is there in the Song of Songs for an appreciation of the place that love and sexuality play in both human and spiritual completion. Seen in its light, the gift of one's self to the other is a free act of surrender, entrustment, and completion, never annihilation. Again, this is opposite of what abuse has been, and so it is sadly the opposite of how a survivor first experienced sexuality. The paradox is this: one becomes more completely one's self in the loving surrender to another that is human sexuality. How can grappling with this aspect of the wound of abuse be a way to grow even closer to God?

FINDING BALANCE

Survivors managed to endure impossibly painful experiences that lasted a day or weeks or months or years. Survival required crisis thinking. Anger offered a possibly protective force. Withdrawal offered a possible removal from the attention of a predator. A fast life with little thought seemed to outrun the predator. Numbing agents dulled the pain. Lying was the perfect disguise for our ugliness.

The surprising thing for survivors is that we actually do outgrow our defenses. Whether they were successful when we used them as children, they tend to obstruct our relationships and fulfillment as adults. Then again, it's not as if they do not have any role in our lives at all.

Anger, for example, can fuel a lot of change; it has been the driving force behind the work of many great artists. The important point is that it must not consume us while it drives our creativity and purpose.

Withdrawal can have led to a rich interior life, which is something that can ground an adult life. It can also be a hiding place, where we miss most of life. Our recovery from an impulse to withdraw is to find ways we can explore beyond our hidden gardens and ways we can identify safe people with whom to share our rich interior lives.

Even as we may need to seek help in addiction programs, we need to learn that numbing agents are not the problem. Our need to be numbed is the problem. Recovery is about unearthing the buried things we fear the most, discovering how little they are in comparison to our great God, and moving into a new life no longer haunted by ghosts we did not even really know.

Balance is needed even in recovery. As we recover, we still live our lives. We still find our joys. We still work and love and learn. We still falter and retrace our steps. Our life encompasses recovery but, except for short periods when a serious focus helps us advance, recovery is not the full life we live. But it does, step by step, if we let ourselves be patient, add a remarkable fullness to life.

―

Salesian spirituality is sometimes described as "inspired common sense" or "good balance." The following expression from St. Francis de Sales captures its spirit well: "Moderation in all things but the love of God."

The old adage spoke of virtue is situated at the mid-point between two extremes. As survivors work in the process of recovery, they often begin looking for the balancing middle between, for example, anger that fuels change and anger that is all consuming; or between withdrawal that leads to solitude and withdrawal that becomes an isolating hiding place from others.

"Balance is needed even in recovery." In practice, balance is proportion, perspective, the apt word, the appropriate gesture, just the right action that is suited to the particular moment or circumstance. Both balance and its lack are best understood in practice.

Most people learn balance through the ordinary give and take of daily life. But that usual process was severely interrupted, halted perhaps, in the child victim's life at the time of abuse. The child's life was devastated, and the family dynamic was altered forever. Balance then becomes another of the countless casualties of abuse. It has to be learned or relearned all over again. Balance is not a "natural fit" for survivors who learned to protect themselves by withdrawal, reserve, and reticence. These defenses further restricted children's participation in the countless little, even daily, opportunities to discover balance through the give and take of trial and error. The same applies to adult survivors. So, balance is not second nature. Rather than finding reactions and behavior at the mid-point between two extremes, survivors can go through periods in their lives when they are given to extremes without knowing how to live in balance.

How can a spiritual guide help survivors find balance? Listening is, as always, the most important step. As a survivor describes interactions, extremes will be revealed, or exhaustion from living in extreme straights. Often survivors can see, for example, a reaction to broached boundaries as out of proportion to the breach itself, but it is hard to imagine alternative responses. Let that be a teachable moment. The guide, in hearing the account, might suggest ways or, better, elicit from survivors various scenarios in which reactions would be more proportionate to the offense, more balanced in keeping with the situation. Here, putting on Jesus becomes a catalyst for imagining ways to be a person who is recovered, rather than a person who is wounded. From there, it takes time and mistakes. Virtue becomes habit through repetition. Good balance is learned in the same way. The guide, along with the safe and accepting environment created with the survivor, can serve as someone who helps survivors rely on Jesus for very practical questions in transforming a way of living.

Trusting Self

No matter how illogical it may seem to everyone else, survivors usually begin their recovery with very little trust in their own judgment. It's not hard to understand why. We were experiencing evil when everyone said the abuser was good, even holy. We were living inside all the lies the abusers and sometimes others were telling to hide what was happening. Reality did not jive with what we knew, and few of us had anyone to corroborate what we experienced. What remains is a potentially fatal self-doubting.

Self-trust is hard won through life experiences that give us practice in making great decisions based on good judgments.

Self-trust is also hard won in therapy, where we take our therapist back as the witness we never had, to see what we saw, to validate the truth no one acknowledged. This is important healing.

Self-trust is won like an interior battle, between a part of us who sees as a victim sees and the growing part of us who sees beyond the constraints of our wounds. Every time we take the difficult step to remove a dangerous person from our life, to change a damaging habit of behavior or thought, to trust someone else, or to pray or seek graces from God, we are earning our own self-trust back with sound choices.

―

The bitter irony in the self-doubt of victims is that they were right all along. They faced the truth of their abuse when no one would believe them. They may have tried to say something but lacked the words or the listeners, or they may have been silenced by the trauma. Yet, they knew firsthand of the evil in their abuser while all others still only saw the pretense of trustworthiness in them. Since no one believed the children, or heard them, over the course of time child victims began to doubt themselves and to mistrust their judgment of things. Why was their assessment of what was true so much at odds with that of so many other older and supposedly wiser people? Their self-doubt now as adults is not the result of any failure on their part, but is rather the sad effect of the betrayal, disbelief, and denial of so many others.

Still, this can leave many survivors unskilled in forming right judgments about themselves and others. They are trained to doubt their own assessment of the goodness of this behavior or that, or the rightness of this practice or the other. Thus, they can arrive for spiritual guidance grappling with many wrong judgments from which they have suffered, it would seem, from deep self-wounding. These can be a plethora of issues, including personal tragedy from alcohol, drugs, people, and high-risk behavior. So, when it comes to making judgments, some survivors begin their process of recovery quite gun-shy, ready to trust more readily in the judgment of others than in their own. And, since some of those others may not be good stewards of their trust, they are vulnerable all over again to re-wounding by trusted others.

The spiritual guide is invited into this juncture with added pressure to be reliable, honest, trustworthy, and gentle. Survivors look for a guy line, which we do become, but we are ever leading people closer to God. One way to do so at this juncture would be to suggest a reflection on the words of Job: "I know that my vindicator lives."[31] Remind survivors that their initial judgments about both their abusers and their abuse were on target all along. Others may have doubted them, but God, their vindicator, did not. Their judgments were, in fact, right judgments, that is, their assessment of the abuser and of his abuse corresponded to the truth of their reality: both were evil. So their instincts were accurate. Those instincts are probably still accurate and may only need practice in honing them once again after years of self-doubt and poor judgments. Leaving behind the self-doubt in this regard is a way of unburying the truth to be heard, believed, and trusted again.

Affirming each small step in right judgment, one after the other, helps survivors rediscover their original wisdom and perceptiveness. Applaud successes and encourage them when they fail. These seem like such basic acts, but for people who have been discouraged or punished for speaking truth, they are

---

[31] Job 19:25

sustenance, and they are a cornerstone in our credibility as people serving God who is Truth. With us, breaking the silence and speaking the truth is a way of honoring how God believed them when no one else did, and how God is waiting for them to turn to Him with all the fallout that remains—and courage and love that emerge in their lives—from the terrible experience of abuse.

OPENING UP

It's hard to be open to a world we learned very early was fraught with danger. The surprise of a birthday party was no memory compared to the shock of how an abuser can carefully groom us to the point of trusting ... all the way to intrusion and manipulation.

Many of us live life like a Japanese garden. We carefully comb the sands in beautiful patterns. People who do not know the sorrows of our pasts might even be drawn to our quiet, our compassion, or our skillfulness. What they do not do, in their admiration, is step into the carefully cultivated patterns around us, and we keep ourselves well inside the perimeter, hidden in full sight.

Breaking out of our cultivated patterns of being with people without people knowing us, is part of recovery. And it is messy. Some people will not be as receptive as we expected, others will be more wonderful than we could imagine. The sands need to be scrambled.

That can be a very long distance. If we look, we may see footprints of God venturing to find us in our hiding places. Or, we may accuse God of abandoning us by pointing at a single set of footprints in the distances we have already covered, but God assures us He was carrying us all that way. It's a timeless story for an endless dilemma of how we choose to walk through life.

There is no perfect solution. Some people are introverted, others extroverted. How we experienced being abused is very tied up in our dispositions as children and our unique natures. Moving through recovery we discover things about ourselves we could not discover when we were still in a post-trauma shock as children. The more we know about our basic needs and dispositions, the more we are able to choose the right people to invite into our treasured spaces and to receive unexpected surprises with the unqualified delight of children.

Adult survivors often hide in plain sight. Through necessity, they have learned how to conceal who they really are while appearing to reveal all that they are. It is not so much a lie as it is the only means they had to protect themselves during their vulnerability as abused children. To appear to others as one thing while in themselves quite another thing: this is how they managed to survive. They had to keep the secret, so they tried to seem "normal." As adults now, they are often at a loss as to how to break this habit of concealment. How they are now is aptly described above as a Japanese garden: "What they do not do, in their admiration, is step into the carefully cultivated patterns around us, and we keep ourselves well inside the perimeter, hidden in full sight."

How can the spiritual guide help them to become for others what they truly are? How can they learn to be congruent or transparent? How can they become truth?

First, of course, there is a spiritual approach to the survivor's shame which is discussed elsewhere. And, there is guidance for maintaining walls against others, as well. There are reasons to be open and to seek to be more open with the right people who are able and willing to love survivors as they richly deserve.

However, the drive to be known can be mistaken, too. One important step is to answer this question: "Does everybody need to know us as God knows us?" Isn't He, as Truth itself, the only one who actually already knows fully the truth of who we are and further, the only One who needs to know that? There are unconscious dimensions or levels of ourselves that are hidden even to us. But, if we can be completely open and transparent to God, that is sufficient. Then all we need to learn is how much of ourselves others need to know for our relationship with them to be authentic, true, and good.

No one ever fully discloses him or herself to another person, nor need they. While there can be a certain loneliness in feeling unknown, especially while grappling with recovery after abuse, there just is no one person who can fulfill the need we have in relationship. All people must confront alone the need to turn to God—and not others—for fulfillment. This is the stuff of spiritual guidance, where we grow strong enough in grace to understand that only Truth itself needs to or can know us completely. The good news is that He already does—and loves us still! Here is the "cure" for shame over time. Here, too, is the starting point for being open with others. We simply need to accept the fact that God already knows us and accepts all—indeed died to save us each—for it frees us to be who we are. There's a place deep within us where only God goes or needs to go. "Full disclosure" applies only to Him.

Spiritual guidance helps us to see all of this clearly and to sort through what we want to disclose to others and how to go about that in such a way that is truthful but not necessarily exhaustive of our truth.

Simplifying Life

Life got complicated the moment a predator began to abuse us in a web of lies and secrecy. What was happening to us was beyond our comprehension. What to do was beyond our decision-making ability at the time. Life as a victim is overwhelming and confusing.

Survivors seldom are sure the abuse has ended. Suddenly it may stop because the predator is taken with a different prey, or it may go through cycles of abuse and then being ignored. Even if a predator was moved to another parish, however, the child does not know if at any moment abuse could resume. If one trusted adult proved so different, any adult could. Some children shut down, become dull to dull the anxiety. Others become hyper vigilant, even hyper, wary, overly alert.

Any of the ways children adapt to a life endangered follows us into adulthood. Research shows that survivors of child abuse retain hyper levels of adrenaline and cortisol (the "fight or flight" hormones) in their systems for their entire lifetimes, although meditation and other practices can help reduce the blood levels. Survivors often have a keen sense of hearing and habits such as sitting close to doors in case escape is needed. Adult life has many hardly noticeable rituals that preserve a sense of alert.

Recovery can be a sense of unpacking the complications. Like emptying an attic of all the things we no longer need, we sort through what helps us and what simply extends the state of anxiety. Prayer, meditating on Scripture, cultivating gifts of the Spirit, as well as exercise, having fun, connecting with good people, and eating well, all are part of finding ways to reverse the gear for anxiety.

One of the things about recovery I resented the longest was the need for added self-care. Self-caring seemed like such an indulgence for someone as driven as I am. But it's additionally difficult accepting that for the rest of my life I will need to be responsible about the many ways triggers can still set off my grief or how events now can set off my anxiety about then. Yet, accepting this responsibility instead of resisting it has permitted me to thrive in ways I would never have expected. With time, I've learned that success is more about skills and practices for self care, and less about losing time or footing in daily life.

I work a lot with Sisters of the Visitation, a monastic Order co-founded by St. Francis de Sales and St. Jane de Chantal. The sisters enjoy a spirituality which favors interiority. It is deep within their hearts that they and God commune, and it is mainly there that the drama of their spiritual lives is played out. They leave there, as Mary did in the mystery of the Visitation, only to carry with them the God whom they have conceived through prayer and meditation, into loving service of those with whom they live in community and share life.

Their monasteries are uncluttered, simple, and clean. The sisters' home is deliberately designed and kept that way in order not to distract them from their interior focus. Without things to distract them, they are forced, in a sense, to struggle to achieve the one thing necessary: loving union with God and the ready accomplishment of His holy will for them from moment to moment as life unfolds.

There are many strategies and techniques that children victims learned over the years in order to keep themselves safe, alert, wary, and vigilant. For a long time, no one else was protecting them. They had to do it all by themselves, or, that is, they lived with the illusion they had the power to take on the responsibilities of adults who should have been protecting them. Adult survivors sometimes find these long-standing habits difficult to break. Something of the vulnerable child can remain with them and will, therefore, need to be protected, guarded, and cared for. The more self-discovery, the more survivors realized that they can never completely forget, or neglect, that child.

For this reason, while the brain of the survivor knows that the threat of further abuse is over, their heart is never quite sure. How can spiritual guidance help here?

The example of the uncluttered monastery and the reasons for it may help a survivor at least want to empty their emotional attic of many of these once-necessary strategies and techniques. Survivors, too, want the one thing necessary. These outdated survival habits take a lot of energy to maintain, often leaving people emotionally exhausted. This prevents them, also, from focusing on God and on his holy will for their healing and wellbeing. So, one approach may be to begin with something that is relatively easy to let go. Work patiently, even intermittently, trusting survivors to know their own pace and enjoying each step toward feeling lightened from the weight of old habits. In a simplified life, survivors find increased energies for the things of God, and a grace-filled momentum begins to enrich their overall healing process.

Detaching as Needed

There is spiritual detachment. Detaching from intense feelings was a really helpful skilled I used with overwhelming feelings. For example, I began to detach from self-loathing. It was like putting a psychic air bubble between me and a feeling that had taken on a life of its own. I didn't even know the degree to which it was undermining my best efforts. I began to watch the hatred ping from one thought to the next, from one daily event to the next, landing on a single detail that it used to tear me down with fresh energy. Detachment permitted me to see my own feelings at work quite independently of how I lived each day. It started to show me how I was not limited to feelings, and my feelings were not a full reality.

Detachment is different from denial. Denial says there is no pain. Detachment watches the pain, over time lessening the pain. There's a big difference.

My favorite image of detachment is geological, where a detachment formation is a huge wedge-like shape that tears out of the building tension between two tectonic plates that just won't give way to each other. There's no return to how things were before once it has been created. Something has to release the pressure of all the forces converging in the broken heart of a survivor of child abuse. The explosion, the crisis, that breaks through is what will release some of that tension just enough to lead us into the help we need, wherever we need to go to find it. Once we make our moves toward recovery, and deeper into recovery, a wedge against the past pressures is in place. Life will never be the same.

―

"It [detachment] started to show me how I was not limited to feelings, and my feelings were not a full reality." I don't think I can count the number of times I have repeated the following sentence to people in spiritual guidance: "You are not your feelings." I usually go on to remind them that their feelings, whether they consider them good or bad, are morally neutral.

They arise in us before our will has had a chance to become engaged. Once our will is engaged, however, do we choose to act on our feelings of, say, anger, or do we "cut them short," doing our best to rid ourselves of them by creatively distracting ourselves in some way? Morally, what counts is acting on our negative feelings of anger or self-loathing or lust; or, for that matter, acting on our positive feelings of compassion or generosity or kindness. Actions—good or bad—flow from the will: we choose to act or we choose not to act. Feelings—good or bad—are just there, uninvited, often unwelcomed. They are not us, but they can offer important insights into ourselves at any moment in time.

"Let go, and let God." As suggested above, this familiar AA principle can be a powerful tool here as well, especially when dealing with the negative feelings associated with abuse. If we are not our feelings, then we need not pay them any attention at all but quickly, decisively, and confidently turn them over to God, trusting that He not only does not judge us on our feelings but is delighted that we try to ignore them and cut them short.

Finally, "Let go" and "let God" are two distinct acts, both involving our will, our choice, our decision. Both are brave and interdependent acts of faith, too—the one an act of faith in ourselves and the other an act of faith in God.

RECONCILIATION

Overview

Reconciliation happens throughout life for survivors of the trauma of child sexual abuse. For example, they reconcile themselves to many losses and much heartache, and they reconcile with people who once failed them but have, since, become able to provide love and support. Reconciliation may involve forgiveness, or it may not. It is part of a process of integrating pieces, the chards of self, if you will. Past is integrated with present, suffering with hope, wound with wellbeing. Reconciliation, in practical terms, is a private marathon demanding tenacity, courage, and growth.

Reconciling with things of faith is particularly painful for some. This is most often related to abuse by clergy or others with authority from our Church or other churches. However, similar wounds may also be inflicted by abusers who were overly religious for neurotic reasons, such as an overly scrupulous parent who hid abuse behind a façade of religiosity. For any survivor who as a child was abused by such authorities, things of faith can be fraught with triggers from past agonies. Even survivors who were not abused by overtly religious adults may still find their connection to God was ruptured, because they lost faith in all authority figures after having been abused by them, or abandoned by them to abuse.

Reconciliation cannot occur safely when wounds are raw or broken hearts remain untended. Personal healing must progress toward reconciliation, which can be found in turning points along the way. Pushing someone toward any reconciliation on our own timing only re-traumatizes them. With a timing that defies our control, reconciliation reveals God's will not ours. We serve His will best when we presume neither to drive nor direct it.

This section has collected together reflections on explicitly Christian and Catholic symbols, traditions, and Scripture. Survivors may decline to read these until they are ready—if they ever are ready. Meanwhile, spiritual guides will see how, because of the evil perversion that is child sexual abuse, sacred things can become a double-edged sword—all the more holy in real-life healing power for one who has endured trauma, but potentially fraught with triggers for painful memories, feelings, and experiences that render them all the more inapproachable. Here spiritual guides must be especially sensitive; what animates us may be what we wish most to share, but such enthusiasm can be hurtful. In this section the need for prayerful discernment is quite clear. The prayer life of the spiritual guide must open to accommodate the idea that, for others, what is holy can seem dangerous because it once was.

Survivors, with the support of prayer, can be ready, at some point, to explore the holy, healing, and triumphant gift of Jesus which can only be obscured but never defeated by evildoers.

RECONCILIATION: A SURVIVOR'S PERSPECTIVE

There are many points in recovery when we come to closure, a sort of release from struggles over feelings, memories, losses, even relationships. In therapy, for me, reconciliation was central. We reconcile ourselves to having endured trauma and all the loss it entails. We reconcile to some degree and in many different ways with parents and family members, friends, and others who failed us as children and as adults—without, for me, needing to reconcile with abusers as I know some survivors have been drawn to do. We also reconcile with people whom we have failed. Life is knitted back together this way quite mysteriously. Grace and faith inspire and sustain the work I otherwise would not have started or finished. Reconciliation does raise the issue of forgiveness, but for me the two were never the same, nor did they happen at the same time. I reconciled with a number of people long before my heart could feel the freedom of forgiveness.

I associate reconciliation with grieving. They share many things, in particular with the misconception that they end. For me, the myriad reconciliations are never done. Their demand for my attention recurs, often when something unexpected triggers old feelings. It's like a wind picks up one leaf from a still pile in the autumn—many are lifted in the swirl. They settle as we observe. I know the hard work I did in therapy has been effective because the swirl settles back into place with little more than a bitter tincture of the full journey that led me through. I've wondered at times if, in its little moth way, the moth grieves the cocoon before—and after—breaking free into flight. I would. I do.

There is also grieving, reconciliation, even closure in faith terms. We survivors have been estranged from our faith and even our God. Sin is rightly described as being estranged from God, but here too is an estrangement due to the sin of another in our vulnerable lives from which we are still left to reconcile with God. For one thing, there is reconciliation with God over what my friend Fr. Lou calls the "theodicy" issue, and what I articulate as "How could You?!" in prayer. There is also reconciling with the Church that failed us, the communities that enabled our abusers, and other Catholics who distained our truth-telling.

There are triggers, too. I have worked to find ways to de-sensitize myself to all the ways precious Catholic images and traditions were triggers for memories of abuse. This is another way I have had to reconcile with my faith. I am not alone in this effort. Many survivors have found ways to manage triggers, or to de-activate them, or to endure them for the sake of their faith. For some, who are drawn to do so, reconciliation restores a sacramental way of life. For me, I kept trying because all the journeys in flight I took away from Catholicism kept leading me back to the simple truth that I live ritually. In relationship to God

I knew that to mean I would thrive sacramentally. For me, for this simple reason (although there are others, too), there was nowhere else to go. For others, it's important to remember that reconciliation with God is possible but only somewhere not associated with so much pain and betrayal.

Being back within the Church will have ups and downs, because life as a survivor includes certain ups and downs unique to our experiences and because for some of us the Church remains a mixture of faith life and traumatic memory. Some survivors recount being able to feel at ease in the Church. Many benefit from continued vigilance to triggers and self-care to navigate the settings of faith. A few make their peace with the Church but move to other churches to find communities of worship where the painful memories don't overwhelm them. What matters is that we have done what we can to remove obstacles to a free and unencumbered relationship with God.

RECONCILIATION: A SPIRITUAL GUIDE'S PERSPECTIVE

For Christians, the life of faith is rooted in ritual. At baptism, for instance, the child enters into the saving waters three times to symbolize faith in the Three Persons of the Trinity as Creator, Savior, and Sanctifier. Water itself symbolizes the washing away of original sin and the bridging of separation from God that resulted. The prominent presence of the Paschal candle represents one's new faith, one's new way of living, in the risen Christ. Anointing with Sacred Chrism symbolizes the new Christian's participation in the triple function of Jesus as priest, prophet, and king. The sign of the cross on the child's forehead at the beginning of the rite by priest, parents, and godparents symbolizes the child's vocation to follow, along with the whole Christian community, the crucified Lord. The white garment each child wears stands for the new creation that she has become through baptism. These are just some of the symbols that ritualize the sacrament of baptism. Every sacrament has its own rituals, its own symbols, and is celebrated at every important moment or turning point in a Christian's life: birth, adulthood (Confirmation), marriage for many, holy orders for some, forgiveness of sin, and diminishments from aging, serious illness, and dying.

In his *Introduction to the Devout Life*, St. Francis de Sales provides a ritual for the moment that one chooses, in a solemn and formal way, to leave behind a good but somewhat lackadaisical Christian life in order to embrace the demands and discipline of a strong and solid spiritual life, that is, a life of prayer, active and full participation in the sacramental life of the Church, and the practice of virtues that are suited to one's age, health, and state in life. As mentioned already, sometimes spiritual guidance for survivors of abuse must focus on fundamentals that are antecedent to such a juncture. Survivors are, and should be, supported as they rebuild a whole life, with God's grace, where abuse has left ruins and ruptured relationships.

However, with adaptations, what St. Francis suggests in the *Introduction to the Devout Life* can serve as an appropriate ritual for survivors who have reached a point when they feel a sense of closure and wish to leave behind, to the extent possible, the woundedness caused by abuse, especially as it pertains to the Church and its representatives, and to embrace once again the fullness of life in the Church. A move toward personal closure is a remarkable point only some are able to observe in their own lives, and it ought to be ritualized.

Francis leads "Philothea" (that is, anyone who loves God) through ten meditations over the course of ten days. The purpose of these meditations is to gradually lead her from her initial desire to lead a devout life to the moment when she elects in a solemn and formal way to follow Christ and to embrace the devout life by taking all the steps necessary for its accomplishment. He helps her to formulate a solemn declaration or protestation to that effect. After a general Confession, the celebration of Mass and reception of Holy Communion, she slowly reads her solemn declaration before God and the entire heavenly court of angels and saints as well as before any representatives of the Church militant who are present such as, for instance, her spiritual guide. Then, Philothea signs her declaration. This series of actions symbolize that she has left behind one stage of life and has entered into a brand new stage.

Survivors may not be comfortable with this particular set of steps. Their memories may be triggered, but, on a more positive note, their creative approaches to healing are likely to offer steps for a ritual they can design with you that helps bring closure to the journey of therapy and to bring God closer into this person's life. No matter what form it takes, the moment when one stage of a survivor's life ends and another begins ought to be ritualized, blessed, and celebrated. This can be an important part of spiritual guidance.

Reconciliation: A Psychologist's Perspective
Frank J. Moncher, PhD

There are two ways in which a therapy process reaches a place of ending or closure. In the first instance, a survivor of abuse achieves enough relief from the symptoms that compelled them into treatment that they desire a break from the work, though it is often recognized that additional help will likely be needed in the future to make more comprehensive life changes. In these situations, it is essential to be respectful of the timing of the person's journey, recognizing that, although we wish flourishing for all whom we assist, for some the risks involved in embracing the vulnerability that this requires is simply not possible at a given point in time. In the second instance, a survivor not only has experienced relief from anxieties and depression, but has taken the next steps towards looking at themselves and their need to change and grow. They have achieved a level of healing where they can objectively look at their own role in relationships and problems, without losing sight of the responsibilities of others for their role and keeping both in perspective.

In this second sense, as a survivor's therapy journey moves towards an end, there is commonly ambivalence experienced by both the survivor and the therapist. As much as both rejoice in the progress and recovery that has occurred, there is a loss that is felt in the victory, because the intensity of the journey has created a very real personal bond, aside from the professional connection. Ideally there is time and commitment spent shepherding the relationship towards an ending that is discussed in as frank and open a manner as discussing the trauma that compelled the beginning of the relationship. All too often with ambivalence comes avoidance, however, and it can sadly happen that the therapy relationship never has a clear ending but simply fades away, without due recognition of the importance each party has played in the other's life.

On the other hand, the opposite extreme can occur whereby both the survivor and therapist collude in keeping the weekly connection interminably, fostering an unhealthy dependence where the survivor gets enough emotional support from the therapist that they don't take the necessary steps to branch out in other relationships. This inadvertently can keep the survivor from moving to the next plateau of flourishing, which involves moving from the ability to embrace a free and unencumbered relationship with God to the challenge and joy of pursuing free and unencumbered relationships with others.

Thankfully, I have experienced many times where the golden mean of moderation has been possible. Neither do survivors fade away with no real sense of closure, nor do we continue to meet regularly in a manner that might inhibit their taking the risks of establishing other relationships. Instead there is the understanding that the therapy relationship, despite any professional trappings, was a genuine human encounter and, as such, it would be artificial to act as if the end of the need for treatment ended the relationship. Of course, the professional aspect of the relationship and boundaries therein should remain, so that the survivor will be comfortable resuming regular therapy in the future if needed. I welcome periodic phone calls, random sessions, or other means of staying in touch in a manner that honors the work done. So, as much as closure in treatment is a positive that should be achieved, and some natural experiences of loss will occur when "same time next week" morphs into "feel free to give me an update on your life when it feels right," the relationship need not be relegated to the past but can remain an active support as the survivor moves into thriving and establishing new meanings in their life.

Prayer

Most of us kept praying, some intermittently, almost all with a feeling of wretchedness.

We have wept. We have screamed. We have groaned. We have trembled. We have cringed and keened and fumed. We begged God, bargained with God, tried to outsmart God, and rejected God. We have assumed that the silent shroud that covers abuse is the sound of His abandonment.

We have recited prayers someone who loved us

taught us, and felt no one answer, and stopped midway. We have looked for signs and seen none. We have felt hurt and even rebuked at the memory of Scripture when prayers were answered miraculously.

We have played music loud enough to cover our crying hearts, and we have surrounded ourselves with noisy people who have, we hoped, drowned out our grief that He abandoned us in our vulnerable innocence. We have cried out to God in bitterness even as we reached for the drink or the drug that would relieve the pain He would not relieve.

And, after all that, we actually believed we did not have a relationship with God.

―

One of the principal aspects of spiritual guidance is prayer. But prayer can be very problematic for an adult survivor of child abuse. They prayed for help at the time of their abuse but there was no help for them. As far as they are concerned, their pleas and prayers for assistance went unheard. For that reason, prayer, especially prayer of petition, will likely be a double-edged sword for survivors. For these reasons, the subject of prayer, so central to the spiritual life, is likely to be a challenging one in their spiritual guidance. So, when you begin to help them find their footing in prayer, it is probably not a good idea to begin with the prayer of petition, at least not until you have helped them grapple with the issue of why their prayers were not answered at the time of their abuse.

Still, they are here. They have come to you for help in renewing their relationship with God and even to explore what will be, for some, a gradual re-entrance into his Church. How to begin? Begin by reducing any obstacles to prayer which is best done with a very simple approach to prayer, or even the idea of conversation. I like how Francis de Sales defines prayer. He says prayer is simply a heart-to-heart conversation with God in which you speak to God and he speaks to you, and you listen to him and he listens to you. It is a conversation, pure and simple. Its subject matter is whatever is on the front burner of your mind and heart and life at the time of your prayer. I tell those whom I guide to pray as you can, not as you can't. There is not one form or type of prayer that is better than any other, the Holy Mass excepted.

Our relationship with God is what the spiritual life is all about. Meaningful and significant relationships call for frequent communication. Prayer, in any form, is that communication, that loving, frank, simple and genuine conversation between two friends who care for one another and who trust one another. They remain in communication despite the ups and downs, the disappointments, and even the setbacks that every relationship may undergo over the course of time. Fidelity is essential in relationship and, therefore, in prayer as well. Friends stick with one another through thick and thin. They talk things over even in difficult and challenging circumstances. They do not give up on one another.

Prayer, in the context of relationship, is all these things. It is not magic. It is communication, loving and sincere, pure and simple. Think about it. What did Jesus invite his first disciples to experience with him?

They lived with him, they ate with him, and they talked with him. They rejoiced in his successes, warmed at his preaching, and suffered in his sorrows and disappointments. All that experience was prayer. All of that can be prayer for us as well. As spiritual guide, help survivors feel freer to open up their whole lives to be prayer.

Indeed, one of St. Francis de Sales' greatest insights into prayer is its intimate relationship to the rest of one's daily life. Francis says that in prayer we conceive what we then bring forth in our daily lives with one another (<u>Treatise on the Love of God</u>, Book 6, chapter 1). I love the image of prayer as conception. Conception is intimately related to the new life that inevitably follows. That's the promise of prayer. It is life-giving, not only for the one who prays but for all those who are a part of his or her life.

One of the most loving things we can do for anyone in spiritual guidance, and especially for survivors, is to demystify prayer. The rosary, the Jesus prayer, the Divine Mercy chaplet, a simple wordless attentiveness to God, the Mass, brief but fervent words such as Jesus or Mary or Savior, the Lord's Prayer—all of this is prayer. They may not be able to pray the prayer of petition for a while, but they can learn to talk things over with God, even the most difficult thing, abuse. "Talking it over with God"—
that is prayer.

Remember, too, that for someone whose relationships have been demeaning as a child or rejection as an adult, this conversation will take courage. Prayer may take courage. It may feel radical to talk anything over with God. Another way to demystify prayer is to help survivors understand that God already accepts them, exactly as they are, even before they may be able to accept themselves. He has already started with the first Word, his Son, and is waiting for their response to the invitation. Now it's up to them to start the conversation any way they are able. He will help them all along the way.

CREATION

As God recreates us from the ashes, there will be some chaos. Growth involves stretching, discomfort, even pain at times. Ask any artist or builder who is creating something what a mess the beginning is— and how impossible it is to see anything vaguely like what the final beauty will be. So it is with recovery graced by God.

There's comfort in God having separated darkness from the light even before He created time. All the conspiracy of lies and triumph of the abusers and their enablers seemed frail by comparison. Creation is redeemed by Jesus already vanquishing death, evil, and suffering. The impact of that victory is still playing out in our day. The battle lines between evil and God are far clearer than they seemed when I was a child. The question then, like now, is on what side we choose to make our stand.

And, so, my salvation plays out including my continuous re-creation from the wounds of my childhood. I am a new creation many times over in a day, but what makes the difference is that I no longer hide in shame from Jesus as my Savior. I experience salvation every day. Do you?

                ⌒

"When the devil had finished all the tempting he left him, to await another opportunity."[32] The phrase "to await another opportunity" sets the stage for a long struggle between Jesus and the Evil One, a struggle in which, as Jesus is hung dying on the Cross, the Evil One seems to triumph, but with the Resurrection we see the victory belongs instead to Jesus.

For the new creation to occur, the first and fallen creation must first be redeemed. This takes place in the cosmic struggle between Jesus and Satan. On the Cross, the axe has been laid to the roots of the tree of evil. But throughout the course of history, the bark, leaves, and fruit of that tree do not yet betray the reality of its death or the definitive nature of Jesus's victory.

This is why it is often difficult for us to find traces of the new creation in a world that is filled with so much evil, hatred, hostility, and sin. And this is why survivors find it almost impossible, for so long a time, to find any light or life coming out of the darkness and death of what they have experienced. It is hard for survivors to find help for their wounds in such a deeply wounded world.

---

[32] Luke 4:13, as found in the NAB translation: "When the devil had finished every temptation, he departed from him for a time."

Faith looks to the Creator to once again create something from the nothingness of near-despair, to bring forth a new light from darkness, and sprouts of new life from the barren and deserted place in which abuse has left its victims.

Only faith, once somehow rediscovered, knows that, in the end, Jesus is triumphant even over the darkness, the death, and the despair of abuse. Therefore, "I no longer hide in shame from Jesus." Still, this is only the beginning, the first step, for "as God recreates us from the ashes, there will be some chaos. Growth involves stretching, discomfort, even pain at times." Faith rediscovered in the Creator-Redeemer can be a source of sustenance for the long journey in recovery.

Job

The most miserable person in the Bible, Job suffered wave after wave after wave of affliction, which is not unlike the suffering of victims of abuse who often relate how the abuse set off wave after wave after wave of trauma in their lives for years afterward.

Job's friends blamed him for what had befallen him and eventually abandoned him. They were escaping proximity to the sheer burden of his grief. How many of us have not experienced that?

We even echo at times with the mix of hurt and anger with which Job questioned God about the random injustice of his suffering. We sympathize with how Job simply could not understand why God would have afflicted him.

What is a key to Job is a key to our own lives. The churning, heavy story of Job's misery and exchange with God is reversed to restoration and unexpected abundance not when Job finally understands, but when Job prays for those who abandoned him. For every abuser in our lives, there were more people who actually abandoned us as victims. Praying for them is a way of opening ourselves to an unexpected resolution of our personal agonies.

Like Marley's heavy chain, abuse drags along with it a whole host of those who failed to help or believe or listen to the victim and who, too often, in some way took the side of the abuser, at least by believing him or by protecting him or even by defending him. In the survivor's account above, these people are compared to Job's friends who, in the end, did not believe in his innocence and abandoned him. It was only once Job forgave them that his fortunes were reversed. Forgiveness brought him abundant blessings.

Simply to return to faith, or to return to God, is an abundant blessing of grace for those who have been harmed as children. This gift of grace is not predicated on the survivor doing something "right" or meeting some criteria. That must include, for your discussions together, a clear understanding that, while survivors may identify with the tribulations of Job, God is not expecting more from them than they have the grace to offer. Forgiveness comes with time, and as long as they are following Jesus, forgiveness will be possible in his timing and with his grace.

It's helpful to remember that Jesus is the new Job, and his personal trauma in his agony and death is far greater than Job's. Alone in death, he feels the pain they feel, and he feels it acutely. Still, he manages even then to forgive all those at whose hands he suffers, both friend and foe alike: "Father, forgive them." He even manages to make excuses for their cowardice, rejection, and hurt: "They do not know what they are doing." (Luke 23:34) Jesus understands we cannot be like him. Our forgiveness takes time and takes shape with his help. The Father rewards His Son's forgiveness with the abundance of His Resurrection. In this, survivors find the insight they need for the fullness of a new life they seek. It is possible with the example of Jesus, on his timing and with his guidance and graces. The path toward forgiveness is one of abundant grace, too, as survivors cultivate an ever-deepening relationship with God. And, the amazing prayer of Jesus as he hung on the Cross won abundant blessings from God for himself as well as for all who will ever come to faith in him. So, it is important to help survivors understand that Jesus has them covered, even long before they begin to grapple with how forgiveness will evolve in their own faith stories.

The standard of forgiveness that Job gives us is high enough; that of Jesus is even higher. Yet, somehow many survivors, in their own time, manage to forgive all the many people there are to forgive—in some unique way. My point here is that not all forgiveness looks the same, and trying to impose an exact approach to forgiving one's abusers can re-traumatize the abused. Instead, we set aside our own preconceptions as we do in many areas of faith, and we help this person follow the guidance of the Holy Spirit in their lives. We help them be open to grace.

There is an abundance of grace available from God to offer forgiveness, and there is an abundance of grace waiting for when forgiveness is offered. Never lose sight, however, that this very heavy chain is not one forged by sins as is the case with Marley, whose lifetime of misdeeds became his eternal burden. Instead, the weights on the sufferers of abuse are forged by sins of abusers and failures by families, and by other caregivers in schools and communities, and by those in authority in the Church which should have offered safe haven. So, the invitation to forgive has an added cast of injustice which, too, must be forgiven. Of course this feels daunting to survivors because it is, and often their choice to forgive will happen a very long time before they do forgive—yet from choice to completion is a Jesus-like transformation surely pleasing to God.

Pushing survivors toward forgiving can re-traumatize them; it's like pushing on very sore bruises, spiritually and emotionally. The bond of trust you are creating can be damaged permanently, for it is right that a survivor should find in you, as God's representative, a place of safe haven and care in which to progress at their own pace. Plus, in time you will come to see that many survivors privately drive themselves very hard to "let the pain go" and to "get over it" too. Perhaps that is why insensitive suggestions in a similar vein from others can hurt so deeply; survivors, wrongly, can doubt they are "trying" hard enough and sometimes turn a viciously judgmental eye on themselves. What survivors often need is encouragement not to forgive as if it is an act of willfulness, but rather to forgive as part of a surrender of will to Jesus, who will help them on a far more gentle pace than they might force upon themselves. Far too often, it seems, the most difficult task a survivor may have is forgiving themselves for their wrong assumption that they bear the fault for what happened.

For some survivors it is even more difficult to forgive those who did not listen or would not help than to forgive their abusers. Indeed, some of these people (often in families, but not always) are still playing a role in a survivor's life, and often this role is not one of love but of judgment, continued abandonment, or even serious dysfunction. Here, a too-general idea of forgiveness can be harmful, for at times one must (for one's safety) forgive from afar or, indeed, forgive without reconciling. In these very sad circumstances, faith and grace are particularly important.

For you, too, forgiveness may prove difficult. You will be a witness in faith to the evil done to this remarkable survivor who shares their story with you. You will witness their struggle toward healing. And, you, too, must take care to forgive in your own heart the perpetrators and enablers lest you assume this person's chains. This is why, for every survivor whom you may have in your care, added devotion to prayer and the Holy Spirit as guide is critical.

Bondage in Egypt

When the Israelites had been brought through the Red Sea to begin a trek into the formidable desert, they were not unlike us as we face the big steps in our recovery process. Like the Israelites, we can long for the bondage in Egypt where we could feel unaware, and safe. But the safety we negotiated to survive an environment of abuse is not the safety we need to negotiate an adult life. We have to walk through the desert, being remade by the crucible, to emerge ready for the Promised Land.

Israel's journey from Egypt through the desert to the Promised Land is a helpful metaphor for what is always a difficult and often a long road from abuse to recovery.

Every Israelite left Egypt in fact but not all of them left it in affection. While enduring the difficulties of a harsh and barren wilderness, some hankered for the known and the familiar of the land they had left behind, for what St. Francis de Sales describes in his *Introduction* as "the onions and fleshpots of Egypt."[33]

The survivor's road to recovery involves leaving the familiar and the known as well. Over time, they must let go of many of the routines and patterns that they have mastered as a way of coping with the dev-

---
[33] Numbers 11:4-6

astating effects of abuse. They have learned to create places, spaces, and behaviors that, while protecting them, often keep them isolated from others or can be otherwise harmful. Thus, though safe, they are often lonely. If they remain there, they may find themselves in another type of Egypt bondage, this one of their own making. To be free, whole, and complete, therefore, they must set out on an unfamiliar road for a land as yet unknown. It is a courageous first step and a brave process. And it is a grace-filled moment at a time when it is usually hard for a survivor to feel very lovable, even by God.

For survivors of abuse, the desert through which their journey to recovery takes them, like that of the Israelites, is a place of both depravation and lack, as well as one of incredible beauty and new faith. Much patience is required. Their willingness to change is constantly tested. There are many stops and detours along the way. It was a forty-year journey for Israel. It may well be a long one for the survivor as well; indeed, many consider the need to overcome abuse to be a lifelong endeavor, vigilance against the dark pain resuming dominance in living.

Still, God was with the Israelites all along the way. He protected them from their enemies, fought their battles, and wrought great miracles in order to provide them with food and water. His was the cloud that led them by day and the fire that guided them at night. He himself wrote out the covenant that forged between them an everlasting bond. God will be with victims as well, leading them, protecting them, loving them, and providing for them. Reflections on the Exodus experience can be very hopeful for survivors for this reason.

The desert formed a new people, provided them with a new law and gave them unfettered access to the living God. Something like those wonders will occur for survivors who set out, with courage and confidence, on the road to recovery.

In a most special way God loves and cares for innocents who have been harmed and sinned against. When, along the way to recovery, they tire from the journey's fatigue or become frightened or discouraged, God himself will take them lovingly into his arms and carry them on. Once they set out, he will always be "Emmanuel" for them, "God is with us."

With Scriptural images like these, the spiritual guide will help to provide victims with a framework with which to understand the course of their own faith journey. As a companion on the journey, the spiritual guide is also the listener. The fidelity across the span of this process becomes a tangible sign of God's faithfulness to them and His desire to lead them from another kind of bondage to a new Promised Land.

Exodus

While Canaan was only a ten-day journey from Egypt, the arduous journey for the Israelites took an unusual route permitting them to evolve into a free people. Every survivor has a recovery journey that will help remake him or her in freedom in a promised new life. It is a process of rebirth we can trust in and believe in. But we cannot rush it. Our recovery journey will take the time it takes. It is an arduous journey. Every step is a decision that affirms our assent to let God intervene, teaching us, reshaping us, healing us all along the way.

Moses was an able leader because, even when the people became disheartened or frightened, he was willing to believe in the wonder of God leading no matter how awful the setting. He seldom was distracted by peripheral matters or emotions. His success was grounded in keeping his focus always on God. Sometimes we will feel like the people in the desert, and sometimes we will feel like Moses. This is the natural process of recovery from abuse.

The Exodus event is peopled with earthen vessels. Take Moses, for example. God knew who He wanted to lead His people and why. Moses was nearly killed as a baby, but God rescued him and saw that he was pampered, very safe, while growing up in Pharaoh's court. Rescued from the harsh life of a slave, he grew up as royalty. But Moses was neither a gifted speaker nor a born leader, and he knew it. Who was he, then, to persuade the mighty Pharaoh to let God's people go? And why was he, of all men, chosen to lead God's people from the bondage of their harsh slavery through the long and demanding trials of a desert journey to the Promised Land? God did choose Moses, because Moses was, in many ways, an earthen vessel. That is, God looked for the broken and imperfect to reflect the glory of His ways.

And what about the people Moses led? Though captive, held in bondage, and burdened with the harshest of labors, they were still not all that eager to leave the familiar and the comfortable and to go through the hell of a desert journey to a promised (but not yet present) land flowing with milk and honey. And, when they were finally on their way, they continually tested to distraction both God and Moses. They complained, they rebelled, and they hankered after what they had left behind. Again and again, they looked back, not ahead. Again and again, after repeatedly saying, "Yes!" to God and His covenant, they turned to the worship of the idols that they had made with their own hands. Survivors often turn to many other sources of comfort only to find these false gods unsatisfying. In that, they are like the Israelites, earthen vessels—willing in spirit but weak as humans.

Precisely because Moses and the Israelites were earthen vessels, they all knew for certain, when they finally reached journey's end, whose victory their arrival really was. It was God's accomplishment in them. In the paradox of grace, over and over again in salvific history, it seems that earthen vessels often make the best vehicles for manifesting God's mighty works! So it can be, too, for survivors who may at times feel keenly attuned to a weakened state in grief, to the weakness as child victims, or to their failings as adults.

The Exodus story, peopled as it is with earthen vessels that become simple vehicles for God's mighty works, can be a great comfort to survivors of abuse. Many will be hesitant to undertake the difficult and unfamiliar journey of recovery. They may indeed be frightened and painfully aware of their own limits and limitations. Still, God prefers His works to be accomplished with people just like them so that they too, like the Israelites of old, will know at journey's successful end, whose victory it is. And, with God on their journey toward healing, they can also be assured that they are not alone. Praise, thanksgiving, and confidence in God—these are all that they need for a successful journey. And these are what the spiritual guide helps them to understand in a deepening relationship with God.

Walking on Water

Every day is an invitation into an encounter with God. We do so in fits and starts, especially during the emotional tumult of recovery when we are reorganizing the clutter of emotions and impressions and assumptions and relationships created by a traumatized and isolated child. One moment we can be confident and even uplifted by our progress, the next crashed in despair and fear. This is a natural way for healing—for walking into the miracle of our new selves. Peter had the enthusiasm of a freshly committed survivor in the early steps of recovery when relief feels possible; it's a time when we feel like we are ready to do anything. Then there are the fears we encounter or obstacles which threaten to overwhelm our progress. At those times we need to cry out, "Lord, save me!" But, at all times, in our recovery, we are responding to our Lord, who is walking toward us with hand outstretched, beckoning us out of the safety of the boat and into the miracle of our real healing journey.

In many ways, St. Peter models for survivors of abuse the complicated chemistry of recovery, with its brave and courageous walk on water coupled at times with its near-drowning through fear and failures.

The beautiful lakeside conversation between the risen Jesus and Peter underscores just how much the Lord is willing to forgive and forget Peter's shortcomings and failures. He does so while at the same time empowering this good, well-meaning but often weak and wobbly man, Peter, who will become the Rock of God's Church. Although directly addressing Peter, Jesus's words are meant for all his followers there, and today. Jesus's words speak especially powerfully to survivors and what may be their frequently uneven road to recovery.[34]

These reflections on the conversation between the risen Lord and the embarrassed disciple are based on those of Pope Emeritus Benedict XVI.[35] The important background to this conversation is Peter's cowardly three-fold denial of even knowing Jesus at the time of his arrest. At a time when Jesus was most in need of a true and loyal friend, Peter had disappointed him and had fled away for fear of his life, leaving Jesus to face his passion alone. At this

---

[34] John 21

[35] From Pope Benedict XVI's May 18 reflections on John 21:15-17 in his *Benedictus* (San Francisco, CA: Ignatius Press/Magnificat 2006), page 157.

appearance of the risen Jesus, Peter's three-fold denial is still a very recent event, and Peter must have felt a profound shame in the presence of his friend and Lord whom he had only a short time before denied even knowing.

Theologian and scholar Pope Benedict studies this exchange between Jesus and Peter in its original Greek. He finds there "a very significant play on words," one that does not come across at all in our English translations. Like Benedict, we will have to make use of a little Greek here.

There are three words in the Greek language for our one English word "love," and this particular passage makes use of two of those words. The Greek word, "fileo" is the love of friendship. It is a love that is tender but not all-encompassing. The word, "agapao," on the other hand, is a total and unconditional love, a love that has no reservations whatsoever.

Now when Jesus first asks Peter, "Simon, do you love me?" he asks: "Agapas-me?"—that is, "Do you love me with a total and unconditional love?" As we know from the Gospels, Peter was a generous and large-hearted man. No doubt prior to his triple denial of Jesus just a few weeks earlier, he would have answered, "Yes, Lord, I do love you unconditionally (*agapo*-se)!" But now that he has known what Pope Benedict describes as "the bitter sadness of infidelity and the drama of his own weakness," he simply replies in all humility: "Lord, you know that I love you: "*filo*-se," that is, "I love you but only within the limits of my poor human love."

Jesus insists and repeats the question: "Simon, do you love with this total love that I desire from you?"

Still Peter repeats the response of his limited love: "*Kyrie, filo-se*," that is, "Lord, I love you insofar as I am able to love you."

But when Jesus asks him the third time if he loves him, he uses the word for love that Peter has been using all along, "*Fileis*-me?" or "Do you love me?" By using the word *fileo* Jesus is assuring Peter that although his love may not be perfect it is nevertheless sufficient.

Pope Benedict remarks that, by using Peter's word for love, Jesus puts himself on the level of Peter rather than trying to put Peter on his level. The Holy Father writes that "it is exactly this divine conformity [to Peter's poor limited love] that gives hope to the disciple who was experiencing so poignantly the pain of his recent infidelity. From here is born the trust that will enable Peter to follow Jesus and to be faithful to him to the very end."

This is a profound meditation! Not only does Jesus forgive Peter his cowardly betrayal. He goes even further, accepting the present limitations of Peter's love and, at the same time, reaffirming his status as the leader of his flock: "Feed my lambs and tend my sheep." Thus, the grace and love of Jesus make up for the shortcomings and weaknesses of his disciple. If only Peter gives all that he is capable of giving, that will be enough. And no matter how often he may fail and disappoint his friend and Lord in the future, as long as he returns to him in sorrow and humility, he will be welcomed and forgiven—"seventy times seven," that is, every time! Jesus's extravagant love for his repentant disciple goes even further. Despite his shortcomings and weaknesses, Peter is commissioned to love and feed both the lambs and sheep—

that is, both the strong as well as the weak ones of the Lord's flock.

This incident is a very comforting one to all who desire wholeheartedly to follow Jesus but whose practice doesn't always measure up to their desire. But, if we do our best, we do enough. Jesus himself will make up the rest!

The idea of such profound acceptance in forgiveness is a double-edged sword for survivors, especially those abused by clergy who were forgiven by their superiors and returned to work only to abuse again. Before survivors may feel comfortable in how such a forgiveness can work wonders in their own lives, it may be necessary (many times over) to acknowledge the difference between forgiveness and toleration. For those in recovery, the difference is best explored as one between forgiveness and enabling. Bishops, intending to forgive, instead enabled for many years. This is not limited to those in authority in the Church. Many survivors are victims of others who might have protected them as children but, instead, enabled abusers in the guise of forgiveness. This perversion of forgiveness is a grave issue and has left wounds in many relationships, but in particular with survivors and their families. It is natural, in fact quite sane, for them to distrust the first mention of forgiveness. We have much to learn from this insight into how forgiveness can be abused.

Yet, these can also be encouraging words to survivors of abuse who come for spiritual guidance. Meditating on Peter they will find someone with whose shortcomings they can readily relate, as they both brave the tumultuous waters of recovery but feel drawn under by their doubt and wavering faith in themselves, their therapists, even God. Peter was, like these survivors are, someone who loved Jesus so much that Jesus himself made up the difference between high aspirations to be like Jesus and limited accomplishments as human beings. Peter's heart was in the right place. That's what matters. Helping survivors understand their hearts, turned toward God, no matter what the circumstances, are in the right place for the Lord to make of them a holy person, a precious friend, and a strength to others seeking God—as he made of Peter. Survivors may need heroes they can imitate on their difficult path toward spiritual healing. In his humanity more than in his strength, Peter can be such a hero.

BAPTISM

After being abused, there is no water that can cleanse the shame that remains. It is hard to sort through how we can be new creations in God while our memories and emotions are so scarred and harmed and while in our hearts we felt so dirty.

Baptisms in our adult lives can be very hard, as can be attending First Communion or Confirmation. Depending on what age we were abused, these events can trigger us. They all focus on something pure, which is quite opposite of what we encountered in similar settings.

Two things are very important in sacraments of childhood and youth. One is to be open to experienc-

ing our own innocence from a now-safe place. Another is experiencing the Holy Spirit, at work in these sacraments, reaching into our own hearts, in the places where we are wounded in relationship to them, and bringing graces to guide us to God's vision for our new lives.

Many rightly speak this comforting truth to survivors of abuse: "It was not your fault." They ought to add its corollary as well: "There is no reason to feel ashamed." For some reason hidden deep within the human psyche, the shame that rightly belongs to perpetrators somehow attaches itself to the victims. They are doubly harmed, doubly abused, carrying a burden of guilt and shame for years, sometimes for a lifetime. This seems to be particularly true in the case of sexual abuse. Survivors cannot easily *not* feel shame for what happened to them. So, whenever those feelings arise, they are important to flag as false ideas. Survivors are well advised to reject them, relying on any number of ways they may develop with their therapists, for example, repeating over and over again to themselves words like: "I am not what happened to me and, therefore, I refuse to accept its shame." Some survivors talk about internalizing another person's voice asserting their innocence, such as that of their therapist or friend or spiritual guide, in some cases the bishop whom they told.

I return again and again to the healing character of grace: *gratia sanans*. It can give what no other assurances can provide: healing at its core, down to its very roots. The presence of the Holy Spirit, or of what theologians call Uncreated Grace, in the hearts of believers recreates them from within, making them into a brand new reality.[36] They are children of God and heirs to his Kingdom; they can rightly claim and lay hold to His power over evil. This is the truth that may need to be repeated again and again for some survivors.

Sometimes the only thing a survivor can manage is to act *as if* one believed the truth of the healing power of grace—especially its healing power in *me*! With time, an inner conviction will match the words and actions. Survivors will come to believe in their own innocence and that they really do not have any reason at all to be ashamed. They are pleasing to God's eye, and always were. Here is the crux of some of the deepest healing, to be freed from the lingering impact of shame from abuse.

Often shame is confused with guilt. From a therapeutic recovery point of view, making the distinction tends to associate guilt with the effect of something a person does, but shame with a sense of something inherently wrong with the person at their core. The wound of abuse reaches that far. To begin to understand God's pleasure in the being of this person is a very effective way to reduce shame. This realization, once it takes hold, frees some survivors in ways impossible from any other source other than God himself. Then survivors can approach the sacraments of their youth with a whole new perspective—these

---

[36] Romans 5:5

are sacraments of welcome and love. Survivors can then reclaim for themselves what was wrongly and brutally stolen from them as children.

"Let the little children come to me."[37] In God's eyes we are all always his little children, innocent, good, beloved, and holy. Let us claim that truth, no matter how old we are!

The spiritual guide will help survivors by continually reminding them that they are not at fault for their abuse. They carry no guilt for this terrible crime. They are not the abuse. They may have felt humiliated and demeaned, but their essential beauty and integrity was not harmed. There is no need for shame, only trust in God's view of them as innocent and wonderful children. It can take a very long time for the truth of this reminder to sink in and take hold. Be patient. There are no quick fixes for healing after abuse.

GETHSEMANE

There is a moment in the Garden when Jesus is praying when He knows of the false judgments, the humiliations, the abandonment, and the physical agony that lies ahead of Him—and He accepts the cup. He still expresses disappointment with the sleeping disciples and still rebukes the false judges and religious leaders. But His first step is to be right with God and to accept God's will.

---

[37] Matthew 19:14

For my part, I started furious with people who were protecting the hierarchy over children. Everywhere from Catholic media to the aisles of churches they were saying that victims should accept abuse as God's will and just move forward. What really irked me was what I thought also: the abuse, indeed, was God's will and I was supposed to surrender to my fate. That would have been a fatal option for my psyche, because from the moment abuse began, I fought in whatever way I could. I lost, but I had not surrendered. To do so now would have been spiritual suicide, or worse.

The hurt from this public Catholic rejection subsided after I met my bishop who told me, with a kind voice, that it was not my fault, I was not to blame. Certainly in recovery I had heard that from many credible people, but I needed to hear it from him, because I needed to hear it from the Church.

There would be, harder yet, the struggle to accept that the abuse was not God's will. God did not want me to be groomed or harmed or isolated or shamed. Something had happened to me that was outside His will. It was very difficult to accept that God had "let" this happen, but I had gotten it right with God first. Everything after that point was a step in the right direction—toward healing, toward Him.

Free will and God's permissive will: irreconcilable? Why does God permit Himself to be, as it were, powerless in the face of evil? Is His gift of free will to the human family so essential to the right relationship between Creator and creature that he must allow bad things to happen to good people, to look away, as it were, when evil people abuse little children? Is human freedom in some mysterious way the equal of the divine? How can that be? Why ought that to be? What is God's will or, better, where is God's will when a human being chooses to impose his evil will on an innocent child?

The Garden of Olives is probably the place where Jesus himself, in the fullness of his humanity, grappled most personally with these series of questions. He definitely preferred to avoid what then surely lay immediately before him. He begged his Father to take away the cup without his having to drink from it. He was aware of his own will. Survivors may very well identify with Jesus begging to be spared from evildoers; indeed, the memory of doing so may trigger very painful memories of when it seemed God had ignored their pleas. As we reflect on Jesus's dilemma in Gethsemane, we see his free will, but quite the opposite in the children who begged to be delivered from imminent agonies. To be abused is to have one's free will overrun by the will of an evildoer.

Yet, there are also comparisons for the survivor considering Jesus's agony in the garden. Could he have known, as human, that the evil of a painful criminal's death was somehow the path to the fulfillment of his mission: the proclamation of the forgiveness of sins, the redemption of the human family, and the arrival of God's heavenly reign? As he struggled with the unlikelihood, on its surface, of such a scenario, he nevertheless said, "Yes." And he did this without knowing how some better ending could possibly be brought about, but he still chose to trust that somehow his Father would be faithful to the promises he had made. Trusting his Abba under those challenging circumstances was not something abstract or merely intellectual. Jesus was prepared to stake his whole person, life, and mission on it, and he did: "Not my will but yours be done."[38]

At that moment, Jesus's act of complete entrustment into the hands of God is how the Savior resolved the theodicy questions. He fell into the arms of God, surrendering his own will and personal preferences and without knowing how God would, under such circumstances, vindicate him and bring about the Kingdom. For survivors, again, to trust any father figure at this juncture is very difficult due to painful, real-world experiences of betrayal, abandonment, and abuse. Yet, as survivors draw closer to God, coming to know him through Jesus, they may see how this Father is very different, and the relationship they can have with God is very different from all those that in their humanity failed. Indeed, in His graces, they will be able, in their new lives on the other side of recovery, find out how God has vindicated them and brought about His Kingdom in their lives and through them in others' lives. This is our work, as spiritual guides, to help point out the distinctions—and the similarities—to help focus on hope.

In this case, this surrender of Jesus is very different than that of a child victim. The surrender Jesus

---

[38] Matthew 26:39, or as found in the NAB translation: "My Father, if it is possible, let this cup pass from me; yet, not as I will, but as you will."

shows us involves assent from our own will. Jesus does not take; he receives, he accepts us. He shows us how to make peace with ways it is hard to understand God. It was possible only within the context of a loving act of surrender into the arms of someone Jesus knew as Father and both loved and trusted.

For survivors, we must be careful when talking about these wondrous truths. For example, for them "surrender" has meant not being lifted up by God but rather it has involved annihilation and humiliation by authority, at times religious authority. Once again, the double-edged sword of healing truth and its perversion are at work in this survivor's faith life. As a spiritual guide, your sensitivity to how the very truths can be painful for very good reason will help you practice the gentleness of St. Francis de Sales.

With the double-edged sword in mind, you may be able to help a survivor struggling with the theodicy issue by reflecting on the part it played in Jesus's agony in the garden. He too was an innocent victim, but he is also a healing example of what it means to surrender to God's life-giving will.

JUDAS

Survivors have, in general, known too many suicides, either by self-murder or by drugs or alcohol. The suicide of Judas, and the lessons preachers more typically draw from his despair, can ring hollow. Most of us have grappled with suicide at one point or another, not necessarily an attempt to kill ourselves, but at least a wish to, or a constant nagging wish to be dead. We know how suicide is thought to be an escape from the pain that will not relent. It is seen as a relief from the blinding feelings of mortal confusion. It is the last act in the play where a child far too vulnerable encounters evil that is far too unbridled.

Suicide is never the answer, in part because it concludes the work of the abuser who was wrong from the start. God is always about starting a new work in us. He is always offering us a new life, not just a patched-up and sputtering good-enough life. The difficulty of recovery is much easier than the pain that leads to suicide. If suicide even seems like a viable option in your life, tell people who love you, seek a professional counselor to help you get some groundwork between your feet and the abyss, and seek God. Suicide for a survivor is, in a way, being Judas to the divine within your own self.

Suicidal thoughts are very serious. The impulse to kill the self is a sign that help is needed immediately, not in a day or a week or sometime in the future. Often a person who has ideas about suicide may only reveal a hint of the greater impulse with which they struggle, so it is critically important to understand, ahead of offering counsel to survivors or others with similar burdens, what to do when suicide becomes part of the dialogue. For that, it is crucial to reach out to resources in your diocese, in particular to the Victim Assistance Coordinator, for policy and procedural clarity.

Yet, offering spiritual guidance to someone who may have been tempted to commit suicide, or who may have attempted suicide, warrants some empathetic reflection. As strange as this will sound, the instinct to suicide in many victims of abuse may, in the end, point to something that may prove very helpful to their recovery. Indeed, there has to be a death of sorts, a definitive ending to the long arc of abuse and the heavy weight of memory, grief, and shame in them before a new life can begin. Obviously, physical death by suicide is not an option. Another kind of death may be happening, however, to make way for life. That is worth celebrating when the person is stabilized and the crisis is well past.

The analogy of a foot race describes well the kind of death that is required of all Christians. When a runner comes to the turning point in the race, he must pause and come to something of a stop in order to turn around and, in reversing his movement, begin the second half of the race. That momentary pause is essential, even though it may at first seem to be a waste of valuable time and the unfortunate slowing down of momentum. Before the second half of life's race, unencumbered, can really get underway in earnest for the survivor, they must let go—let die—the heavy and painful baggage that is the detritus of abuse. How does this happen? Most commonly this happens with the help of professional therapy, but where it happens is in the course of living. A natural next question is *when* does this happen?

When a survivor comes to something like the rock bottom powerlessness of the alcoholic, it is then that they finally recognize two vital truths:

their own powerlessness and their very real and personal need for a Savior. Once an adult survivor comes to the realization that, on their own and even with the best of help, they cannot totally free themselves from the heavy weight that abuse leaves on their shoulders, they are ready for that weight to be lifted off by another, but not just any other. They are ready for the Lord's help.

Judas's sin is unlike what the survivor faces in some important ways. Mainly, Judas sinned through his own free will. Survivors, with respect to the trauma with which they are struggling, are carrying the burden of the sins of others, largely of abusers but also of enablers and others who failed them. Yet, here the double-edged sword of truth is at work. Judas was heavily burdened with despair because he knew that he could not lift the weight of his betrayal of Jesus from his own shoulders. Judas did not choose to ask for help. On the other hand, Peter, also knowing he could not lift from his shoulders the heavy weight of his denial of Jesus, reached out instead to Jesus for help. And in the very act of reaching out to Jesus, he discovered that the hands of Jesus were already reaching out to him in turn. If Jesus was so ready to help Peter in his guilt, surely Jesus is ready to help survivors in their innocence. If Judas's real failure was not in betraying Jesus but rather in not asking for Jesus to help, then survivors can know there are no obstacles to their asking for Jesus's help beyond the despair born of sins they did not commit.

Again, we find ourselves at the heart of our faith—forgiveness from God. Two models are placed before every Christian, including every Christian survivor of abuse. First, there is the example of Judas, not the example of his sin (for the survivors are innocent) but the example of his failure to reach out for help because he did not believe the truth that no guilt or shame in his heart could separate him from Jesus. Then there is the example of Peter, again not the example of his denials and sin, but the example of his humility and good sense to reach out to the Lord and, in reaching out, to be saved, and indeed loved for his shortcomings. Choosing Peter will make all the difference!

These two central examples are complicated for survivors who have been wounded by a perversion of forgiveness, yet they are nonetheless part of the faith that can enrich their lives as it is freed from the effects of abuse in the past. Your role is to be able to understand the distinctions and choices, trusting that the survivor can make the choice in time with God's grace. As Peter had to wait for the Lord after the point of denial, and as Judas might have done too, all of us, including survivors, must wait on the Lord's timing for the examples offered in the life of Jesus to take root and bear fruit in our own lives.

Holy Thursday

Many liturgical seasons draw us back to the faith of our childhood, and many of us respond like moths to a flame. But these times are also rife with triggers for some of us. So often we flee before finding safety that waits for us in these grace-filled events.

It may be Stations of the Cross, it may be midnight Mass on Christmas, or may be Gregorian chanting. Holy Thursday, with its high services and incense, has a distinct challenge. It marks, after all, the establishment of the priesthood in the same service that people expose feet for a priest to touch.

Offering tools for how to deal with triggers is one of the best gifts of professional psychological counseling. It takes a mix of these tools and choices about the pace at which we can re-engage to ensure our homecoming is safe and uplifting. These tools, and smart choices, are important to help guide us through a gradual, gentle return home to our faith.

Holy Thursday has a role in that. It can be seen as the feast of the truth of our abuse. Despite all the efforts to cast the truth in some other light, we better than anyone know exactly what a priest is not. He is not a predator. And, what's more, many of us know as part of our healing story how the right word from a devoted priest catalyzed our recovery, bringing into focus the contrast between priest and predator. Holy Thursday in that sense is a moment of graces all around the truth of our abuse, both its perpetrators and its antidote.

It is sobering to read above how so moving and solemn a feast as Holy Thursday often carries with it many potential triggers even for survivors who may be well along the road to recovery. If their perpetrators were priests or if those who refused to listen to their accounts or to be helpful to them were priests, for survivors Holy Thursday is likely to be a very ambivalent celebration. This feast recalls the institution of the Eucharist and priesthood, while highlighting the poignantly tender moment when Jesus, on his knees, washes his disciples' feet. If drawn to the Eucharist, the survivor may also be rattled by the focus on priests. At the same time, the Eucharist here or at daily Mass can remind survivors that priest predators also consecrated the Eucharist. They may remember how priests who were perpetrators washed feet on Holy Thursday and even be discomforted by people baring their feet in a church.

Brutal abusers to child victims, these same priests were for others the esteemed representatives of the all-holy Jesus, priest and servant. For some survivors, the abusers were more exalted than anywhere on this solemn feast. No wonder, "Holy Thursday … is a moment of graces all around the truth of our abuse, both its perpetrators and its antidote." This line continues to highlight the double-edged sword of reconciling with one's Catholic faith.

The example of triggers associated with Holy Thursday is a helpful reminder to spiritual guides to be on the alert for the real possibility of triggers even in venues or circumstances in which they would be least expected or anticipated. Triggers are like mine fields. They lie hidden beneath the earth, unseen, and unexpected. When triggered, they may cause immediate and great harm, especially for survivors who have not yet mastered managing their responses to triggers. Those less practiced survivors may suddenly find themselves back "there," once again a vulnerable and frightened child, confused, hurting, helpless, and outraged. This is not necessarily a stirring of memories or even conscious for the survivor. It is often just a surge of inexplicable feelings. It can be, I am told, like a slap to a bruise. Survivors may, as a result, suddenly become silent and non-communicative, once again seeking safety and sanctuary within.

At those moments, understand the natural impulse to regroup. Who wouldn't, considering everything the trigger may have awakened? Simply trust yourself to be with them while maintaining an emotional, respectful, and discreet distance. Do not crowd their space or attempt to talk them out of it. This is not something to be solved or changed by anything you can utter. In fact, do not fill quiet space, which may be quite holy, with talk of any kind. Wait patiently until they themselves are ready to talk. And when they do speak, gently follow their lead, not yours. Meanwhile, in the silent interim, pray silently to the Holy Spirit for guidance. He knows what triggered this reaction, what horrors they are now sensing or even remembering, and how you can comfort them without making an already difficult moment even worse for them. All this is a delicate dance, more art than a science. There is no script for any of this. The pain does not disappear in any one session. Your role is to help them develop an ability to rely on the very wise, gentle, and powerful Guide, the Holy Spirit. This work will develop the same ability more deeply in you. Trust Him while you both follow his lead in this person's life.

Good Friday

Good Friday in our lives can be mixed with triggers and with a keen sense of Jesus very close to what we have suffered. If we understand nothing else after abuse, we almost all appreciate suffering.

But, Jesus was no masochist. He did not delight in the suffering; if He had, it would not have been suffering, really. Living lives that deeply reject what we have suffered, finding a way to accept the suffering without accepting its condemnation is important work. So is our recovery work to heal so that we do not move into the future thinking life cannot be well lived without feeling terrible. Jesus was accepting but not complicit with the abusers in His agony.

When Jesus gives up His spirit to God and dies, the curtain in the Temple is torn in two, top to bottom. The dividing line between God and His people is gone, and nothing will ever be the same again in all of history. Survivors understand how, in a single moment, time can be torn asunder, because we each experienced the first shocking moment of abuse and how everything that followed was changed forever. But the change wrought by abuse was all about wounds and suffering, yet it also opens us in a particular way to understanding the permanent changes in our own lives affected by the crucifixion of our Lord. The more we bring his Cross into our lives, the more we step to the other side of the grave, where the stone is gone and our lives are resurrected.

What was Jesus thinking of during the three hours of agony on the Cross? According to St. Francis de Sales, the more accurate question is this: *Who* was Jesus thinking of during those painful hours of abandonment and suffering? He was thinking of each one of us "by first and last name,"[39] that is, he was thinking of each of us in our own particularity, uniqueness, and personal history.

In order to truly grasp the saving significance of the Cross of Jesus, St. Francis encourages every Christian to grapple with the truth of the Cross in a very personal way. Jesus died for *me*! He suffered for *me*! I was as close to him during those hours of suffering and passion as I am to myself at this moment, even more so. While enduring bitter sufferings at the hands of violent men, Jesus took me and my whole story to himself—all of it, including especially the pains and humiliations of a violent abuse against an innocent victim. He took to himself my sufferings and, in doing so, he made them his own. At the darkest moment when there was no sun on the earth, Jesus and I became, together, victim. In shouldering my sufferings, his were deepened, mine lessened. Only his Cross can heal me; only his sufferings can make me whole again. Innocent and without sin—as I was when abused as a child—the crucified Jesus took to himself not only the moments and hours of my abuse but all the pains, sufferings, rage, confusion, and isolation that were to pile upon me from that time to this. Only from his Cross can love destroy the death I died.

---

[39] St. Francis de Sales's *Treatise on the Love of God*, Book 12, chapter 12

From there can I, and others like me, live again. For survivors whose suffering as children was marked by abandonment, this understanding of the Cross can be healing, but only when they are ready to take a deeper step into His suffering, that is, only after they have had time to grapple in practical terms with their own.

The truth of Good Friday awaits them. Good Friday is "good" only because the Cross of Jesus saves us all. For survivors, to be saved means much more than to be saved from sin. It also means for them to be saved, rescued, and eventually healed from the devastating and lasting effects of having been sinned against. Making distinctions between having their own sins and having the burden of being sinned against is very important in the process of healing.

Holy Saturday

The empty church that remains after everything is emptied or covered on Good Friday has a certain comfort for survivors. There was a mix of repentance that even affected our abusers. Holy Saturday is also a "space in between" one state and another, between agony and Resurrection. It is a special moment of reflection for all Christians, but for survivors is marks a place that is very much like the process of recovery.

Sometimes words are both impossible and unnecessary anyway. Holy Saturday is one of those times. An ancient Christian writer describes the whole world on that solemn day as clothed with a great silence and stillness. The mighty Lord, crucified, now lies shrouded in death and hidden within the darkness of a tomb. A hushed awe lies with the heaviness of a pall over the earth.

On this day, this universal silence and unvoiced awe is liturgically depicted in every Christian Church. Altars are stripped, the vigil light snuffed out, holy water vessels drained, and sanctuaries empty. Throughout the world no Mass is celebrated on this sacred and silent day of vigil. Only the dying, that is, only those who bodily identify with the dying Christ are permitted to receive the sacraments of *Viaticum*[40] and Anointing on this day. Taken together, empty churches, bare sanctuaries, and minimalist liturgies represent a collective held breath, our vigil of awe and expectation that arcs from the horror of the Lord's death to the dawning of new life.

For all these reasons, Holy Saturday is a fitting symbol for victims who are starting to realize they are survivors, and for survivors who are ready to move beyond survival mode and into a thriving life. In a real sense, this is their day. This day of silence and awe, these hours of expectation and waiting, this moment that separates the horror of what was from the promise that is to come—this is their day in ways never anticipated by those whose task it was to design our liturgical calendar. Because of the absence of priests who may represent their abuser, and the lack

---

[40] *Viaticum* is Eucharist when it is given to a dying person. In Latin, it means that the Lord Jesus accompanies the person who is now ready to pass through death to new life.

of sacraments and sacramentals that can trigger bad memories, survivors talk about finding comfort in being alone with the One whose death has destroyed their own kind of death and whose awaited resurrection is their promise of a new kind of life. What, therefore, is true for every Christian on Holy Saturday is true in a unique manner for survivors of abuse.

Let it, therefore, be appropriated by them in a special way, for it symbolizes who they are at this crossroad between death and life, at this solemn moment when their former identity as victim is replaced by a new identity, that of survivor. You can offer your own special prayers this day for survivors in your care, or in your own family or parish or community. You can encourage survivors to appreciate, even ritualize, this solemn day of vigil in a new way, one that speaks directly to their situation of transition from victim to survivor, from the death of an abused childhood to the fullness of life as a child of God.

Easter

One of the favored readings at our survivor prayers services and Masses is the story of Mary and the other women coming upon the tomb of Jesus worried about who would roll away the stone for them. It was an impossible stone for them to move, yet they went to the grave anyway out of love for Jesus. When they got there, he had provided—and more! They came to serve him in death, but he had new life to offer.

Like Israelites through the desert, wandering uncharted desert as the process remakes us, moving from bondage to freedom, we survivors face our own Via Dolorosa, moving through memories of the death of abuse and all it causes ... and into a life resurrected in Jesus.

That passage isn't what I expected. When I began therapy decades ago, I wanted to be fixed. I wanted to be restored to what I would have been if I had not been abused. Therapy was supposed to offer me a reset button. So, here I am with my wounds still part of my life after decades in recovery. Certainly I've grown adept at caring for them and managing for safety for myself. But the wounds have changed. They do not dominate my life, but they have also become sources of wonder, having transformed from the self-absorbed cringe of agony into the love and service of others.

Ultimately, Jesus offered me Resurrection, not restoration. I was not always happy about that. Yet, it took a while before I could appreciate how his risen hands kept their wounds but were transformed into something remarkable, transformative for us, and redemptive for all of Creation. New life would not be without its scars.

Now, I won't say I'm glad for the wounds of abuse. It would be a delight to live complacently ignorant of all that I have had to learn. Yet, the wounds in my healed life serve beauty, truth, light, and hope in others. They aren't just wounds anymore. They are resurrected with Jesus. It is a wondrous place to live.

"Yet, it took a while before I could appreciate how His risen hands kept their wounds but were transformed into something remarkable, transformative for us, and redemptive for all of Creation. New life would not be without its scars."

Jesus could have risen from the grave with all traces of the wounds of his Passion healed and erased, but he chose not to do that. Indeed, for all eternity the blessed in heaven will never look upon the glorified body of Christ without seeing there the marks of his wounds and, in doing so, being forever reminded of the length to which his love for them once took him.

Why does the risen Jesus refuse to hide those wounds from us even in glory? St. Francis de Sales gives us what is perhaps its principal reason: "O Jesus my Savior, how worthy of love is your death, for it is the supreme effect of your love! Live Jesus, live! Your death upon the tree shows all your boundless love for me!"[41] Thus, the most powerful witness to Jesus's tender and saving love for us is the death that he willingly endured for each of us, even by "first and last name,"[42] that is, even in the unique specialness that each of us is.

For survivors, Jesus's saving love embraces in a particular manner the horror of their abuse and all the years of pain and woundedness that followed. The presence of the wounds of his Passion in the risen Jesus is the concrete, personal, and very tangible sign of his great love for each of them. His "glorified"

---

[41] St. Francis de Sales, *Treatise on the Love of God*, Book 12, chapter 13
[42] St. Francis de Sales, *Treatise on the Love of God*, Book 12, chapter 12

wounds are a perpetual sign of the divine compassion for each of them, not only during the abuse itself but all along the many dark and painful corridors of its effects in their lives. The wounds in the risen body of Jesus testify as no words can to the compassionate presence of Jesus in the death of abuse as well as its seed of new life, even in the throes of that hell.

Words fall short. So Jesus lets his wounds speak for the depth of his love for them. When a survivor is finally able to lay hold to this truth in a very personal way, Easter Sunday follows Good Friday, death yields to new life, and the victim becomes a survivor. You, as spiritual guide, will help the survivor personalize what new life is, how it can be born into their present lives, how they will change to make room for all the blessings that come from a deepening relationship with a God who so loved the world that He gave His only begotten Son.

Pentecost

Survivors encounter the failure of language in more than the ascendancy of lies that hid the trauma in their childhood. The dominance of lies and secrets filled the world with incomprehensible babble of abusers and enablers who were assuring us that what we knew wasn't true.

Certain we were abandoned by God along with others, we have cowered in fear. We have lived in hiding. We hide in full view because, contrary to media caricatures, survivors can be highly functioning, with a locked chamber filled with memories and hurt. We are all like the Apostles in the upper room after Jesus had ascended, fearful. The most daring of us even admit a part of us is waiting.

Yet, when the Holy Spirit roared through the fear, the babble disappeared; those who could not speak to be understood, did, and those who could not hear the speakers were moved. The caricatures can fall away, because the breath from our own Creator arrives as Spirit to renew us.

―

Following the horror of the Cross, frightened disciples gathered together in a locked upper room, frightened, confused, and uncertain about what to do next. There is a state in which many survivors, even with friends or family members, find themselves in hiding from imminent harm. That may be from the emotional storms that often erupt when one or more family member begins to face the abuse in the past. It may be from a sense of emotional danger that can occur when first confronting behaviors that can run amok in a survivor's life. Or, it may be simply, by speaking the hitherto unutterable truth of abuse, a survivor feels the same dread and fright that the abuser used to keep them silenced as a child victim.

Yet, into this hiding place, the first one to break through those locked doors is the risen Jesus himself. He comforts them, relieves them of the burden of sins, and he shows them the wounds of his Passion in hands, feet, and side. They see the evidence of what he has endured so that they are not alone or abandoned, even if that not-aloneness and that non-abandonment looks and feels differently from what they might have imagined. Then, Jesus breathes upon them the Holy Spirit of his Shalom. Among all the many images of Jesus's rescue of humans in hiding, here is one which survivor can imagine again and again. They have such a room or space to which they withdraw when startled or triggered. It is not you who will open those doors and not them. Your role is to help them invite Jesus in.

When Jesus stands before the disciples, he doesn't stop at reaching into their deepest hiding and fear. He also commissions them to bring his healing peace and reconciling love to the world.[43] For the Apostle and evangelist St. John, Resurrection and Pentecost occur on the very same day. It's his way of suggesting that they are but two sides of the same coin. The first is new life for the crucified Jesus himself, and the second is new life for his followers and for all those who believe from that day forward. Thus, the gift of the Holy Spirit is the Easter gift of the crucified and risen Jesus to his new Church and to every member of it.

Many survivors experience release from hiding and shame in a way that reveals the life-giving work of grace, for they start to want to help other survivors escape the constraints of the past on their lives and spirits, too. The gift of the Holy Spirit brings a new and heavenly peace to all who receive it, propelling them out into the world to undo both its personal and

---

[43] John 20: 19-23

communal babble. This is true of survivors as well. They respond to the mysterious commission in different ways, in family or personal circles, in larger work supporting survivors seeking to reconcile with God or faith. What they do, however, is receive and seek to share by words and actions that speak and do the Lord's peace, a peace that the world cannot give.[44]

For survivors of abuse, the gift of the Holy Spirit also can destroy the babble and lies that they were told by their abusers as well as by those who refused to believe them or ignored them or, worse, excused or enabled the abusers. In ways that are perhaps even truer for survivors than for others, the Holy Spirit gives a peace that the world cannot give. Therapists teach survivors how to deal in a creative and freeing way with the wounds of abuse, and spiritual guides help them to reestablish bruised or broken relationships with God and his Church. All this is helpful, but it does not heal at the roots and from the deep down death that is abuse. Only God's healing grace can reach to such depths, into these inner rooms. This healing grace the crucified and risen Jesus breathes upon every survivor when He gives them the Holy Spirit of his very own Shalom.

Like those first disciples, survivors may be hiding behind doors that they themselves have locked for their safety and sanity. They have wisely built inner rooms where they can hide, for there has been much to hide from. Their recovery is venturing out to discover a world that is safer than they thought, or

---

[44] John 14:27

to build a new life that is finally safe in ways they had not imagined possible. Yet, those doors can be opened in one of two ways: either by those who locked them in the first place or by the risen Jesus as he passes through them just as he did on that first Easter night. The paradox of grace is this: these, too, are but two sides of the same coin. It is the gift of the risen Jesus, the Holy Spirit, who can pass through the toughest defenses and can also enable survivors themselves to dare to throw open locked doors and pass through them to a new life.

Thus, Pentecost is never just a past event, formative of a new people and a new Church. It occurs every time the risen Jesus appears to brokenness of any kind and breathes upon it his very own Shalom, healing what was broken from deep down within, and sending those now healed out into the world to undo the babble that evil once spoke. This is particularly hopeful for survivors. They know more than most the power of the Pentecost encounter—and rescue. Their blossoming new lives proclaim the power of God's peace, love, and new life over every form of death, even that of abuse. This is not necessarily or principally through words but through the witness of their new way of living. That is, by living from a peace that the world cannot give but one that, through the grace of the risen Lord, they have now received.

The spiritual guide naturally helps survivors unlock the saving significance of mysteries like the Pentecost by inviting them to prayerfully reflect on what those mysteries say to them and to their experiences in a very personal way. Yet, you also must understand the double-edge sword at work. For example, the safety represented in this survivor's hiding may be a fragile and precious thing indeed. The person may be far too aware of the frightful experience of an adult breaking into hiding places in the past for this encounter with Jesus to be simple. It is important to take time to talk about how the Lord will not break through the boundary of defenses to add to vulnerability or to overwhelm this loved child of God. Making the distinctions is very important. Jesus works with our will and surrender, not so the abuser or those who failed child victims.

The Pentecost encounter is one that the Holy Spirit knows how to unfurl in each life to add all his gifts, not to reduce one's humanity. With your help, prayerful imaginings such as these will help faith become safer and less fettered, helping the Spirit work God's transforming power in these survivors' lives.

Mary

Many, many survivors tell me that Mary played a central role in sustaining them, both when they were children enduring abuse alone and when they were adults estranged from God and isolated from the Church. There are many stories of Mary's role in the lives of survivors of abuse. This little essay cannot begin to express them.

Mary in her role as mother, however, can also be difficult for survivors who were either abused by mothers or abandoned by them. Some still find solace in Mary's care as the true mother she is, but others find the image of mother triggers the worst of their pain. Her role as mother can suffer like the role of a priest suffers from confusion with the predator priests I knew.

Mary is not just the Mother of God. She is also the first Christian. Mary accepted Christ before there was Christianity, in fact before there was Church. Her surrender was a leap of faith that is like our own. We are drawn, even called, home, but we are encumbered by false truths of our faith. We need to leap beyond what we know.

Mary's leap of faith shows us something about what we miss as adults grappling with childhood abuse. Not just we, but all adults come to a juncture in life where the faith of their childhood is like a seed cracking open, even dying. In our case, this death is of something that is in part, maybe entirely, dark. For others, it is a real loss of comfort. Nonetheless, there is the watershed moment when we need to choose Christ in a way so fresh, so unexpected, that we are stepping into a new life, into an unknown. Saying "yes" to Christ here remakes the meaning of Church in our lives. It can become what it never could be before. For this moment, whether we feel safe with Mary's love as a mother or not, we can follow her as the first Christian.

There is also Mary's cloak, as she showed in Guadalupe, which she uses to embrace and protect people whom the Church may struggle to accept. Whether Juan Diego was even a full person under European law was still in dispute when Mary appeared to him and protected him. The children of Fatima and Lourdes suffered also in a disbelieving

Church. Mary takes special note of those who turn to her but whom the Church has failed to embrace fully. Through all of Mary's intervention in history, she has led people closer to Christ by ignoring judgments made by people without mercy.

And, in the Pieta, Mary's grief at the suffering and death of her son makes her a perfect refuge for the mothers, fathers, sisters, brothers, other family members, and friends of victims of abusers. Many tell of how they were able to sense her solace as they gazed on that great work depicting secondary victimization.

I like to think of Mary as the first teacher of her child Jesus in the ways of faith. The adult Jesus tells us in both words and deeds that God's will is everything to him: "I have come to do the will of the one who sent me."[45] "Your will be done."[46] One of the petitions of the Our Father is that God's will be done on earth as it is in heaven.[47] Where did he first learn such total dedication to the divine will except from his parents? He must have particularly learned from his mother's "fiat!"—her "yes!"—to the angel's invitation to her to become the Mother of God: "May it be done to me according to your will."[48]

---

[45] John 6:38, as in the NAB translation: "I came down from heaven not to do my own will but the will of the one who sent me."
[46] Luke 22:42, or the NAB translation: "Father, if you are willing, take this cup away from me; still, not my will but yours be done."
[47] Matthew 6:10
[48] Luke 1:38, or the NAB translation: "May it be done to me according to your word."

Mary's "yes" at the Annunciation was perhaps the most beautiful moment of her "fiat disposition," that is, her total openness and receptivity throughout life to God and to the ways and will of God for her. I often picture her on her tip toes, arms outstretched, reaching up eagerly to do or to embrace whatever God asks of her. But before such a total union of wills took place, Mary must have first fallen deeply in love with God so that, between them, there was a loving union of hearts.

This image is very different from what survivors experienced. This was not God forcing his decision on Mary, as a child victim might understand best the idea of being forced to do what authority wants. Some survivors struggle to imagine there is a distinction between the two, between what authority (even priestly authority) taught them as children and what God asked of Mary and of all of us. Mary's willing abandon to God, for some, this imagery may be too confusing at first, or for their lifetimes. Indeed, the role of mothers and fathers in the story of each person's abuse can be very complicated, even harrowing. So, it is not unreasonable that these ideas trigger emotions on the cutting, not the healing, edge of the double-edged sword I've mentioned.

Yet, for many survivors, precisely because of these difficulties, Mary's image helps them let go of the false lessons of abuse and reveal a loving union in which a young woman flourished. It opens them to understand, even seek, the fulfillment that comes of their free choice in surrender in seeing Jesus as a son who, in his human nature, first learned the lesson of truth from his earthly mother, Mary. In her "yes" he learned and we can learn everything about his loving and faithful relationship with his heavenly Father. Your role as a spiritual guide is to permit each survivor to find the meditations that open them to the Holy Spirit.

An alternative way survivors may find Mary helpful is how she was also the first disciple of Jesus or, as described above, the first Christian. When she told the servers at Cana's wedding feast to "do whatever he tells you,"[49] she was giving wise counsel to all who would ever become his disciples. She was speaking to survivors, too, assuring them that her son is safe to trust. As the first disciple, Mary also trusted that Jesus would somehow save the newly married couple from the embarrassment of running out of wine on their wedding day. In that way she prompted his first miracle, the first "sign" of the messianic abundance of God's reign that he was bringing about. It might seem like a mundane need, to preserve wedding day festivities, yet Mary will do no less interceding for whatever we ask, and for whatever survivors need as they come to grips with the harm caused them. Mary will take an interest in even the smallest matter, which can be overwhelming to survivors as they work through memories and emotions.

Mary took her own counsel to heart. She continued to listen to, to follow, and to believe in her son, not only when everybody else did, but especially as more and more people pulled away from him and

---

[49] John 2:5

began to desert him, and even as religious leaders plotted and then carried out his violent death. Standing against religious leaders in their power, Mary is a powerful beacon to survivors of abuse by clergy and others with some claim to spiritual authority (which can even be a parent). At her son's Cross Mary stood, resolute and strong despite the pronouncements of the holy men in power. In her arms she tenderly held him in death, still trusting, still believing, still loving. She cried a mother's tears while holding him close to her disciple's heart. She above all felt the pain of his Cross, so the pain of our suffering that he carried. And she continued to believe in her son and to trust in her God even when everything around her was darkness and death. This is a personal characteristic, a steadfastness that speaks to survivors who have, in one way or other, had to exercise very similar fortitude.

Of all the images of Mary presented here, the one of her tenderly but sorrowfully holding her dead son may speak most powerfully to survivors of abuse. At that moment, all must have seemed lost, dark, and without hope to Mary. Certainly, survivors can relate to those sentiments as well. Yet, Mary continued to trust, to hope and to love even then. That is what she brings to survivors, even to them when they are still child victims. She held on to Jesus, no matter what befell her or him. They were as inseparable in suffering and death as in life. This was her choice as disciple even though it was her mother's heart that was breaking. While his disciples betrayed, denied, and abandoned him, she did not. In this meditation, the cowardly disciples find their echo in Church leaders today who for so long failed to believe—or ignored—victims' stories. In the end, there were only mother and son, both broken in some sense by the Cross and by the crosses of the little ones. Yet, from that moment of death, sorrow and union, arose new life, resurrection life! These are just some reflections which a spiritual guide can use to help survivors find a mother in Mary. Remembering how painful a wound that can be inflicted on a survivor's relationship with one or both parents, the spiritual guide can gauge how Mary might be most helpful. What is true and particularly important for survivors is that Mary stood by Jesus. She stands by them as well. She was the first to believe in him and to follow him, no matter to what hell of suffering her path of faith led her. In every survivor, Mary finds another only child whom she loves tenderly and in whom she believes totally, and by whose side she stands, resolute and strong.

Yet, some survivors might find this love painful. Its perfection may cast light on the failures of parents. Mary's absence during childhood trauma may feel like abandonment, too. So, as rich as Mary will be in the life of survivors, so too will their relationship with her need care and sensitivity. Remember, that even during a survivor's often long and at times uneven return to Church, Mary is grieving as a mother for her children and is protecting them. Helping survivors find a place for Mary in their lives is a great service to their healing.

Rosary

Enough can never be said about the rosary. Praying the rosary has helped many survivors I know when any other contact with the Catholic Church would have been impossible. The rosary sustained survivors who were otherwise rejected, even persecuted, by the Church, its representatives, or Catholic families. The rosary has been in many pockets of survivors too wounded to pray at all, but who held their rosaries through many dangers and snares.

The most treasured possessions I have are rosaries. I have the rosary my mother prayed many times a day, to Mary and as the Divine Mercy, in her final years when our love had deepened in a freedom possible only through my own recovery and our reconciliation. It's hanging in a special box next to rosaries my father carried in his pocket for years. I only heard him recite the rosary when we were traveling places; it was something I loved to do because it meant we were out of the range of the predators. The box also has the rosary I clutched through all the difficult and frightening procedures and recovery following my first brain surgery, and the rosary I carried with me to a Marian shrine during a visit I promised myself to take when I was lying in my hospital bed. At the Marian shrine, we recited the rosary with crowds speaking in many different languages, all at once, with the same meaning. I was reminded of the Pentecost when everyone was speaking in different languages but it was no barrier to understanding or love.

The rosary box is in my prayer room, where I sit and cultivate openness to God every day. When I pray the rosary there, I realize my words are flowing into a current around the world, praying the same prayer simultaneously. This solidarity is something that far exceeds the wound of my childhood and makes me grateful for all the struggles I endured to find some place of my own in the faith of my childhood.

I love the image of the words of the rosary "flowing into a current around the world." That current is made up of many languages and cultures. It also includes many experiences, some happy but probably many more that are sad and some even tragic and at times despairing. The painful and isolating experiences of young abuse victims as well as their still-wounded adult selves form part of that same current. Joined to the prayers of so many others, their words of faith, however halting or listless, can take on a depth and hue not otherwise possible.

Spiritual guides will help survivors look for connections between the mysteries of the rosary and their own past experiences and present feelings, showing them in that way how to find healing balm for what they suffer still and the promise of a better future. Yet, it is important to be ever mindful of the double-edged sword created by the impact of abuse on the truths of God in a child's life.

Take, for example, the birth of Jesus. There, God discloses himself to those who, like the shepherds and wise men, seek him still. He is revealed in that mystery as an innocent, vulnerable, and powerless babe but also as someone who is very approachable, smiling, and warm. The very idea of a vulnerable child can be distressing for some survivors, depending on their experience of abuse. Also, associations with Christmas can be terribly difficult for some survivors whose abuse took place in homes where traditions like Christmas were disrupted by dysfunction and abuse. No amount of your reason can wipe away this pain, but the Holy Spirit can help to heal the past associations and open this person to new and healthful Christmas and nativity associations that are not fraught with the pain of abuse. So, be open to how a survivor feels about the scene of the nativity, find ways this defenseless image of God can help survivors be open to the Holy Spirit.

For survivors, the babe at Bethlehem may also bring to mind the young innocents who, at Herod's hands, suffered violence for Jesus. Tiny martyrs, they now sing with him forever the joyful songs of heaven. Innocents who suffered at the hands of violent men are the witnesses to the horror of young victims of abuse. Many adults failed child victims, beginning with the abuser, but, in ever wider circles, others have failed them as well. They were in their abuse as alone and as powerless as were the Holy Innocents. They were all unprotected. The Holy Innocents understand the experience of death in childhood. They are now, in a very special way, patron saints for survivors of abuse, their heavenly protectors, those in whom they see dimly a mirror of their own experience. Survivors may not have died bodily from what they suffered as the Innocents did, but they certainly died in other ways—emotionally, spiritually, and relationally. In the Holy Innocents survivors may find solace of kindred spirits.

In the Joyful Mystery of the Lord's baptism, survivors may find comfort from the Father's words, "This is my beloved Son." God speaks those same words to each person at the moment of their own baptism. Survivors, so demeaned by authority for so long, may need help from someone like a spiritual guide to be able to hear those words or to believe that they actually include them. But once they do they can begin to lay claim to all the power, love, and happiness that these words of God imply. We don't have them in Scripture, but surely Jesus must have said similar words to his Father at that very special moment: "You are my beloved Father!" If a survivor can begin to echo those words, a whole new world opens up for them.

These are some suggestions as to how survivors can, from the mysteries of the rosary, find connections to their own experiences, past, present, and future.

LOURDES

Lourdes and Fatima were encounters with Mary that involved children. For some survivors, the famed sufferings of these children, who still held staunchly to their connection with our Blessed Mother, were hopeful signs. On one side there was a dubious and punishing hierarchy, with its tin ear. On the other side was one child, or three children, not believed and punished for their truths. For me, the story of these children was like a letter found in a bottle cast into the sea, from God to me, for later discussion. My love of Mary, and reading about her appearances to the poor and disenfranchised, played a guiding role in my own faith story, no matter how dark the time.

"Woman, there is your son … There is your mother."[50] From being first disciple in the Joyful Mysteries of the rosary, Mary was called to be a disciple as a mother for eternity. From the moment the dying Jesus entrusted Mary to John as his mother, he gave her as mother to all believers as well. Indeed, Mary is our mother in both name and in fact. She loves and treasures each of us as a mother loves and treasures an only child. As any good mother, she hastens to comfort. In Mary, survivors can find the loving and protective mother (or father) whom they might never have had to comfort them. Or, they may find a mother who can walk them by the hand through reconciliations with parents and families they never thought possible. To do so, they may find they need time to resolve painful associations with mothering and parenting.

There are other dimensions of Mary in relationship specifically to children, as we see in apparition sites such as Lourdes or Fatima. One dimension that may speak directly to some child victims and survivors of abuse: Mary suffers whenever her children suffer. This meditation can dispel, for some, the sense

---

[50] John 19:26, 27, or in the NAB: "Woman, behold, your son. Behold your Mother."

of isolation as they return to, and make peace with, the actual memories of being abused. With Mary, that unflinching witness to evildoing began with the life of Jesus. The sword that passed through his side, piercing his heart, passed through her heart as well. As discussed earlier, between mother and son, there was but one heart, one will. What Jesus suffered, Mary suffered. It was her choice; it was her "yes." And whenever any of her children suffer, Jesus suffers, and she does not look away as so many others do. She remains steadfast and suffers as well. In the presence of any hurting child, Mary is truly their Sorrowful Mother. So, too, for families of survivors of abuse can Mary's sorrow join with theirs, helping healing. Yet again, this is a double-edged sword for those struggling with how abandoned they feel—and were—in human terms. Yet again, as spiritual guide, you follow them at their pace as you explore facets to devotion to Mary.

More to the point here, Mary suffered with Bernadette at Lourdes as well as, later, with Lucia, Jacinta, and Francisco, the three children at Fatima. Mary is the sorrowful and suffering mother of every child who is a victim of abuse, some of whom were and are suffering in plain site with no human person to witness the wrong or acknowledge their agony. What they endure, she endures as well. Their hell is her hell. So often children suffer without witnesses, and so often Mary has appeared to children who seem to offer the same face as her son in the manger—vulnerable, guileless. What does she, as mother, teach from this close proximity to our suffering? Mary spoke no words at the foot of the Cross. She just stood there, silent, comforting her son just by being near him in his pain, lessening it for him by sharing it with him. Her role was not to look away as so many do. She did not succumb to denial as many in our Church have done about the child abuse. She remains beside her suffering child. And, then, with her son, she waits for God to keep his promises. In this she is teaching children to trust their Father's promises, and she teaches those who would look away from child victims and wounded adult survivors what we must do.

Trusting God, as mentioned often in this book, is very difficult for people who have survived trauma. Indeed, people who have suffered catastrophic loss of any type will grieve, and in their grief question God over and over. One thing survivors grieve is the breaking of the implicit promise to keep a child safe. That was broken long ago, as may have been many promises since that time depending on how disrupted families became from the effects of the abuse. Mary's faithfulness may serve as a dependable alternative, offering solace but also insight into the wondrous outcomes trust in God's promises can offer. Mary can, in other words, dare survivors of the worst abuse nonetheless to trust again.

Looking at Lourdes and Fatima, and at other places where Mary has appeared to children or young people, we see the visionaries often suffer for the gift of her presence she has bestowed on them. Family members, local authorities, and Church authorities were cruel to these little visionaries. So, to those familiar with the stories, the fate of children in Mary's special care may seem dangerous, not holy. The old, familiar confusion left by abuse can surface, seeing proximity to Mary and her son as painful and not something of spiritual joy. Yet, Mary chose each visionary for a particular reason, and each visionary in very different ways brought messages to an often stiff-necked world. In their faithfulness to Mary over their persecutors, the children were choosing, exercising their will, quite unlike a child victim. And, unlike this victim, the visionaries were given the purpose of their lives, no matter how short, at a very early age.

It is true that their messages were carried with pain, from Jesus and Mary in pain, to the children sharing in that pain, as a world remained uncomprehending, even hostile toward what the children said. No one would wish on a child victim such pain; it was not a pain ordained by God. The gift of messages to visionaries was ordained by God. When and however survivors find a way to offer God their own assent, they too will offer messages, all different from each other, each uniquely purposeful in survivors' lives. In their own "fiat," survivors can welcome the grace of God into their stories and allow their own lives to be a message for their families, friends, and communities in how they permit their suffering—as child victims, as adult survivors in recovery, as people grappling with all of life's struggles—to reflect the work of the Holy Spirit.

Mary's messages through visionaries were consistent through the ages. She asked people to come back to God, to reject mistaken ways, and to convert more deeply to dependence on God. As spiritual guide, you are asking the same of survivors, to come back to God, to turn away from false lessons from abusers and enablers, and to convert into a deeper reliance on God as part of their healing. You can help survivors understand how Mary was at the Cross of her son's sufferings and is there at the cross when any of her children suffer. She may not speak but her presence comforts. Her presence in their lives may not be as sensational as an apparition, or as discombobulating as it was for Bernadette. Maybe one day there will be a new verse to the Litany of Mary: "Mary, Sorrowful Mother of abused children, pray for us!"

Sin

Many of us emerge from abuse feeling a range of emotions, from confusion through humiliation. What we do not happen to feel in the early days often catches up with us through the following years. And, what also catches up with us is the staggering reality that no one could save us.

We emerge from feeling like we sinned. For some of us, we were told we were the ones who sinned or were to blame for causing the abuser to abuse us. In a world rife with people ready to blame the victim, this reversal of guilt onto a victim could be found in many corners and only fed our sense of rage or shame.

As one survivor described it to me, we all carry the weight of our own sins, but some of us have had to carry the weight of terrible sins committed against us by others. Putting down those sins we did not commit can be very hard.

In our shame, sin is a complicated issue. Sometimes it's harder to say what we have done right than what we have done to sin. Sometimes admitting we are sinners is very hard, because we can be struggling to maintain our innocence against all the internal voices that blame us for being abused.

Sin is theologically defined as estrangement from God. How odd that the core of our own estrangement has been someone else's sin, against God through us. What's important to remember is the puzzling line Felix Culpa, *or happy sin. The idea is not that sin is happy. It's not that our pain and suffering are happy. It is, however, that we can be happy precisely because of our estrangement from God, for whatever reason I am in flight from God is the reason God sent His son to find and save me. He knows, like I know, I cannot find the way back, over these terrible obstacles of pain and memory, alone, without His help.*

Even before we have sorted it all out, understanding our own sins as something separate from what we have suffered as children while we seek recovery, we can be relieved of the pressure to protest our innocence to avert the deep-seated sense of mistaken guilt for what happened to us. We have a way to be saved from the heavy burdens bearing down on us. We can let God figure it all out. In the very real, life-and-death terms of a survivor, God has sent Jesus to save us. We are freed already, before we even know what it means to be saved.

Adult survivors of abuse often struggle long and hard with the question of their own guilt or complicity in their abuse as children. They ask themselves how they could have stopped or avoided certain incidents, and they often conclude, without having any idea how they might have exercised some control over the abusive adult, that they are at fault to some degree.

Even those who knew right from the start that they were truly victims, and thus innocent, often encountered skepticism or unbelief in those they told of their abuse or, worse, reactions that implied that they were in fact guilty. Told that often enough, especially by authority figures, many victims became confused, even became convinced of their guilt. They bring all that baggage of guilt and, worse, sometimes assign themselves the impossible task of sorting it all out.

Survivors may know and believe in their heads that they are innocent of any guilt at all, but their feelings and their hearts cannot believe. Add to that situation the spiritual dilemma of feeling such guilt, and you have a mix that becomes all but impossible to sort out. This is a very heavy burden. Yet again, the damaging effects of abuse leave their marks deeply embedded in the psyches of survivors for many decades.

While an oversimplification, one way to understand this misguided sense of sin is that, as children isolated by abuse, child victims had no adult to help them understand what happened. They were left to understand with the very limited experience of a child something so evil that wise and learned adults cannot comprehend it. So child victims can grow up with a very wrong sense of their own power in the situation. They can be entirely unaware of the disparity of power between abuser and abused. This is natural for people grappling with what happened in abuse.

In fact it is not at all uncommon for survivors (even of clergy abuse) to venture back into a first adult encounter with the Church in confession—to confess the sin of being abused. While the idea seems preposterous to an outsider, it is important to be prepared to help survivors understand gently but firmly that, first and foremost, this is not their sin to confess. From there, like anyone in a position to be approached by survivors of abuse, you should have contact numbers on hand to offer. And, you should also be open to receive the gifts of a very powerful dialogue with this person that may continue over time.

There is here another double-edged sword. By forcing the survivor to reject one kind of preposterous guilt, the wound of abuse might also deny them the joy of being a sinner saved. It may create an impasse to their own Exsultet, or Easter Proclamation, "O happy fault, that earned for us so great, so glorious a Redeemer!" Certainly, many are estranged from God by the obstacle placed in their lives by another's sinfulness—their abuser's evildoing. In other ways, everyone has committed sins which keep them estranged from God. This can be a complicated web. It cannot be sorted out too quickly without creating more harm.

As the survivor struggles to find their own innocence, they may feel unusual anxiety, even resistance, to a sense of sin. Yet, they are at that very time also moving through their own Paschal Mystery, which is the arc of their abuse and recovery. Their new life is hardly full without the Divine Mercy. Offering guidance we are also reflecting God's mercy in everything we do, including in our patience and regard for this person. It has indeed been an unmerciful world for them. They likely arrive in your care at the price of estrangement, even cruelties, from some or all family members, parishes, friends, and communities. Don't push to focus on sin, but don't deny them the right to be sinners saved, either.

Survivors' confusion and doubt about their own sense of guilt and innocence can be a very great weight. Sorting through what sin really is can take a very long time for someone who has been the victim of many layers of other people's sins. You need to understand this is not rational. If the survivor could have figured their way out of this box surely they would have—without turning to you! With our role representing the Church and Christ, we need to assure survivors again and again that they are not guilty of their abuse and that any doubts to the contrary are actually the tragic effects of the abuse itself. They need be assured that they have the Holy Spirit to help them understand what can seem impossible to believe: their own innocence. And the Spirit will help them see and be freed from their own sins. For this, it is okay for survivors to turn what is confusing over to God, to "let God figure it all out." This is actually both a very wise thing to do as well as a courageous act of confidence in His love for them. It will take time.

One meditation that may be helpful is for a survivor to reflect on the words of Jesus: "Come to me, all you who labor and are burdened, and I will give you rest."[51] In these words the Lord wants to address and relieve every kind of suffering and burden. The survivors' long and ultimately impossible struggle to "figure it all out" is truly exhausting. Though innocent, they have had to

---

[51] Matthew 11:28

bear the weight of another's guilt for far too long. They can begin to lay this burden down, now. To the extent that you can help them do so is a healing process itself, as a survivor gradually is able to receive from you the Lord's own comfort and rest. None of this is likely to be resolved easily or quickly. The nature of this person's recovery can be slow and halting. You may both agree on things as obvious as their innocence, but then their own heart must catch up for them to be really free. Comfort these resilient people often, and learn from them, and let the Spirit guide them to the Lord's healing.

Since we are in some way representing God or at least authority, we can offer assurances that "it is not your fault" from a unique vantage point. Living up to our reflection of God and authority, we can help lift from survivors a burden that they did not earn and ought not now to bear. "It is not your fault" needs to be repeated over and over again; never assume it fully sinks in to the wounded survivor. As these heavy and down-pulling feelings subside, survivors grow stronger psychologically and spiritually.

Confession

One trait many survivors share is being confessional. Some of us remember it as a phase when we told our abuse story to anyone who would listen, seeking somehow a key that would unlock us from the bondage of its grip, or some final relief, or some eureka solution however we might imagine that to be. Because no single key or relief or solution existed, we kept telling—anyone. In the process, we encountered rejection, partly because people failed to know how to respond with loving kindness and partly because we were overwhelming people ill-equipped to handle such truths. We may have even traumatized empathetic people vicariously or re-traumatized other victims. This was not a confession that could work.

And many of us felt we were carrying the weight of the abuse on our own souls. It is not uncommon for survivors of abuse to try to confess their role in the abuse to a priest in the sacrament; that is what I did, only to encounter a priest who, wisely, told me that was no sin. He suggested we speak about what happened outside the confessional, and my own progress returning to the faith of my childhood took a leap forward.

"We can let God figure it all out." The Evil One is wily. He tempts us to sin in the first place; then, he often leaves us with the nearly impossible task of assigning the true weight of our guilt in sinning. We know that we have committed the sin, but we are not always so sure about how free we really were in sinning. Many factors, some unknown even to our conscious selves, cluster around the sin, factors that could mitigate not the fact of the sin, but its true guilt and, thus, our full responsibility before God. How often do penitents, frustrated at not being able to determine the full weight of their consent in a particular sin or habit, confess it "as it stands before God"?

In this, just like survivors did above, they "let God figure it all out."

Confession promises among other graces a greater closeness with God. In that, it is like all sacraments an intimate moment between God and his child. Learning ways to approach confession, and the great mercy and divine intimacy it offers, can be good work for spiritual guidance, just as can reassuring a survivor that the crippling shame that can remain after abuse has nothing to do with what they must confess.

In that intimacy of confession, do not underestimate that anxiety of exposure and vulnerability survivors may feel. This sacrament, something many Catholics find as a treasure, can be for some survivors an act of courage taken with trepidation. For that reason, timing confession must be carefully discerned. A confessor might meet with the survivor—and possibly with a supportive friend—beforehand to establish a sense of safety. Ideally, confessors will be advised in advance of the gravity of this step for this person, and better have a general sense of the issues discussed in this book. It is in confession that the closeness to God can be healed but also most wounded, particularly if an uninformed confessor fails to reinforce a healthful sense of guilt—and innocence.

Telling one's story can be very helpful for survivors, but discovering how best to tell one's story can be a very great obstacle. For example, the confessional is no place for receiving good care for the stories they have to tell. Much as they seek to be heard, some survivors don't know how to find ready and able listeners. By the time you meet them, some survivors will have shared their stories, with mixed results. Others may never have uttered the fact to anyone before speaking to you.

People often confuse the need to confess sins with the need to be heard overall. This is not limited to survivors. Both are true and good needs, but they are different. It is very important for survivors to be heard, and if they turn to you to be heard it is very important you do not recoil or reject them—lest you fuel the shame and increase the burden they carry. Yet, it is also important they are heard in the right way by the right people. One step may be moving them from the confessional to an office appointment. Or, from a brief encounter on the street to a setting that is comfortable for you both.

Then, you will play a role. If you are not able to provide what is needed, it is important to have alternatives at the ready. In our diocese, for example, we encourage survivors of child sexual abuse to connect with one of our Victim Assistance Coordinators who ensure they have options for therapy and spiritual direction as well as prayer services, Masses, discussion groups, and fellowship with other survivors. In this setting, if you are not prepared to offer spiritual guidance to a survivor, you can be sure they find a wealth of options to support their recovery.

If you do offer spiritual guidance of any kind, formal or casual, you will learn how the needs vary greatly. For some survivors, being heard involves telling their whole story. For others, it may involve something more limited, such as being acknowledged as a survivor of abuse with unique struggles in the present day. Each person's need is unique.

We are likely to hear about similar issues they are discussing in therapy with a trained professional, and can find ways to encourage them to let God, prayer, their faith, and sacraments help them. Over the course of time, as survivors work through their past with the help of therapists their needs evolve as well. We must be flexible and open, as ever, to each person's specific needs.

There are risks in this work to be mindful of. For example, we can, in respecting the reticence of some survivors, overlook their need for more open communication about their pain. Or, as we listen to a survivor's story in the acknowledged presence of God we can help them let go of a past, or hang onto a past, which harms them. This is a very important reason why we need to be sure survivors understand our role is helping them deepen their bond with God to sustain and enrich their healing journey, but not playing trained therapist who can help people challenge themselves to do painful work resolving the past.

Here is where a spiritual guide can be helpful firstly by knowing what our role is—and what our role is not. We listen, and when we listen we listen with the Holy Spirit. We listen with the ears of our hearts. For people who as children suffered invisibly, to be seen, heard, known, respected, and accepted is a healing experience. We are honored to serve this woundedness, and we are sure to learn from these people a sensitivity that helps us help others—in a sense, passing along the gift born of their suffering.

CROSS

The Cross is one of the realities in our faith that speaks directly to survivors. Most people think our cross is defined as what we experienced as children. For most survivors, it is that, plus trauma that followed either as a consequence of abuse directly or of its effects on our ability to live free and well lives.

Picking up our cross and following Jesus is not about accepting anything about the abuse, but it is about understanding that no one can carry this burden for me. If I recover from it—or from the addictions or self-harming behavior that follow it—it's because I will take responsibility for myself recovering. No other person can carry this responsibility for me. Resisting this cross is much harder and more damaging than accepting it is there for me to lift so I can move forward.

Something our loved ones need to understand is what our crosses mean. It is important for us to permit loved ones the freedom not to own our pain. They will suffer a wound from the trauma by one degree of separation, and they will need care, too. Ultimately, our loved ones need to focus on the moment when Simon of Cyrene foisted the Cross back on the wounded shoulder of Jesus. At the end of the day, when all the rage and hurt and grief and confusion subside, we are left to carry this trauma forward—through recovery and healing, into new life.

All who wish to follow Jesus are commanded by him to take up their cross daily and follow him. The cross takes shapes in a unique way for every Christian. It is weighted by the circumstances that make up each person's unrepeatable life. Thus, my cross is not your cross, nor yours mine. And no one can carry another's cross either. Loved ones might want, like Simon of Cyrene, to shoulder our cross completely and to carry it all the way. Indeed, love often wants to do more than it in fact is able to do. But the command of Jesus is directed to each person, even by name. For that reason, one's cross can and must, in the end, be carried only by the one for whom it has been fashioned.

What has gone into the shape and weight of a survivor's cross? Certainly, it is partly the result of the actual abuse. But it is much more than that, and much of what follows bears the imprint of the abuse. The survivor's cross is also all the damage and detritus that has followed the abuse: the grief, the addictions, the isolation, the wrong turns and detours, the harmful friends, the self-doubt and self-hate, the failure of others to protect in the first place or, afterwards, to hear or to help. Very sadly, the list is legion. But collectively, all of these things, not just the trauma of abuse, constitute what is now the cross that the adult survivor must pick up daily and, alone, carry.

The spiritual guide is nonetheless a companion for this wounded person. We do not pretend we can carry their cross, and we must be mindful of our own impulses to recoil from its injustice by trying to offer unhelpful things like pep talks ("You can get on with your life") or solutions ("This is an experience to process, not a problem to solve"). Survivors will spy our discomfort with their cross in any suggestions we make that the process can be sped up, shortened, or minimized.

As they find better ways to carry this cross, what we can do is remind them that they are always in the company of Jesus. Indeed, he leads. He is the Way. They can choose to follow just one step behind, as he carries his Cross. People understand a suffering path shared, and in time they may comprehend a suffering melded. Through prayer and reflection, survivors find very personal ways to acknowledge that the Cross of Jesus has graciously incorporated into its own shape and weight the shape and weight of their heavy crosses as well. This does not reduce the reality of their burden, but it does reduce the difficulty of bearing it. Then, what Simon of Cyrene had been for Jesus, Jesus now becomes for the survivor—more so, because Simon could only help for a small moment in Jesus's path, but Jesus has never left this survivor's side.

Saints

If anything embodies how Catholicism is a wide road that welcomes people with every kind of gift and every kind of foible, it is our saints. With angels, I have grown to treasure their presence in my life, most especially during the Eucharist when the altar is full of their presence. Saints are often what draw us home to Catholicism, and they have a role in any faith story of any survivor of abuse whom I have ever had the honor of knowing.

For me, there was the mosaic of St. Anthony in a shrine in the basement chapel of a church tucked into blocks of skyscrapers in midtown Manhattan. I spent many hours during my first ventures back into a Catholic church staring at the mosaic, outraged that anyone would display, given the scandal that was always in the media, a friar holding a child in his hands. Over time, the image went from angering me and frightening me, to soothing me and reminding me that some safe relationships still existed. People speak of that shrine as one of many healings. I believe mine began there, which is the same place where a bronze statue of St. Francis of Assisi kneels in an open courtyard where thousands of nameless commuters pass daily and touch him, leaving a golden sheen.

There was also the sacred icon of St. Therese of Lisieux which my mother hung in the hallway outside my bedroom. At night, I was too afraid to sleep and would, in my ramblings, stumble upon her looking at me when everyone else in the house of my childhood was sleeping. She never slept. She felt, to me, like a witness more than a portrait. An early therapist dismissed as magical thinking my memory that a portrait could see what adults should have and did not. She was not wrong about the failure of adults, but, in time, I came to understand the icon was reflecting what was also true: saints and angels were witness to what others in the Church refused to see for a very, very long time.

The saints stand behind the survivors as supporters. "I believe in the communion of saints." This very comforting line from the Creed speaks to the ultimate victory of human freedom that is forgiven and graced. Men, women, and children of every age, race, tribe, and nation are now enjoying, and will forever enjoy, the unimaginable happiness of heaven. They were parents and children, kings and farmers, wealthy and poor, soldiers and homemakers, husbands and wives. And, yes, no doubt some of them were likely victims of abuse as well. Saints intercede for us. Having crossed the finish line themselves, they now urge us on, encouraging and supporting us, no doubt at times they even run interference for us.

Specific saints can play singular roles in survivors' lives—and in their recovery. At times throughout this book we have singled out saints who might well serve as patron saints of abuse victims. We already noted the very young boys, the Holy Innocents, who were martyred at the birth of Jesus by agents of Herod. Their story and the power of their intercession may well provide much comfort to survivors, but we also noted how aspects of such stories may prompt unforeseen triggers as well.

For instance, there is the young Italian preteenager Maria Goretti. This girl suffered attempted rape as a youth. She was killed resisting her would-be rapists. Her courage has inspired some, yet, her decision to fight off her young attacker is something that some survivors may mistake as a reproach for not fighting off their adult abusers.

After returning from a failed experience in a crusade, St. Francis of Assisi is known for his experience of a state much like what we call "post-traumatic stress" now. Post-traumatic stress disorder is a common therapeutic diagnosis for survivors of abuse. How this St. Francis dealt with his psychological darkness, and how it shaped him into the friar now loved by so many, can be a very helpful story for reflection.

What is important for the spiritual guide is to remain alert to each survivor's state of mind, to take time to appreciate their disposition and proclivities, before suggesting saints. It is, as always, best to take the lead of the survivor in finding what is comforting and what is a trigger for pain.

The very diversity of the saints can help give hope to survivors. As noted earlier, St. Francis de Sales describes saints in this way: "They once were what we are now."[52] They represent every personality type, profession, state, and stage of life. Some were once unbelievers who converted to Christ, early or late in life. Some were notorious sinners who eventually found their way to Jesus. Many were once just Christian or Catholic in name only but, surprised by grace, became strong in the faith, generous in charity, and firmly rooted in hope. In many of them, grace transformed mediocrity into heroic virtue. The weak and wobbly became paragons of virtue; earthen, clay vessels were transformed into channels of God's goodness, forgiveness, kindness, and compassion. In their world, saints were the caring hands and gentle smile of God Himself. One thing we notice as spiritual guides is the heroic virtue practiced by these powerful

---

[52] St. Francis de Sales, *Introduction to the Devout Life*, Part 5, Chapter 12

people who are survivors who come for our care. So often our work is simply to point out that they have already been walking closely, if perhaps wordlessly, with God all along.

On a closing note, if saints were once what we are now, in all probability there are saints in heaven who were once victims of abuse. Until the last decade or so, this sad and tragic side of the human condition was simply not openly acknowledged, written about, or spoken aloud. Abuse in families, whether physical, sexual, or emotional, used to be considered largely a private matter. Much has come to light and thus the possibility of healing has become more prevalent in the wake of the recent scandals of abuse. The point I wish to make here is the likely fact that some who were once abused as children are now among the saints of God. Though their names may be known only to God, these holy ones are now most certainly the very special protectors, friends, and advocates of today's survivors—and child victims. The spiritual guide will contribute greatly to the spiritual healing and growth of survivors if these heavenly friends are part of the dialogue, invited to pray for their ready assistance in their challenging efforts at recovery.

Forgiveness

Forgiveness: It is a word that has far more facets than most would think. Mostly, forgiveness became enabling in those who chose to protect abusers over children. Forgiveness in abusers was simply a matter of permission. Later in life, survivors hear "forgive" in the context of a person making the recommendation to "get over it" so they can avoid facing the depth of a survivor's pain. Forgiveness as expedient does not work; it neither heals us nor anyone else. Christ's death on the Cross was not about expediency.

Whole movements talk about forgiveness in recovery, and most psychological programs rightly seek to help survivors find a way to forgive—or to let go, to release, to move beyond, or even to integrate. So, we set our little paper boats in the ocean or river and watch abusers float off into the current. We buy a helium balloon and let it go with a paper list of names tied to the tail. We burn a list of names in the Hibachi. I even buried a list of names under a rock at a rest stop on a highway when I was 800 miles from home. These are all good and sound symbolic gestures, but when they are done it still remains for the heart to release something.

Sometimes we just aren't ready to release the indictment, sometimes we fear the hollow that will remain when we do. Often, we're pushing too hard for forgiveness to happen, like the flick of a switch, when it takes the same slow time recovery does.

For my part, I'm not sure I forgave. What happened was that my healing and recovery have moved so deeply into Jesus that, once I was sure my abusers had been identified, I just didn't have any more space in my thoughts or heart for them anymore.

In the Salesian tradition, we have this saying: "Make room for Jesus within." In order for Jesus to come alive in our daily actions and behavior with others, we have first to make room for him to live and reign within our hearts. We want for ourselves what St. Paul describes of himself in Galatians: "The life I live now is not my own; Christ is living in me."[53] This will involve a challenging asceticism as it did for St. Paul: "I have been crucified with Christ."[54]

The simple truth is this: the presence of Jesus within our hearts displaces whatever is not compatible with his love. Therefore, making room for Jesus within must occur before forgiveness is even possible. Indeed, forgiveness of one's abusers or of their enablers, or of those who would not or could not listen to survivors—things like this come most often at the end of the recovery process. And, even the willingness to forgive eventually is not solely or principally the result of one's own efforts, however hard one may try. Forgiveness, in all its phases and ways, is the fruit of the healing power of grace. Nothing negative or angry or hateful can co-exist within the same heart where the Lord resides. So, the more he reigns there, the more the resistance to forgive is displaced: "Let go; let God!" As you help a survivor to let God reign in their heart more and more, deepening their relationship, you are letting the Holy Spirit work in ways that will make forgiveness possible when God ordains.

These words from above seem to witness to this very thing: "For my part, I'm not sure I forgave. What happened was that my healing and recovery have

---

[53] Galatians 2:20, as translated in the NAB, "... yet I live, no longer I, but Christ lives in me."
[54] Galatians 2:19, as translated in the NAB, "For through the law I died to the law, that I might live for God. I have been crucified with Christ."

moved so deeply into Jesus that, once I was sure my abusers had been identified, I just didn't have any more space in my thoughts or heart for them anymore."

It's critically important, meanwhile, to remember that forgiveness was used as an excuse to keep sending abusers back into place, where they could prey on more children. This was true of our Church for far too long, and it remains true in too many settings today. A survivor's resistance to forgiveness has many layers, one the simple and understandable difficulty of forgiving one's abuser. But, also, there is a well-founded fear that to forgive is to tolerate or enable. This hesitance is grounded in a moral good, to never forget children suffering now. There are ways different survivors have found to move that moral intent into good action, from parenting of course, to caring for younger siblings, to volunteering as a Big Brother or Sister, or promoting child safety. In prayer and in time, survivors can discern ways to help others, if they wish, that also help them let go of any doubts about forgiveness.

In offering spiritual guidance to survivors of abuse, work first on helping them to make room for Jesus within their hearts. The rest will follow in time.

Praise

So often in the Psalms, David lists all the woes and seemingly unbeatable foes he faces and then, in the middle of the verse, proclaims that he will praise the Lord. The Book of Lamentations is the same. Even Job interrupts his litany of suffering with statements of wonder about God. To anyone who is suffering, this abrupt switch can be mistaken for primitive verse or a rough-hewn translation. For survivors it can seem, well, like the writer is shutting down on a very emotional circumstance.

The nature of the process of recovery may distract us from what is at work here. Recovery safely delivers us up on the shore when we do not fight the current, but rather work with it and let it take its time. Yet, so many places in Scripture, well before any good reason is obvious, people step out and praise God in the midst of suffering.

In a similar way, praise has been a catalyst for some survivors at unlikely moments of despair or grief. Praise doesn't erase or ignore the darkness, but it orients our hearts to the Light we know prevails. Praise, as a recovery exercise, is the opposite experience of abuse.

In his *Treatise on the Love of God*, St. Francis de Sales describes a ladder of praise of God that ends in silence and "unvoiced awe." Like the psalmist, he first invites all of creation to praise its Creator, but he soon realizes that, however beautiful and fitting such praise is, it cannot measure up to glory that is God's. He then invites Mary, the greatest and most beautiful of all of God's creatures to render God adequate praise. Still, even her praise falls short of God's infinite grandeur. Then he invites the Sacred Humanity of Jesus itself, personally joined to the Logos, to give praise that is truly worthy of God. But even the praise of Jesus, given his finite human nature, does not fully measure up to the infinite and uncreated being that is God. This is when St. Francis finally calls for the silence of all creation, inviting us to listen with unvoiced awe to God praise Himself. Only God's praise of Himself is truly worthy of Himself: "Glory be to the Father and to the Son and to the Holy Spirit." The human effort to render worthy praise of God must in the end yield to God's praise of Himself. It must end there, for only God is truly worthy of God and only His praise is fully commensurate with the divine glory. This is a sublime meditation, which may in time help survivors approach the wonder and mystery involved in praising God.[55]

For a while, survivors may not be ready to even attempt to praise God with a full appreciation until they have somehow been reconciled with His apparent silence and distance from them when they were in the throes and horrors of their abuse. Even once that reconciliation has taken place, however, praise may not be the first form of prayer that comes naturally to them. They may need first to pray the prophet's prayer of a lover's complaint: "Where were you when I needed you most?" Moving beyond that, they may feel called to the prayer of petition, begging that God, who has helped them to begin at last on the road to recovery, will see them all the way to its end. As a preparation for the silent prayer of praise and unvoiced awe, they may be content for a while with the simple prayer of presence in which they are silent

---

[55] St. Francis de Sales, *Treatise on the Love of God*, Book 5, Chapters 9-12

and alone with the Alone. In time and inevitably, praise will follow, perhaps even along the rungs of the ladder of praise suggested by St. Francis de Sales. The progress would be that they can imagine themselves part of the praising and glorifying creation, freed from the shame that keeps them isolated even from these.

In any case, just as the disciples asked Jesus to teach them how to pray, at some point survivors may make that same request of their spiritual guides. Always begin with where they are. It is in that place where God is pleased to find them seeking Him. Discern and follow with them the Spirit's lead as they move from one form of prayer to the next. In the end, both of you will fall silent before the living God and in unvoiced awe be content simply to listen to the Triune God praise Himself. And, you will likely find yourself giving praise to God for the opportunity to be a spiritual guide and companion to this resilient and courageous survivor of abuse.

Eucharist

Even while we were being abused in our churches, schools, home, and other "safe" places, there was one place that remained safe because it was untouchable, even where the hands of a predator priest held it high over the congregation.

Even while we were alone trembling and grieved without words to speak or witnesses to speak for us or advocates open to our complaint, back when we were too small to be deemed competent witnesses in courts of law on our own behalf, this Presence was Truth, able to gather and protect our truths until we grew and were old enough to return, adult witnesses on behalf of the silent victims we were.

This Presence is the only Word an abuser cannot corrupt for evil ends. This Presence is the rebuke to those who have been complicit with the lies. In the staggering silence that surrounds this Presence, we are safe, indeed safest on our knees.

Adoration has been, for many of us, a safe place. The church is empty enough to spy any potentially dangerous priest or person approaching. The words of an entire Catholic church chattering with opinions about the abuse scandal are usually unheard. There isn't even a priest or other official in proximity of holiness. It's a place where some of us even receive the graces for the internal patter of self-loathing and shame to be hushed by the tenderness of our Savior staying with us always in the simplicity of consecrated bread and wine.

Before the abuse, the priest abuser represented Jesus to his victim. The abuse thus greatly damaged their image of God. For child victims, for adult survivors, the predatory priest may become the personification of evil itself while, for others, he remained undiscovered and was long-touted as a holy vessel of God's grace. It was a confusing contradiction, to say the least. The victim found evil in the person in whom everyone else suggested they would find God. Where, then, was a child to look for and find God? Where does the adult survivor seek God? In what safe and holy place can He be found without, at the same time, the unsafe presence of his corrupted vessel?

As noted above, some survivors—even as child victims—found protection and love in the safe and secure place of an empty church. Its burning vigil light witnessed the presence of the living God under the form of Eucharistic bread. Others recount being drawn into a silent, almost-empty church with people sitting in Adoration. Even without realizing it, their search for Him had been God's own handiwork in them. It was His searching grace that led them to Him. They found Him in an empty church, waiting for them behind the doors of its Tabernacle.

From childhood this calling to child victims exists. "Suffer the little children to come to me." Jesus spoke those words to his disciples but, in the case of child victims, he speaks these words to his angels. Those heavenly and good spirits surround and comfort the little children, while gently leading them to the quiet and safety of their Lord, who waits in the Eucharist.

Later, as adults on the road to recovery, survivors can still find comfort and safety with Jesus in all manner of ways, but particularly in the Eucharist. How to approach Adoration, how to relate to God in the Eucharist, may provide the basis of profound discussions in spiritual guidance. Mostly, devotion to the Holy Eucharist offers access to the presence of the only One who comforted, protected, and loved them when they were all alone and all seemed so very dark. In its silence with them, they may recognize old feelings of isolation, but discern more closely His presence in silence. Here again is that double-edged sword, but too here is a place where no human stands between a survivor and their God.

As part of spiritual guidance, it is not uncommon to seek a deeper understanding of the nature and reality of the Presence as well as the bread that heals broken lives, soothes wounded spirits, and repairs scarred hearts. As people comforted by angels at times when they were unaware, survivors may want to delve into the connections between the angels and the Eucharist with its familiar designation as the "Bread of Angels." Some survivors struggle terribly with habits of self-care; even eating well is problematic for people whose shame makes them feel unworthy of attention. Yet, there is the Eucharist, given by God, so simply bread, so mysteriously so much more, with the reminder even God puts care for them at the center of His concerns. In many ways, meditating on the Eucharist, with its centrality to our faith and to creation, can play a major role in survivors' recovery and new life as well. It is one of the primary reasons many, including survivors, find their return to the Church.

Your role can be to help find ever new ways to encounter the Eucharist, for it is a powerful way to deepen love of God and to understand His love for us.

Storytelling

Few of us were able to tell our story when we were young. Some did, and parents or other caretakers of some of us took protective action, including telling a hierarchy that did nothing more than move an abuser elsewhere, doubtless seduced by the predator's persuasive assurances that a fresh start near children would have different results. Even parents' stories were not heard.

As we grew, few places within the Church were hospitable to our stories, which were mistaken for stories of something other than faith. Some were willing to listen, but few had the training to manage the impact of our stories, and some showcased our stories for their own agenda.

That's why I was surprised to meet the De Sales Oblate priest who told me, "Tell your story." He assured me it would help heal me and might help heal others.

Storytelling is, after all, the nature of our faith. We believe in God, despite all the unbelievers, because we are told by others of His Word and redeeming actions. The Apostles were told about the Resurrection before they experienced it. Our stories of encountering evil can slowly reveal a deeper encounter with Christ, if we are willing, despite all the unbelievers.

Storytelling is about choices. How will we go about revealing the full truth of the tale? How much will we ask the listener to experience one thing over another? What I decided, as I described my own cross to myself, was that I did not want to traumatize others with my story of trauma. Over time I found different ways to recount it to different people. A few people are professionally prepared to handle all the details I may want to share, but most people are not. There is no reason for them to experience the full impact of a secondary trauma simply because they listen to my faith story. Neither is there any reason I would retell my story in a way to trigger another survivor with memories and references to the pain we share.

In the end, my storytelling was about my cross— my power to understand it in a way that permits me to carry it with the most freedom and love, my mastery to share it as I wish, my hope to find it can be a creative and not destructive force in my life anymore.

Most of all, storytelling expresses how wonderfully we are made, because each healing story is distinct and remarkable for its resilience and its brokenness, each faith story has a signature of its own love that no one else can replicate. That's why Jesus died on the Cross to save each and every one of us. No one of us is expendable to God. No one of our stories can be reduced to a list of survivor characteristics. We are truly, truly wonderfully made.

Telling one's story is healing. For many survivors, the first time they told another person what happened was their first step toward, finally, putting the abuse behind them. That first step, however, was too often met with incredulity or skepticism or worse. A negative reaction of any kind probably meant many more months or years when they could not or would not tell their story to another person. Tragically, in some cases it also meant more abuse. To the horrible pains of the abuse itself, then, were added the anger, even the rage, at not being helped.

When, finally, someone was able to both hear and help, a huge boulder began to be lifted. Healing had begun. Obviously, they thirsted for more healing and, thus, began to tell more and more people their story. They soon learned that not all people could hear their story and that many, hearing it, did not know how to help them heal. At first, when survivors are particularly vulnerable, this can be very hurtful. Over time, as they gain some distance from their early steps in recovery, they begin to see how some people were simply not prepared to receive the gift of knowing this survivor.

What is needed from the start is a supportive environment in which they can tell their story as often and with as much detail as they need to share, while still being heard and helped. The various elements of Victims Assistance Program of the Diocese of Arlington, Virginia, provide survivors with that supportive environment and, this, on several integrating levels of healing: therapy, support groups, and spiritual guidance. The relationships fostered here encourage storytelling, sharing, and listening among people who want and who are prepared to hear and help.

The spiritual guide in this environment knows that he or she is one important part of a multi-level system of support for survivors of abuse. Stories are told in pieces, a little at a time, sometimes over years. The relationships, the fellowship that lasts and is ready to hear more and care more form a strong support system that lasts beyond early recovery and well into a thriving, new life. Health care professionals, social workers, trained spiritual guides, and other "veteran" survivors are all part of an integrated diocesan approach that helps that whole person, and their loved ones, too.

What many survivors had long prayed for, others had never imagined possible, but here is this program, helping many to deepen their relationship with God and with the Church.

A SURVIVOR'S PRAYER[56]

God, let me be the person
You created me to be, and let me be that well!

Re-create me into that beautiful person You know to be,
Whole once again and holy in your sight!

I am loved and I am loveable!
This is my true identity: this is me.

I claim it!

---

[56] "Survivor Prayer," by Fr. Lewis S. Fiorelli. Copyright © 2013 All Rights Reserved

A PRAYER FOR GATHERINGS[57]

He found them in a wilderness, a wasteland of howling desert. He shielded them, cared for them, guarded them as the apple of his eye.[58]

> Come, Holy Spirit, to rest in our broken hearts and tend to our broken lives.
>
> Bear us up on wings of eagles when our hope lies crushed below the cross of our past. Release us from the shame and grieving that hobble our pursuit of joy in our Redeemer, Jesus Christ.
>
> Comfort our pain.
>
> Help us trust in Christ's complete victory over evil, so we may endure what we have suffered until that day when all we cannot see and cannot know is finally made clear.

---

[57] "Praying for Survivors," by T. Pitt Green. first published on usccb.org March 2013 Copyright © T. Pitt Green All Rights Reserved

[58] Deuteronomy 32:10

Heal us with a fuller understanding God's grace, so we may be open to sustenance to continue our recovery. Help us discern the sure direction of God's whisper when noise and confusion threaten to send us on mistaken pathways.

Provide us generously with Your counsel, so we may not be lost in a wilderness of sorrow, doubt, and despair but, rather, are able to hear over our shoulder which way to go, what way turn to choose, which time to rest and which time to push forward.

We ask in the name of Jesus Christ, Our Lord. Amen.

The LORD alone guided them. He suckled them with honey from the crags and olive oil from the flinty rock.[59]

Grant us the courage to persevere through deserts of heart, mind, and body.

Be there to remind us gently how, each time we reach the end of our own strength and abilities, we may surrender the next step to Jesus, who will take our cross and stretch us into new levels of faith, hope, love and life in him.

---

[59] Deuteronomy 32:12-13

Help us keep our minds set on our true destiny which trauma, abuse, and grief can so easily obscure.

Be our constant companion as we move toward that time when we will witness all of Creation restored and in resplendent adoration of the One True God Who, for love of us, gave His only Son to die on a Cross that we would not be abandoned forever to the one who prowls the world seeking our ruin.

Cultivate in us the wisdom to know the difference between weight from carrying the sins of others and from bearing our own sins. Through Your graces help us let God show His great strength in our recovery from the latter and in our redemption from the former.

Unlock psychological defenses against our past and present that can make surrender seem dangerous, so we may be free to receive the peace that surpasses all understanding.

We ask this in the name of Jesus Christ, Our Lord. Amen.

(continued next page)

So you also are now in anguish. But I will see you again, and your hearts will rejoice, and no one will take your joy away from you.[60]

> Guide us into a piety born of healthful surrender that completes but does not harm us, that fosters in us humility but does humiliate us, that releases in us a forgiving spirit neither enabling nor denying the work of evil in our lives or the lives of others.
>
> Shine Your light in our hearts so we are able to able to fear God with freedom and without fright, with awe but without terror. And, heal our wounds and the wounds of our broken world as the wounds of Christ have been healed, by grace through faith, as visible signs of renewed life.
>
> For ourselves, for our fellow survivors of abuse of any kind, for those wounded through their empathy for our wounds and love for us, for those offering us care and seeking to heal wounds in our Church, and for those who have wounded us, we ask this in the name of Jesus Christ, our Lord.

---

[60] John 16:22

Then they set out and went from village to village proclaiming the good news and curing diseases everywhere.[61]

---

[61] Luke 9:6

RESOURCES

Reading

Encouraging survivors to develop faith stories is an important part of the process of listening and offering spiritual support during recovery from abuse. Books have traditionally played a powerful role in recovery and in spiritual growth. However, books that are scholarly or abstract, such as exposes of child abuse or the scandal of abuse in the Catholic Church, may have value in general but do not support developing an open relationship focused on speaking "heart to heart."

Below are the authors' top suggestions. You'll note these works encourage seeking God's hand in one's own faith story.

Acts of Recovery, by Michael D. Hoffman (Chicago, IL: ACTA Publications, 2013) is a brief but powerful account by a survivor of child sexual abuse by clergy. It describes a process from first breaking the silence, through work with a Review Board and a highly personal pursuit to create experiences of restorative justice.

Beauty for Ashes: Receiving Emotional Healing, by Joyce Meyer (Nashville, TN: FaithWords, 2003) is written by a renowned evangelical preacher who was, herself, a victim of child sexual abuse. This book heartens abuse victims who are struggling with personal issues and even mental illness, assuring them that they can turn the ashes of their lives over to God, Who returns beauty as Scripture promises.

The Courage to Heal Workbook: A Guide for Women and Men Survivors of Child Sexual Abuse, by Ellen Bass (New York, NY: Harper Perennial 2003) is half of the classic set of abuse recovery literature which many therapists use as a starting point for therapy, or as "extracurricular assignments." Neither Catholic nor Christian, this book covers a full range of topics and approaches a survivor will face. It may provide useful insights into a process that may be evolving in parallel to spiritual guidance.

The Exodus Experience, by Maureena Fritz (Winona, MN: St. Mary's Press, 1989) offers a retreat-like walk through the journey from bondage through salvation on an individual basis, by traveling through the Exodus relying on Christian and Jewish texts. Although out of print, copies of this book are available through the website www.teresagreen.org.

Introduction to the Devout Life by St. Francis de Sales, translated and edited with an introduction and notes by John K. Ryan (Garden City, NY: Image Books, 1972) is an excellent introduction to Salesian spirituality which has proven helpful to survivors because of its gentle and pastoral approach. A popular shorter and modern interpretation of the *Introduction to the Devout Life* is found in Bernard Bangley's **Authentic Devotion** (Colorado Springs, CO: Waterbrook Press, 2002). Two other very helpful readings for survivors seeking simple, basic principles in the spiritual life are **Treatise on the Love of God** (two volumes), by St. Francis de Sales, translated with an introduction and notes by John K. Ryan (Tan Publishers: Rockford, IL, 1975) and **Francis de Sales, Jane de Chantal, Letters of Spiritual Direction,** by Wendy M. Wright and Joseph F. Power, O.S.F.S., translated by Péronne Marie Thibert, V.H.M., with a preface by Henri J. M. Nouwen (New York, NY: Paulist Press, 1988). A basic and readable overview of Salesian spirituality can be found in **Inspired Common Sense: Seven Fundamental Themes of Salesian Spirituality**, by Rev. Lewis S. Fiorelli, O.S.F.S. (Stella Niagara, NY: De Sales Resource Center, 2012). Many books and recordings related to Salesian Spirituality are available through De Sales Resources and Ministries at desalesresource.org or directly from desales@desalesresource.org

Life of Christ, by Archbishop Fulton J. Sheen (New York, NY: Image Books, 1977 reprint edition) uses Scripture and tradition to present a chronological story of the life of Christ. It is a faith narrative that can inspire individuals to know Jesus more intimately—and to discern how their own faith stories are entwined with his.

My Peace I Give to You: Healing Sexual Wounds with the Help of the Saints, by Dawn Eden and Agnes Mary Donovan (Notre Dame, IN: Ave Maria Press, 2012) offers insights into relying on the lives of the saints during recovery from abuse. One of the authors is a Catholic survivor of childhood sexual abuse (not by clergy).

The Practice of Spiritual Direction, by William A. Barry and William J. Connolly (New York, NY: The Seabury Press, 1982) is a classic which surveys approaches for offering both formalized and casual programs of spiritual direction.

Restoring Sanctuary, by T. Pitt Green (Indianapolis, Indiana: Dog Ear, 2012) is the co-author's chronicle of how her recovery from sexual abuse by priests progressed through encounters with Catholics and other people who challenged and sustained her faith.

Online Resources

RestoringSanctuary.org is a website where you will find many resources, including copies of retreats and seminars we have given together, and also videos on topics such as basic concepts in spiritual dialogue with survivors of abuse. Here too are free articles you may use, interviews with Catholic scholars, and other information for survivors, their families, priests, sisters, deacons, and others.

USCCB.org is the website of the United States Conference of Catholic Bishops. Here, under "Issues and Action/Child and Youth Protection" are excellent resources for finding local Victim Assistance Coordinators, for learning the history and current state of the Church's reforms in the wake of the abuse scandal, and for finding the seminal documents by which the bishops have charted a course to protect all children and youth in their care and to tend to the needs of survivors of clergy abuse. From Teresa, there is a nine-minute tutorial on much of this information posted on her YouTube survivor channel: search YouTube for "Church Amends: 5 Things 2 Know."

ArlingtonDiocese.org is the website for the diocesan program with which both authors work most commonly. Here, under "Outreach/Victim Assistance" are many free resources and much information about the variety of offerings offered to survivors of child sexual abuse by clergy or others—and to anyone who has suffered abuse or violence. Contact information is available, too, for those who may wish to ask for more individual dialogue.

BibleGateway.org is a great resource on translations of Scripture, as well as maps and other citations in Bible history.

St. Jane de Chantal

Hold your eyes on God and leave the doing to Him.
That is all the doing you have to worry about.

INDEX

12-Step programs, 207, 209-210

Abandonment, 108-112
    as recurring issue, 185
    assurances against, 92-93
    at Jesus's Crucifixion, 53-54, 163-164, 280, 293
    being believed versus, 209-211
    by authority figures, 117, 210-211
    continued, 266
    defenses linked to, 147-148
    depression after, 117
    God's seeming, 92, 109, 111, 160, 162-163, 209-210, 238, 256-257, 213-214
    independence after, 110
    Job's experience of, 262-264
    needy friends and, 89
    others' shortfalls and, 160
    relationships developed after, 89, 162-164
    reliability as response to, 26, 63, 65, 105
    survivor's worry and, 146
    with trust on Cross, 53-54
Abba, 282
Abjections, 168-170
Abuse scandal, statistical detail about, 23-24
Abusers
    child chosen by, 52
    child's focus on, 150
    Church represented by, 138, 228, 209, 247-248
    clergy as role of, 24, 25, 26, 71, 290
    compared to God's creative power, 260
    confronting, 71, 86, 225
    confusion used by, 52, 125, 164, 170, 342
    cycles of, 240
    domination by, 68-69, 282
    Eucharist consecrated by, 290
    families as setting for, 222, 223, 225
    finishing work of, 61, 125-126, 128
    first thing destroyed by, 67
    forgiving, 193, 337
    God as opposite of, 94
    God misrepresented by, 238, 290, 342
    God rejected by, 94
    spiritual guide's need to forgive, 266
    guilt assigned by, 205
    lies and, 52, 299-65, 205, 299-300
    other than clergy, 11
    perversion by, 136-137
    prayer for, 263
    power of, 21 34 52-53, 66
    profiles of, 26, 45
    relocation of, 125, 240
    returned to ministry, 45-46
    spiritual guide's need to forgive, 266
    still active, 225
    survivor's carrying sin of, 130-131, 196, 202, 204, 234, 235, 287, 313, 219, 322-323
    threats by, 49, 98, 99, 196
    victim as seen by, 171, 138, 171
Acceptance
    angry comments and, 116
    healing graces in, 191
    of others' flaws, 160
    of suffering versus abuse, 292, 329
Accountability, in child protection, 8-9, 10

Achievements, survivor's, 44, 182-183
Acts of Recovery (Hoffman), 357-358
Acts of the Apostles, 72, 224-225
Actualization
    caricatures versus, 172
    unburying self and, 131
    see also Creativity
Adaptation, 28, 44, 139, 241
Addictions
    help for, 28, 127
    ministry for, 28
Admiration, 237
Adoration, Eucharistic, 342, 343
Adrenaline, chronic elevation of, 241
Adults, child victim's attempts to tell, 99, 125, 195, 235, 245
Advice, 58, 115, 330
Advisory Board, 9
Affection
    child's need for, 204
    imbalance of, 225
    molesting under guise of, 137
    survivor's distrust for, 138
    survivor's skills for, 107
    see also Grooming
Affirmation
    boundaries supported by, 158-159, 219-222
    confidence built by, 221-222
    dialogue based on, 79
    of every step, 235-236
    God's love as, 191-192
    inherent goodness as, 159
    ministry of, 16
    for personalizing Gospel, 63
Aftermath, 136-137, 262, 319, 320
    Cross as image of, 329
    end of abuse and, 125-126, 240
    lasting nature of, 42, 43
    tumult in, 54
    see also this whole book
Aging, 55
Air bubble, psychic, 243
Alchemy of grace, 169
Alcohol use/abuse, 119, 122, 123, 196, 235, 245, 257
    enabling, 169
    insomnia and, 175
    limited effect of, 183
    rock bottom in, 286-287
    suicide by, 284

Alcoholics Anonymous, 123, 245
Alert, high, 145, 165, 240-241
Alignment, 43
All in your head, 203
Allegations, standardized review of, 8-9
Alone, The, 144-145, 200, 341
Altar servers, 46-47
Amazing Grace (hymn), 129-131
Ambivalence
    about God, 111
    about therapeutic closure, 255
    about touch, 51
American Psychological Association, 23-24, 26
Anchor, 73
Angels, 343
    Bread of, 344
    comfort from, 144
    evil witnessed by, 332
    Mary's yes to, 306-307, 308, 316
    Philothea to, 253
    saints and, 331
    sleepless with, 177
    struggle with, 145
    support from, 73
    Tobias helped by, 173
Anger or rage, 52-53, 112-117, 330
    boundaries defined in, 219-220
    breaking silence met by, 195
    Church vs. God and, 53-54
    creative distraction from, 245
    creative force of, 113, 114, 231
    depression and, 117
    faces of, 113
    identity based on, 113, 190-191, 192-193
    judgment of, 221
    misdirected, 116
    moral dimension of, 112
    numbness versus, 113
    positive uses for, 231
    prayer and, 147
    secrets and, 99-100
    self-protective use for, 113, 115, 231
    starting with, 147
Annihilation, 137, 221
    choice to surrender versus, 227
    sexuality and, 230
    surrender as, 284
Annunciation, 307
Anthony, Saint, 332

Anxiety
    cognition dulled by, 240-241
    control and, 151
    dealing with sin and, 322-323
    desire to let go of, 166
    normalcy of, 86
    powerlessness as cause of, 130
    praying and, 175
    shame and , 89
    sharing prayer and, 148
    simplifying life versus, 241
    stories as spark for, 58
    wavering confidence in, 192
    wishes for homecoming versus, 165
    worry and, 146
Apologies
    by Church leadership, 85
    Church's early lack of, 46
    guilt by association and, 83
    truth statements with, 170, 186, 202, 207-208, 209, 278-279, 281, 320, 323
Apostles, 300, 345
    see also Disciples
Apostle's Creed, 91-92
Appointments
    importance of keeping, 66
    moving from confession to, 327
    survivor's commitment to attend, 190-191
    survivor's failure to appear, 81-82
    time between, 63
Arguments
    distraction created by, 225
    prayerful listening verses, 128
Arlington (VA), diocese of, 80-82, 83, 47-48, 347, 401
ArlingtonDiocese.org, 361
Art, spiritual guidance as, 66
Articles, survivor's stories in, 11
Artistry, anger channeled in, 113, 114, 231
Artists, 97, 231, 260
Ashes, recreated from, 260, 262
Attachment, 187
    see also Detachment
Attention, danger in, 52, 231
Attics, 241, 243
Attorneys, complicit role of, 55, 65, 98
Aunts, 108
Authentic Devotion (Bangley), 359

Authority figures
    abandonment by, 117, 210-211
    complicit, 66, 108
    failure to be trustworthy, 104-105
    naivete of, 45-46
    no alternative to, 52
    past versus present, 66
    personal flaws of, 210
    personal sense of truth versus, 203
    perversion of, 137
    self-protective distrust of, 138
    triggers associated with, 210
    wounds inflicted by, 50
Automatic pilot, 179-180
Autumn leaves, 250
Avoidance
    ambivalence as, 255
    hiding secrets by, 152-153
    worry as, 146

Baby Jesus, 312-313
Babysitters, 26
Background checks
    policy requirements for, 10
    priests routinely checked by, 46
Backsliding, 62, 87, 124
Balance, 231-234
    boundaries in, 157-158
    connections in, 108-109
    saint's inspiration for, 118
    social needs in, 212
    unhealthful lack of, 153
Balloons, , 336
Bangley, Bernard, 359
Baptism, 251-252
    Jesus's, 314
    triggers in, 277-278
Barry, William A., 360
Bass, Ellen, 358
Battles, desert, 268-269
Be who you are…., 128, 173
Beauty, 34
    final (ultimate), 260
    God in, 27, 97
    self-loathing and, 127
    survivor's, 58, 131, 239-240
    see also Creativity; Faith
Beauty for Ashes (Meyer), 358
Bed, 121

Belief by others, 186, 206-211
    by Church, 208
    damage in absence of, 206
    failures in, 208
    lies and, 64-65
    Mary and, 310
    by medical doctor, 203
    by priest, 207-208
    as retrospective, 234, 235, 236
    self-trust relying on, 234
    survivor's need for, 209
    by therapist, 49, 202
    triggers and, 210-211
    see also Self-belief
Benedict XVI, Pope Emeritus, 228-229, 273-275
Bernadette, Saint, 316
Bethlehem, 313
Betrayal
    fault and, 13-14
    paths to God harmed by, 211
    self-doubt due to, 235
Beverages, 151
Bible, Holy, 199, 200, 262
BibleGateway.org, 361
Bird nests, 220
Birth of Jesus, 312-313
Birthday celebrations, 133, 237
Blaming
    guide's role with, 105
    Job, by friends, 262-263
    self for abuse, 202, 204-205
    self-distrust and, 107
    siblings for victim's sorrow, 226
    victim for abuse, 27, 43-44, 130, 170, 204-205, 206, 207, 319-322, 323, 324-325
Blind spots, 157
Blink, 175
Boats
    grief released to, 336
    Peter's leap from, 218-219
Bondage, psychological, 267-269
    to another's sin, 130-131, 196, 202, 204, 234, 235, 287, 313, 219, 322-323
    harm leading to, 59
    shame as cause of, 90
Book of Lamentations, 338
Bossiness, 150
Bottle, letter in, 314-315
Boundaries, 51, 156-159, 169, 219-222
    before abuse, 138
    destruction of, 219
    discovering, 219-220
    emotions as cues for, 219-220
    intimacy as needing, 228
    isolation and, 93, 94-95, 158-159
    on sharing, 33, 58, 196, 239-240
    personal balance and, 233-234
    self-imposed, 74
Boys, abuse of, 24
Bracelets, 218
Bread
    of Angels, 344
    breaking, 72
    see also Eucharist
Bridges, spiritual guides as, 165-166
Brokenness
    as caricature, 171
    God's use of, 170
Brothers, 26
Bruise, slap to, 291
Builders, 260
Building up from zero, 105
Burial
    of frightful things, 231-232
    of memories and emotions, 130-131
    of names, 336
Buried treasure, 129-131
Busyness, 117
    as avoidance, 152-156
    cloistered heart in, 155-156
    praying in, 179-180
    survivor's shortcomings in, 190
    Wordsworth on, 153

Cana wedding feast, 308
Canaan, 269
Candles, 200, 342
Canvas, 219
Car backfire, 134
Car mechanics, 43-44
Carefree, 138
Caricatures, 28, 34, 58, 171-174, 192, 223, 299-300
Cataclysmic thinking, 89, 159
Catholic Charities, 9, 63, 127
Catholics
    called to action, 17, 23, 26-29
    faith as safe for, 103

help offered by, 9. 16, 24, 25, 28-29, 101, 209, 331, 360, 364
media, 281
mistaken understandings of, 7, 226-227
negative reactions by, 65, 111, 210, 223, 250, 281,
311
opinions of, overhead, 342
outreach by, 8-9
praying with survivors, 11
reforms unknown by, 10
sacred things loved by, 134, 248, 250, 326
saints as, 360, 334
spiritual imagination of, 38
survivors distained by, 223, 250
in therapy, 13-14, 18, 34, 149
useful skills for, 26-29, 34
wounded by scandal, 24
Caves, 144-145
Center for Applied Research for the Apostolate, 24
Centering
    prayerful, 201
    walls and, 220-221
Centers for Disease Control, 24
Chains, Marley's, 263, 265
Chairs, 151
Change
    anger as fuel for, 113
    healing versus, 60, 70
Chanting, 178-179
Chaos
    creativity in, 262
    order restored after, 173
    power of, 149-150
Character defects, 140
Charter for the Protection of Children and Young People (USCCB), 8-10
Check-ups, therapeutic, 189
Chemical dependencies, 124
Child protection programs, 9-10, 24
    Church as new leader in, 10
    priests scrutinized in, 46-47
    reading for, 34
Child protective services, 9
Child victims
    abuser loved by, 204
    abuser's access to, 109, 222, 223, 225
    abuser's sin borne by, 130-131, 196, 202, 204, 234, 235, 287, 313, 219, 322-323
    abuser's view of, 137, 138, 171
    balance denied to, 232-233
    before abuse, 137-138
    confused in isolation, 52, 125, 131, 164, 170, 196, 202. 204, 234, 235, 313, 233, 342
    de-humanized, 52, 126, 127, 226, 228, 230
    detachment of, 122
    distance as protection for, 123
    end of abuse unknown to, 6, 125-126, 136-137, 199, 240
    futile cries for help by, 99, 125, 195, 235, 245
    powerlessness of, 161, 206
    sense of guilt in, 27, 130, 170, 204-205, 206, 207, 319-322, 323, 324-325
    surrender of Jesus versus, 283-284
    see also Survivors; Victim
Childcare workers, 26
Childhood
    healthful lessons in, 137
    loss of, 129, 132
    murder of, 67-68, 131, 138, 313
    re-encounter with, 122
Choice, 58, 67-71
    accepting healing grace, 191
    anger relying on, 113
    breaking silence and, 195-196
    comforting aspect of, 149
    domination versus, 68-69
    at end of self, 184
    entirely new, of Jesus, 305
    every day, 70
    forgiveness as, 186-187
    free, God's value for, 94, 281-282
    God, with or without, 260
    healing as, 171, 172
    identity by, 190-191, 192-193
    intimacy and, 227, 230
    Jesus's wounds as, 126
    life-and-death, 68
    making, skills for, 69
    Peter's versus Judas's, 287-288
    returning to Church after, 289
    sacred space and, 200-201
    sharing as, 74
    spiritual growth starting in, 184-186
    step-by-step changes in, 124
    storytelling and, 345
    survivor-specific courtesy of, 81, 151-152
    see also Decisions; Freedom

Chrism, Sacred, 252
Christ, Body of, 224
    see also Eucharist; Jesus
Christmas
    Incarnation, 229-230
    triggers associated with, 289, 313
Church hierarchy
    abuser as representing, 138, 228, 209, 247-248
    being believed by, 208
    child victims dismissed by, 99, 125, 195, 235, 245, 345-346
    credibility of, 55, 209
    disciples' failures and, 309-310
    enabling by, 45-46, 98, 194, 298
    forgiveness vs. toleration by, 276
    forgiving, 82-83, 266
    historic reforms by, 8-10
    Marian apparitions and, 314, 317-318
    Mary's unflinching witness and, 317
    secrets kept by, 98
    special healing words from, 170, 186, 202, 207-208, 209, 278-279, 281, 320, 323
    survivor's faith tenacity and, 210-211
    truth silenced by, 65
    victims unprotected by, 203, 218, 265, 310, 345-346
Church, Roman Catholic
    abuse beyond, 17
    desire to return to, 164, 165, 166
    exposes on, 357
    recovery programs and, 209-210
    rejection of, 28
Churches
    difficulty walking in, 102-103, 178
    empty, 295, 342, 343
    isolation in, 95
Chutes and Ladders (game), 44
Clinging, 108, 109-110
Cloak, Mary's, 305-306
Cloistered heart, 155-156
Closure
    forgiveness and, 186-187
    therapeutic, 254-256
    see also End; Forgiveness; Reconciling with Church
Clothing
    baptismal garment, 252
    high priest's robes, 207
    neat appearance of, 70
    priest's, 209-210
    religious habit,
    Roman collar, 237
    self-protective use of, 89, 90
Clutter, 152-153, 241-243
Coaches, 26, 108
Cocoon, 250
Codes of conduct, standardized, 8-9
Cognitive dissonance, 53, 117, 207
Cognitive tools, 183
Come Home program, 16
    see also Reconciling with Church
Comfort, 29
    false, in desert journey, 270-271
    God's removal of darkness as, 260
    repeated, 323
    resting with God, 201
    retaining faith as, 44-45
    triggers and, 291
    truth assertions as, 170, 186, 202, 207-208, 209, 278-279, 281, 320, 323
    unhealthful, 186
Commitments, keeping, 63, 105
Common sense, as inspired, 232
Communication
    between friends, 258
    see also Prayer; Stories
Community, 72, 242, 252, 296
    God as, 96-97, 161
    spiritual guidance as, 73
Companionship, simple gift of, 118-119
Compassion
    for depression, 118-119
    for grief, 133
    intrusion versus, 329, 330
    little acts of , 106-107
    loving abjections as, 170
    survivor's, 237
    in therapy, 55
Complaints, taken to God, 56-57
Complications, simplifying, 240-243
Complicity, 108
Compulsions, *see* Habits or compulsions *and specific types*
Computer macro, 178
Consecrated life, 26
Conception, prayer as, 259
Conference of Catholic Bishops, United States, 8-10, 24-25

Confession, 16, 28, 47, 324-328
    abuse first revealed in, 205, 207, 322
    need to be heard versus, 326-327
    safe setting for, 326
    survivor's misguided guilt in, 324-325
Confidentiality, 127
Confirmation, 277-278
Confronting
    abuser, 71, 86, 225
    God, 56-57
    inclination for, 150
    secrets, 98-99
    self, by survivor, 190-191
Confusion, 330
    abuser's use of, 52, 125, 164, 170, 342
    boundaries as source of, 156-157
    breaking secrets and, 98
    cognitive dissonance and, 53, 117, 207
    complicating effect of, 240
    delayed reactions due to, 142-143
    disbelieving self and, 202
    family member's feeling of, 223-224
    grace and, 60
    hardened knot of, 205
    lies behind, 65-66
    memories numbed and, 123
    misguided sense of sin, 27, 130, 170, 204-205, 206, 207, 319-322, 323, 324-325
    mortal, 285
    pretzel-thinking as, 205
    professional unity and, 62
    reclaiming life and, 86
    rejecting caricatures and, 173
    self-reliance and, 212
    in sexual intimacy, 227
Connolly, William J., 360
Consent, 226-227
Consistency, constancy, 134-136, 166
Consolation, 123-124, 144
Contradictions, God's role in, 109, 111
Control, 149-152
    grief versus, 133
    issues with, 150
    personal limitations in, 182-183
Conversion, 16, 72, 86
Coping mechanisms, 49, 86
    see also Defense mechanisms
Cornelius (Roman centurion), 224-225
Cortisol, chronic elevation of, 241

Counseling, see Psychotherapy
couper court, 120-121
Courage, 27
    abuse revealed in, 99
    in breaking silence, 196
    control issues versus, 150-152
    for conversation with God, 259-260
    of family members, 223
    for first steps, 41, 268
    for letting go, 245
    for reconciling, 247
    for rejecting caricatures, 172
    therapist's regard for, 189
    in therapy, 50
    for turning burdens to God, 323
    in unlearning process, 139-140
Courage to Heal Workbook, The (Bass), 358
Courtesies, 151-152
Covenant, forged in journey, 269
Crayon box, 118
Craziness, preference for, 202
Crazy feelings, 123
    see also Emotions or feelings
Crazy-makers, 152-153, 183, 216
Creation, 260-282
    God's kiss to, 229-230
    praise as joining with, 341
    silence as praise in, 340
    see also Creator; God; Holy Spirit; Jesus
Creativity, 26, 70, 184
    anger channeled in, 113, 114, 231, 245
    cloistered heart exercise for, 155-156
    couper court in, 120-121
    distractions devised by, 121, 245
    God's, 121, 229-230, 260-261, 262
    holy spaces for, 200
    joy and, 121
    new paths to God through, 211
    survivor's proclivity for, 121
    unlearning process as, 139
    see also Imagination; Stories
Creator, 199, 211, 251, 339
    inspiration from, 199
    re-creative promises of, 94, 215, 262, 282, 300
Credibility
    of Church hierarchy, 55, 209
    of spiritual guide, 26-27, 236
Crisis
    avoidance through, 152-153

child's unseen, 52
continuing abuse by, 61
distraction created by, 87
faith during, 75
growth restrained by, 62
interior shifts build to, 244
prayer during, 180
price for healing, 71
wounds recurring in, 43
see also Trauma
Criticism, 89, 113
Cross, 292-294, 329-331
disciples' fright after, 300
evil's seeming victory in, 261-262
Mary at foot of, 309, 316-317, 319
survivor's personal, 329, 330, 331, 329
see also Crucifixion; Jesus
Crossroads, faith, 165-166
Crowds, safety among, 201
Crucifix, 200
Crucifixion, 53-54, 163-164, 280, 292-294
abandonment memories as, 163-164
baptism and, 252
Church trappings around, 207
see also Cross; Jesus
Crusades, 333
Crying, 183
praise and, 185-186
see also Grief and grieving; Sadness
Culture or society
children's pain and, 318
danger in, 138
elite enablers in, 55
hyper-sexualized, 227
stigma assigned by, 194
survivor caricatures in, 28, 34, 58, 171-174, 192, 223, 299-300
traces of new creation in, 261-262
as wounded, 261

Danger
abuse extended in, 61
abuser moved and, 125
colors in, 118
control issues and, 149-152
delayed responses due to, 143
early in healing, 71-72
estrangement and, 164
ideas as precursors to, 44

Jesus prayer during, 176
sleeplessness and, 176
trust and, 102
world fraught with, 138
Dangerous people
as avoidance technique, 152-153
breaking connections to, 216
as numbing, 123
as proxies for abuser, 61, 125-126, 161-162
safety after, 198
self-trust versus, 234-235
Darkness
difficulty finding light in, 261-262
God's removal of, 260
praise in, 339
sudden onset of, 14-15
David, 338
De Sales Resources and Ministries, 359
Deacons, 12, 13, 16, 26, 28
Death
of childhood, 67-68, 131, 138, 313
Jesus's victory over, 261-262
of loved one, 133
of seed, 305
of self, 112, 183-184
suicide versus, 285-288
Debate, 163
deCardi, Adlin, 363-364
Decision
healing as, 171, 189-194
letting go, letting God as, 245
modesty as, 227-228
self-trust earned in, 234, 235
turning point as, 185-186
vigilance as, 216
see also Choice; Freedom
Defense mechanism
coping and, 49, 243
delayed reactions due to, 142-143
detachment as, 122
detachment from, 141
exhaustion of, 184
giving up, 147-148
Holy Spirit's reach through, 303
outgrowing, 231, 243
reconciling with Church and, 211
Defensiveness, 134-136
De-humanizing victims, 52, 126, 127, 226, 228, 230
Delayed responses, reasons for, 142-145

Demeaning attitudes, 89, 90-91
Demons, 145
Denial, 198
    abuser's access due to, 225
    as defense, 86, 196
    detachment versus, 244
    family changes in, 225
    Mary's truth versus, 317
    Peter's, 218-219, 273-274
    self-, 221-222
    self-doubt due to, 235
    as tradeoff for love, 212
Dependence, 109-111, 254-155
Depersonalizing, 109-110, 254-255
    boundary violations, 158-159
    overreactions, 135-136
Depression, 117-121
    anger in, 117
    asking for explanations of, 118-119
    couper court in, 120-121
    daily choices in, 70
    joy co-existing with, 120
    normalcy of, 86
    self-doubt in, 192
    spiritual sadness versus, 119
Depth, personal, 142-145
De-sensitizing process, 134-136, 250
Desert mystics, 144-145
Desert, spiritual
arduous journey through, 268, 269-270
    identity forged in, 269
    Israelites in, 267
    prayers in, 121
    recovery journey through, 267-269
Desire, growth beginning in, 184-186
Despair, 284-288
    caricatures of, 171
    praise during, 339
    temptations to, 44
Detachment, 140-142
    abuser's harm and, 61
    childhood and, 67-68, 131, 138, 313
    sense of safety and, 145-146
    turning point in, 243-244
Detours, personal, 171
Deus caritas est (Pope Emeritus Benedict XVI), 228-229
Devil, Jesus tempted by, 261
Diet/nutrition
    anxiety reduced with, 241
    mood disorders and, 117-118
Dignity, 131, 171
Diocesan victim assistance, *see* Survivor ministry
Disabilities, shaming of, 227
Disappointment
    friendship despite, 258
    in Gethsemane, 280
    in God, 211
    to Jesus, 38
    as trigger, 160
    very extreme of, 183
Disaster, inklings of healing in, 43
Disbelief, family member's feeling of, 223
    see also Belief by others; Self-belief
Disciples
    echoed in Church leaders, 309-310
    as friends to Jesus, 259
    Jesus's command to, 99
    Mary's counsel to, 308
    prayer learned by, 213, 258-259
    rejection endured by, 72
    see also Apostles
Discipline, ritual for accepting, 252
Discouragement, 142, 192
Discussions
    courtesies before, 151
    debate versus, 163
    delayed responses in, 143-145
    during day of Recollection, 84-85
    mistakes in, 162
    room or setting for, 151
    support found in, 73
    support person at, 12
    survivor guidelines in, 11
    theodicy issue in, 162-163
    topics chosen for, 33, 149
    triggers covered in, 135-136
    unpredictability of, 165-166
    see also Appointments; Listening and dialogue
Disguises, 57-58
Disinterest, 117
Disrespect, 89
Disruption, distress over, 149-152
Dissolution, 58
Dissonance, cognitive, 53, 117, 207
Distractions
    creative use of, 121, 245
    Moses unmoved by, 270

numbness as, 196
secrets kept by, 196
self-wounding as, 127
simplicity versus, 241
in therapy, 87
Distress, 86
Distrust, 52-53
for affection, 138
protective nature of, 138
self-blame and, 107
see also Self-trust; Trust
Divine Mercy chaplet, 179, 259, 322-323
Divorce, 43, 222
Dogs
triggers experienced by, 134
walking, 121
Domestic violence, 29
Domination, 282
free will versus, 68-69
spiritual guidance versus, 69-70
see also Abusers
Donovan, Agnes Mary, 360
Doors
policy on, 46
survivor sitting near, 241
Doubts, *see* Belief by others; Faith; Self-doubt; Trust
Dreams
death of, 131
nightmares, 117
wish for, 183
Drug use and abuse, 119, 122, 123, 175, 196, 235, 257
abuser's opportunity in, 222
criticism and, 89
limited effect of, 183
numbing in, 125-126
safety and, 61, 198
suicide by, 284

Earthen vessels, 38-39, 170, 270-272
Earthquake, 154
Easter, 16, 296-298
Easter Proclamation, 322
Eden, Dawn, 360
Educators, 34, 47
Egypt, slavery in, 267-269
Elephant in room, 152, 154
Elijah, 154, 155
Email, 212

Embrace, 51
Emmanuel, 268
Emotions or feelings
after abuse ends, 125-126
annihilation of, 137
avoidance of, 153
burden of another's sin and, 130-131, 196, 202, 204, 234, 235, 287, 313, 219, 322-323
boundaries defined by, 219-220
detaching from, 243
distinct acts of abuse and, 204
estrangement from, 142
family members' range of, 223
free will in relation to, 245
God working through, 221-222
God's effect on, 124
insomnia driven by, 175
kept at bay, 86
range of, 167
sacred items and, 32, 88, 134-136, 200, 248
secondary wounding and, 222, 223, 224-225, 230, 306, 309, 319-320
sewn into remembered images, 202
sin and, 319-324
spirit higher than, 120
surge of, 100, 124
survivor's identity versus, 123-124
survivor's observation of, 221-222
triggers as spark for, 135-136, 290-291
unmatched to circumstances, 122
like walking on water, 272-277
you are not your, 244-245
see also specific emotions
Enablers, 137, 216, 290
choice to heal and, 71
encourager versus, 169
forgiveness and, 194, 266, 276, 337, 338
inadvertent, 127
lies of, 52, 65, 205, 299-300
prayer for, 263
reconciliation and, 250
refuting, 53
secrets involving, 98
spiritual guide's need to forgive, 266
survivor's resisted by, 196
tolerating evil, 276
Truth unchanged by, 55
weakness of, 260
Encouragement, 70

after backslide, 62, 87, 124
    enabling versus, 169
    familial rejection and, 72
    God's simple requests as, 106
    survivor's need for, 265
End
    of childhood, 67-68, 131, 138, 313
    of relationships, 216, 217, 220
    of self, 182-183
    of therapy, 186-187, 189, 253-255
    unclear in abuse, 6, 125-126, 136-137, 199, 240
Endearment, terms of, 70
Energy
    consumed by defenses, 150-152
    drained by outdated habits, 243
    gradual increase in, 243
equilibrium
    child's, 138
    regaining, 189
Escape, 164
    as coping mechanism, 86
    first steps as, 61
    music as, 257
    suicide as, 285
    survivor's positions for, 241
    turning point in, 183
    worry as, 146
Essential Norms (USCCB), 8-9
Estrangement, 37, 165-, 250
    drawn out of, 53-54
    God's patience during, 125
    Mary and, 304-305
    price involved in, 71
    recovery hinged on, 44
    sin and, 320
Eucharist, 341-344
    abuser's consecration of, 290
    Adoration of, 342, 343
    companion to attend, 142
    feast of institution of, 290
    inherent safety of, 341-342
    saints present near, 331
    in spiritual guidance, 343-344
    as trigger, 141
    union with God in, 141
Evangelization, 15, 23
Events, survivor skipping, 81-82
Evil
    anxiety and, 58
    authority as false in, 65
    battle lines against, 260
    child's false sense of, 66
    experience of, 55
    free choice and, 94, 281-282
    good misrepresented as, 234
    Jesus and survivor's experience of, 126
    Jesus's victory over, 15-16, 176, 261-262
    pathology versus, 55
    sacred perverted by, 248
    seeming triumph of, 53
    storytelling and, 59
    survivor's judgment of, 235-237
    survivor's testimony against, 189
Excuses, 55
Exercise
    anger channeled in, 114
    depression treated with, 117-118
    hyper-vigilance reduced by, 241
    insomnia lessened by, 175
    less strain, more gain in, 140
Exhaustion
    in depression, 117
    from insomnia, 175
    from living in extremes, 233-234
    outdated defenses as source of, 231, 243
    shame as cause of, 89
    spiritual guide's, 76-77
Exhibitionism, 227
Exhilaration, 117
Exile, 68
Exodus, 267-272
Exodus Experience, The (Fritz), 358
Expectations
    of hurt, 162
    of protection for child, 218
    of roles, 61
    of spiritual guide, 123-124
    of therapy, 186-187
    unrealistic, 170
Experts, enabling role of, 55
Exsultet, 322
Extremes, balance versus, 233-234
Extroversion, 238
Exuberance, 119

Failure
    berating self for, 182
    fear of, 192

God's seeming, 55, 111
of protectors, 129
Faith
    abuse not related to, 248
    deepening, 36, 97, 76-77, 326
    Holy Spirit working through, 120
    in new life, 86
    joy as, 120
    loss of, 129
    retaining, 44-45
    shared prayer and, 148
    speaking with God as, 56
    stretching, 191
    survivor's depth of, 105-106
    survivors' range of, 209
    taken personally, 128
    triggers connected to, 36, 248
    worry replaced by, 146-149
    see also Grace
Fall, The, 67
False gods, 271
Families or family members, 222-226
    abuser among, 26, 71, 72, 223, 225
    abuser as, 224
    arguments in, 225
    before child's abuse, 138
    breaking silence in, 195-198
    broken, 138, 222
    choice to heal in, 71-72
    Christian, 224
    in crisis, 28, 222
    destruction of, 87, 131, 164
    dynamic transformed in, 233
    enablers in, 194, 224
    faith in ties with, 210-211
    forgiveness vs. toleration by, 276
    forgiving, 193-194, 266, 337
    healing shared by, 224
    helpful workbook for, 17
    isolation in, 95
    loss of, 129
    managing relationships in, 187-188
    Mary's care for, 316, 318
    ministry for/by, 34
    needs unmet in, 222
    new, choices for, 73
    Pieta as image for, 306, 309
    prayer for, 48
    resistance in, 68
    secondary wounding in, 222, 223, 224-225, 306, 309
    secrets kept in, 98
    shared abuse in, 196
    shared wounds in, 222, 319-324, 329
    support from, 49-50
    survivor as help for, 224-225
    survivor rejected by, 218, 223
    survivor's concern for, 12
    testing before trusting, 101
    see also Support network
Family functions, abusers at, 71
Family therapy, 224
Father of lies, 65-66
Fathers, 307
    as abuser, 26
    desert, 144-145
    difficult feelings toward, 108, 283
    St. Francis story about, 109-110, 111
Fatima, children suffering in, 305-306, 314-319
Fears
    common, 50
    desire to let go of, 166
    reclaiming life and, 86
    of sexual intimacy, 227
    trust versus, 50
    of trusting, 166
    walls to contain, 220-221
    worry and, 145-146
Feast day, survivor's unique, 289
Feet, Jesus's washing of, 289, 290
Felix Culpa, 320, 322
Fiat disposition (Mary's yes), 214, 306-307, 308, 316
Fight or flight response, 145, 241
Financial strain, 222
Fingerprinting, 46
Fire, 154, 184, 336
First Communion, 277-278
First steps, 31-32, 41-77, 171
    choice in, 67-71
    compelling drive in, 49
    courage in, 41, 268
    first inklings of, 41
    first tough encounters, 79
    God's failure and, 54-57
    lies and, 64-67
    personal abandonment and, 52-57
    prayer during, 57
    price for, 71-73

safety in, 61-64
safety steps in, 61-64
self-blame and, 107
shame in, 57-60
spiritual guide's perspective on, 45-49
for spiritual guides, 49
starts/stops in, 43, 87
survivor's perspective on, 42-45
theodicy issue in, 57
therapist's perspective on, 49-52
in trust, 54
as vague longing, 61
Fix, addictive, 183
  child as, 136-137
  see also Abusers *and specific addictions*
Fixing the system, 58
Fix-it impulse, 58
Focus, spiritual guide's, 62, 75, 110-111, 112, 140-142, 230, 302
Foes, overestimated, 183
Foot race, 286
Footprints, God's, 238
Footstool of God's mercy, 168
Forget about it, 14
Forgetfulness, 154-155
Forgetting self, 187-188
Forgiveness, 335-338
  from afar, 266
  of all authority, 210
  for common shortcomings, 160
  communion with God before, 213
  enabling versus, 194, 335-336, 276
  at end of self, 183
  by God versus others, 54-55
  God's plan for, 282
  as gradual, 263, 264, 265, 336
  Holy Spirit's gift of, 193-194, 265, 266, 337
  hope needed for, 188
  Jesus's fulfillment and, 336
  Jesus's, of Peter, 219
  by Job, 263
  later in recovery, 186-187, 192-193, 213, 265, 336
  perversion of, 137, 276, 288, 336, 338
  psychology of, 186-187
  reconciliation versus, 249
  of self, 167, 266
  by spiritual guide, 266
  as surrender not assertion, 266
  survivor's, of others, 193-194

survivor's distrust of, 338
survivor's request for, 193
survivor's sensitivity to, 82-83
survivors' unique approaches to, 85, 264-265
toleration versus, 276, 338
too-general ideas about, 266
without reconciliation, 266
Francis de Sales, Jane de Chantal, Letters of Spiritual Direction (Wright, Power), 359
Francis de Sales, Saint, 284
  on abjections, 168-169
  anti-worry prayer of, 147
  on bird nests, 220
  on detachment, 140-142
  on Exodus, 267
  father-daughter story of, 109-110, 111
  on friendship with God, 179-180
  as gentleman saint, 114
  gentleness of, 284
  on gift of Holy Spirit, 193-194
  hot temper of, 113-114
  on interiority, 217-219
  Jesus prayer of, 177
  on Jesus's agony, 293
  on ladder of praise, 339-340, 341
  on moderation, 232
  monastic order co-founded by, 241
  on personalizing Gospel, 63
  prayer defined by, 258-259
  on Providence, 151
  on putting on mind of Christ, 214
  on reducing burden, 102
  on Resurrected wounds, 298
  on retiring to Sacred Heart, 201
  ritual by, for faith commitment, 252-253
  on saints, 334
  Song of Songs loved by, 228-230
  on spiritual sadness, 119-120
  success as defined by, 191
  on Tobias's angel, 173
  on truth of the Cross, 293
  writings by, 358-359
Francis I, Pope, 85
Francis of Assisi, Saint, 332, 333-334
Franciscan confessor, 207
Francisco Marto, Blessed, 316
Free will
  abuse as opposite of, 282
  evil and, 94, 281-282

feelings in relation to, 245
intimacy as, 227, 230
Jesus's wounds as, 126
Judas's exercise of, 287
rediscovery of, 129-131
sexual nature of abuse and, 226-227
Freedom, 145
abuser's destruction of, 67-68
desire for, 166
forged in desert journey, 269-270
from another's sin, 130-131
God's grace in, 141
progression in, 143, 187-188
sorting through sinfulness and, 169-170
storytelling and, 59
truth needed for, 188
Friday, Good, 292-294
Friends and friendship, 67, 161
attention needed by, 180
blaming in, 262-263
breaking silence in, 195-198
on call, 212
chaos of recovery and, 173
choice to heal in, 71-72
clinging to, 108
as community, 96-97, 161
forgotten victims in, 223-224
God's, as best, 136, 213
helpful book for, 17
with Jesus, 38, 99, 258
ministry for/by, 34
new, finding, 73
psychotherapy and, 49-50
resistance in, to listening, 68
revelations in, 187-188
risks in, 104-105
Salesian, 70
secrets shared in, 100
survivors' caring in, 12
testing before trusting in, 101
therapy versus, 74
troubled persons in, 89
see also Help and helpers; Support network
Fritz, Maureena, 358
Fulfillment, source of
God as, 239-240
other as, 230
Fun, 241
Funerals, 71

Garden of Gethsemane, 280-284
Garden, Japanese, 237, 238
Gears, rewiring, 216
Generosity, spiritual, 79
Gentleman saint, 114
Gentleness
of God's grace, 141
in reconciling with Church, 211
self-loathing confronted with, 127-128
as self-trust develops, 236
success measured by, 145
survivor's choice for, 191
survivor's lack, toward self, 266
therapist's, 50
of voice, 81
while being tested, 104-105
Gentleness, 67, 70, 193, 284
Geographic detachment, 244
Get on with your life, 330
Get over it, 27, 34, 58, 265, 336
Gethsemane, 280-284
Gift
ability to forgive as, 193-194, 265, 266, 337
anger as, 113
grace as, 38
healing as, 65
from Holy Spirit, 191, 193
from the Lord, 39
self as, 187-188
survivor's story as, 187-188, 341
Girls, abuse of, 24
Glacier, 122
Glorified body of Christ, 128
Goals, 48, 70
God
apparent abandonment by, 92, 109, 111, 160, 162-163, 209-210, 238, 256-257, 213-214
abuser as proxy for, 138, 290, 342
abuser versus, in viewing child, 137
alone with, 201
bigger than any problem, 191, 192
bridging separation from, 251
brought into pain, 135
child's versus adult's view of, 56
communing with, 201
as Community, 96-97, 161
confronting, 56-57
as constant, 121

creative power of, 121, 229-230, 260-261, 262
as delighted with us, 245
disappointment in, 211, 270-272
earthen vessels sought by, 38-39, 170, 270-272
as failsafe, 110, 111
focus fixed on, 270
footprints of, 238
friendship with, 179-180
gave His only begotten Son, 299
growing reliance on, 124
handiwork of, 108, 124, 128, 151
heavy lifting by, 106
human burdens vs. might of, 231-232
human imperfections and, 167
human weakness and, 117, 271
image of, 27, 79, 107, 127, 128, 171
Job's questions put to, 262-266
as journey companion, 60
junk not made by, 128
as Love, 120
negotiations with, 44
nondenominational sense of, 210
as nourishing, 144-145, 200, 341
as only healer, 302
perverted image and, 138-140
praise of, 338-341
promises of, 317
reconciliation with, 250, 251
rejection of, 256
relationships remade by, 95
relationships used by, 161-164
running after, 226, 229-230
saints as hands and smile of, 334
seeing back of, 136
self-discovery as, 203
self-esteem grounded in, 128, 138-140
spiritual guide as proxy for, 93, 111
spiritual sadness and, 119-120
as still small voice, 154, 155
as sure footing, 61
survivor accepted by, 260
survivor lost by, 129-131
survivor prompted by, 151-152
survivor's need for, 209
survivor's shortfalls and, 121, 271
survivor's faith in, 210-211
survivor's testing, 146-147
trust in, 108-109
as unfailing, 136, 160

unfinished business with, 54
as vindicator, 236
waiting with welcome, 41, 125, 191, 200-201, 217
without trappings, 207
God's kiss to creation, 229-230
God's love, 92
control needs softened by, 150, 151-152
as firm footing, 192-193
heart-to-heart with, 133, 148, 163, 214, 258, 357
humiliation and, 128
mistakes possible in, 159
as personal, 107-108
revealing, opportunities for, 147
self-recrimination versus, 205
self-wounding and, 127
spiritual sadness and, 120-121
as surprising, 191
see also Grace
God's will
abuse misrepresented as, 281
alone with, 144-145
as life-giving, 284
creativity in service of, 121
Jesus aligned with, 280-281
Jesus's struggle with, 282-283
Mary's openness to, 306-307
pace of healing as, 248
self-care before discerning, 62
sisters in union with, 241
survivor's healing as, 243
survivor's openness to, 214
Good Friday, 16, 240, 292-294
Good Shepherd, 206
Good to better, 102, 106
Goodness, decision to seek, 138
Goretti, Saint Maria, 333
Gospel, 63-64, 84, 129-131
Grace, 198
12-Step program and, 210
alchemy of, 169
anger and, 114
being found in, 129-131
in cloistered heart, 156
in confession, 326
creating a safe setting with, 151-152
in decision to heal, 192
detachment and, 140-142
for discipleship, 38

faith inquiry and, 7
forgiveness and, 263, 264-265
God's pacing in, 174
grief and, 112
healing, 67, 117, 278-279, 302, 337
helping work of, 79
imitation of Jesus and , 115
for internal patter, 342
nature built upon by, 62, 112
opposing sentiments in, 54
outreach for help and, 8
paradox of, 271
praise welcoming, 179
in process, 76
running ahead, 226
in sacraments, 141
saints' cooperation with, 114
in self-discovery, 112, 203
shame and, 92
sharing , 26
sleeplessness and, 176-177
at start, 59-60
state of prayer and, 179
surprised by, 334
survivor's cooperation with, 171
in survivor's life, 106
for therapy, 14
in time with God, 215
true self found with, 139-140
unfreedom broken by, 130
won in powerlessness, 130-131
see also God's love; Holy Spirit
Graces all around…, 289, 290
Greek translation, 274-276
Gregorian chant, 178, 289
Grief and grieving, 29, 52-53, 131-135, 330
In breaking silence, 195
buried, 55
defenses against, 43
difficulty believing in, 56
feeling buried in, 130-131
first step in, 132-133
frozen, 122
grace for, 112
hope in, 271
ideal lost and, 217
as identity, 190-191, 192-193
Job's, 262-266
lack of, 133

as normal reaction, 86
other's shortfalls and, 160
pace of, 131, 132-133
praise during, 339
reconciliation as, 249-250
in relationships, 216-217
self lost and, 112
at St. Francis prayer, 147
unresolved, 44
Grooming, 137, 164, 281
memories of, 237
of parents, 108
secrets and, 98
trusted adult and, 26
see also Abusers; Lies
Growth
arrested, 138
backsliding versus, 62, 87, 124
danger in, 111
sacred space for, 201
setbacks in, 191, 258
spiritual, 62
stretching for, 262
in therapeutic breaks, 111, 112, 254-256
Guidelines
for survivor discussions, 11
for spiritual guidance, 63
for therapy sessions, 51
Guilt, 322
priest's, by association, 47, 83, 115, 320
priest's, abuser's versus, 46-47
shame versus, 279-280
spiritual sadness and, 119
survivor's mistaken sense of, 27, 130, 170, 204-205, 206, 207, 319-322, 323, 324-325
Guy lines, 236

Habit, religious, 153
Habits or compulsions, 57, 124, 152-156
concealment as, 238-240
healing impeded by, 153
hyper-vigilance as, 80, 145-146, 165, 240-241
mood disorders and, 118
in meetings, 151
needed by child, 242-243
safety preserved by, 198-201
self-trust in changing, 234-235
self-wounding as, 127-128
simplifying life and, 241-243

virtue in, 233-234
worry as, 65, 145-149
rejection of, 68
return to, 183
self-wounding as, 128
sexuality and, 230
see also specific types
Hair, combing, 70
Handiwork, God's, 108, 124, 128, 151
Handshakes, 51
Happiness
    heartbreak during, 122
    prayer in, 180
Hawk, 132
Healing
    change versus, 60, 70
    choice required in, 188, 189-190
    communion with God before, 213
    decision to, 171, 189-194
    fits and starts in, 62, 86, 166, 171, 192, 211, 272
    forgiveness later in, 186-187, 192-193, 213, 265, 336
    as gift not achievement, 65
    price of, 71
    reconciling later in, 248
    secrets as opposite to, 222
    self-image set in, 190
    as shared experience, 224
    shared in families, 224-225
    in sexual needs, 230
    see also Creativity; Forgiveness; Freedom; God's love; Grace, Jesus; Joy; Reconciliation; Stories; Survivors; *and just hang in there*
Health Care Professionals, 7
Hearing, 241
Heart, 97, 101, 104, 146, 167, 185, 249, 266, 277, 321, 324, 336, 338
    broken, 7, 17, 122, 138, 171, 205, 244, 247, 248, 257, 334
    cloistered, 155-156
    of faith, 287, 288
    God in, 141, 180, 213-214, 242-243
    grace preparing, 226
    handled with care, 171
    Holy Spirit in, 120, 193, 211, 278-279
    Jesus and, 217, 219, 336-337
    lifted to God, 180
    meek and humble of, 114-115
    mind versus, 163-164
    Sacred, 201
    shutting off, 167
    silence broken first in, 195
    see also God's love; Prayer
Heart speaks to heart, 133, 148, 163, 214, 258, 357
Heartbreak, happiness during, 122
Hell
    past as, 202
    shame as, 89, 91
Help and helpers, 139-140
    asking for, 212-215
    for attending Eucharist, 142
    balance in, 212
    confidence developed with,
    discerning approach to, 212
    gift from, 53
    help for, 7-8
    immediate, for suicidal thoughts, 285
    phone list of, 61, 62, 212
    as quilt, 41, 61, 62-63, 75, 160, 216
    safe, 61, 62
    shortcomings in, 212-213, 216-217
    survivor's confession and, 326
    testing before trusting, 105-106
    USCCB *Charter* and, 8-9
    varying gifts of, 61
    withdrawal reduced with, 231
    workbook for, 16-17
    see also Angels; Friends and friendship; God; Holy Spirit; Jesus; Saints; Support network
Hibachi, paper burned in, 336
Hiding
    behind walls, 220-221
    cloistered heart versus, 155-156
    as coping mechanism, 86
    disciples, on Pentecost, 300
    in full sight, 237, 238, 239, 299-300
    from God's radical love, 92
    God's clear view into, 239
    God's re-creation and, 262
    healing grace despite, 302-303
    as imbalanced defense, 231
    as okay, 60
    no place for, 199
    protective nature of, 238-239
    reducing in recovery, 49, 143
    in shame, 57-58
Higher Power, 207, 209-210
High-functioning survivors, 14, 110-111

Hoffman, Michael D., 357-358
Holiness
    attachment to, 140-142
    perversion of, 137
    triggers associated with, 32, 88, 200, 248, 134-136
Hollow, The, 336
Holy Innocents, 333
Holy Saturday, 294-296
Holy Spirit, 96, 192-193
    celebrating child with, 139
    creativity working with, 121
    decision to heal stirred by, 225
    depression open to, 120
    in disciplines' prayer space, 301
    draw of, 64
    as Easter gift, 301
    forgiveness as gift of, 193-194, 265, 266, 337
    gifts from, 191, 193
    human rejection versus, 72
    identity enriched by, 191
    as lead in healing, 73, 136
    lies destroyed by, 302
    love and joy from, 120
    on misguided sense of sin, 323
    on Pentecost, 300-304
    as re-creative force, 279-280
    residing in heart, 120, 193, 211, 278-279
    simplifying life with, 241
    spiritual guide and, 73, 128
    sustenance from, 76, 192-194
    triggers soothed by, 278, 291, 313
    trust for, 64
    virtues revealed by, 117
    whole families converted by, 224-225
Holy Thursday, 288-291
Homecoming program, 164-166
    see also Reconciling with Church
Honesty, 26, 66
Hope, 23
    at end of self, 183
    family support and, 223
    in Jesus's acceptance, 275-276
    limited availability as, 171
    reason for, 16
    survivors as gift of, 187-188
    for thriving life, 172
    trust and, 105
Hopelessness
    caricature of, 28
    in depression, 117
    in prayer, 121
    see also Depression; Isolation; Loneliness
Hormones, chronic elevation of, 241
Horror, responses of, 58
Hospital workers, 34
Humiliation
    during Crucifixion, 280
    God's love versus, 128
    humility versus, 137
Humility, 193
    humiliation versus, 137
    about identity, 168-169
    as truth, 168
Hurt
    survivor's, by others, 167-170, 330
    survivor's, of others, 190-191

Ice floe, grief as, 122
Identity
    abjections and, 168-170
    anger as, 113, 190-191, 192, 193
    choosing, 190-191, 192-193
    defined in relationships, 160-161
    de-humanized by abuse, 52, 126, 127, 226, 228, 230
    discerning, 160
    emotion as, 190-191
    enriched with God's Spirit, 191
    as hurt, 167
    powerlessness over, 168-169
    quest to find, 221-222
    rediscovery of, 187-188
    religious habit as, 153
    shame as, 190-191, 192-193
If only (no abuse), 44
Illness (physical), 28
    choice to heal in, 189-190
    therapy and, 87
Illusion
    child's, of power, 242
    in grooming process, 164
    loss of, 99
    some victimhood as, 184
    of worry, 145-146
Imagination, 37
    accurate memories versus, 202
    animated through grace, 172

exercise for, 154-155
God's work served by, 201
healing in, 41
Jesus as catalyst for, 233-234
of safety in Christ, 206
in sleepless nights, 176
spiritual retirement in, 180
see also Creativity
Impatience, 113, 117
in survivor's drive to heal, 168-169, 174, 265, 287
Imperfections, 168-170
God's work through, 169
media shaming of, 227
as normal, 167
Imposter, feeling like, 89
Impulsive acts, 87
Incarnation, 229-230
Incense, 289
Independence, 109-111
Infant Jesus, 312-313
Inner child, 112
Innocence, 14
coming to believe in, 278-280, 320
grieving for stolen, 132
guilt for abuse versus, 190
Jesus's clarity on, 205
of self-defining sin, 169
sin against, 130
survivor's acknowledgement of, 192
survivor's need to hear, 170, 186, 202, 207-208, 209, 278-279, 281, 320, 323
survivor's sense of guilt verses, 27, 130, 170, 204-205, 206, 207, 319-322, 323, 324-325
Innocents, Holy, 313
Insignificance, sense of, 90
Insomnia, 117, 175-177, 332
Inspired Common Sense (Fiorelli), 359
Instinct, 150, 235-236
Integration, 44, 74, 247, 347
anger with self, 190
faith with recovery, 12, 13, 16, 23, 37, 47, 74, 80, 91
forgiveness through, 336
past with present, 187, 227
Integrity, 156
Intellect or understanding
abuse as beyond, 240
abuser's influence on, 205

of adults' missteps, 165
child's lack of, 52, 125, 131, 164, 170, 196, 202, 204, 234, 235, 313, 233, 342
futile efforts in, 322, 323
God's vs. human's, 322, 323, 325-326
heart versus, 163-164
innocence as seen by, 322
Job not saved by, 263
memory in body versus, 228
safety from abuse known by, 242-243
self-indictment via, 205
shame circumventing, 278-279
of slowing down, 155
worry and, 146
Interconnectedness, 224
Interdependence, 212-213
Interiority
boundaries set within, 156-157
cloistered heart and, 156
of cloistered sisters, 241
delayed reactions due to, 143
positive role of, 231
psychic battle in, 234-235
quieting practices for, 153-156
sacred space drawing on, 148
St. Francis on, 217-219
Intimacy, 226-230
free choice in, 227, 230
God's intention for, 228
self-esteem in, 227-228
Introduction to the Devout Life (St. Francis de Sales), 220, 252-253, 358-359
Introversion, 238
Intuitions, 122
Invisibility, 105
Isolation, 93-97
abuser's use of, 52
behind walls, 220-221
boundaries and, 93, 94-95, 158-169
caricatures of, 172
child left in, 52, 125, 131, 164, 170, 196, 202, 204, 234, 235, 313, 233, 342
companionship after, 187
disbelieving self and, 202
due to shame, 93, 94
end of powers in, 183, 184-186
false messages in, 14
as hiding, 57
independence versus, 111

Jesus's silent Presence versus, 344
  as numbing technique, 123
  rage as factor in, 113
  as reaction to danger, 94
  as resistance in therapy, 87
  self-reliance in, 212
  tendency toward, 95-96
Issues, familiarity with, 48
It was not your fault, 52, 125, 126, 131, 164, 170, 186, 196, 202, 204, 207-208, 209, 233, 234, 235, 278-279, 281, 313, 323, 342

Jacinta Marto, Blessed, 316
Jacob, 56
Jane de Chantal, Saint, 241
Japanese garden, 237, 238
Jar, prayer, 199
Jeepers, 402
Jesus
  abandoned by Peter, 273-274
  acceptance "as is" by, 284
  baptism of, 314
  beckoning outside boat, 272-277
  birth of, 312-313
  buried, 15-16, 292, 294
  as catalyst for imagination, 233-234
  at end of self, 183-184
  change based on, 114
  comfort in Presence of, 343-344
  Cross dragged by, 58
  Crucifixion of, 163-164, 280, 293
  in decision to heal, 194
  disciples taught by, 258-259
  evil vanquished by, 261-262
  final victory by, 260
  fixing eyes on, 207
  following, toward forgiveness, 263
  glorified body of, 128
  grace needed from, 130-131
  as heart of our heart, 217-218
  heart seen by, 219
  help finding, 7
  human weakness completed by, 275-277
  imitating, 190, 141, 174-175, 214, 217-219
  Incarnate, 229-230
  Infant, 312-313
  joy from faith in, 120
  killers forgiven by, 263
  like us, 54
  locked doors give way to, 300-301, 303
  on losing/gaining life, 203-204
  making room within for, 336-337
  meditating on life of, 214
  as model for change, 114-115
  name of, 177, 259
  as new Job, 263
  new walk with, 106
  obscured gifts from, 249
  Peter and, 218-219, 273-275
  prayer as command of, 179
  in prayer with Father, 213
  proclaiming as command of, 99
  rest offered by, 201, 323
  Resurrected wounds of, 298-299
  secrets shared with, 100
  self-emptying by, 91
  struggle in garden by,
  surrender by child victim versus, 283-284
  surrender to, 266
  survivor accompanied by, 211
  survivor as sibling of, 124
  survivor's burden born by, 91-92
  survivor's closeness to suffering of, 292
  triggers related to, 134-136
  triple function of, 252
  as Victor, 65
  as The Way, 185-186, 331
  wounds of survivors versus, 126
Jesus prayer, 176
Job, 236, 262-266, 338
John, Saint, 301
John Jay College, 24
John Paul II, Saint, 80
John, Saint, 315
Journaling, 33, 100, 183, 203
Joy, 23, 119-120, 232
  abjections as constraining, 168
  childhood, 138
  creativity and, 121
  as faith, 120
  feeling found and, 130
  God's, 125
  growth leading to, 111
  in intimacy, 228
  shutting out pain and, 150
  sorrow co-existing with,
  spiritual sadness versus, 119
  surprise by, 121

Juan Diego, Saint, 305-306
Judas Iscariot, 284-288

Kindness, 104-105, 106-107, 193

La Salette Lay Associates, 15
Ladder of praise, 339-340, 341
Lamentations, Book of, 338
Landings program, 16
    see also Reconciling with Church
Last Supper, 218-219
Laughter, with God, 156
Law enforcement, 9
Lawsuits, 46
Lay ministers, 16, 26, 47, 75
    workshops for, 12, 13
Leadership, 270
Leaf pile, autumnal, 250
Leaps of faith, 305
Learning, 232
    balance, 233-234
    being true to self, 202-203
    building support while, 61, 62, 212, 216
    false lessons and, 137-140
    by listening, 148-149
    needs and, 221-222
    new rules, 68
    numbness and, 123
    one's goodness, 106
    slowing down as dangerous, 155
Legislators, 55
Letting go, 173, 245, 336
    abandonment and, 108
    in grieving, 112
    hollow after, 336
    letting God, 245, 337
    practice of detachment and, 140-142
    of self-development, 168-169
Lies, 64-67
    abuser's use of, 52, 299-65, 205, 299-300
    complication of, 240
    fragility of, 260
    paths to God harmed by, 211
    self-trust lost in, 234, 235
    under guise of truth, 65
    victim dismissed as, 99
Life of Christ (Sheen), 359
Lifestyle changes, 68, 118, 121
Limitations, human, 117, 167, 212-213, 216-217, 271

    of human love, 274-275
    identity and, 168-170
    survivor's, 167
    at turning points, 181-182
Linear progress, 31
Listening (and dialogue), 8, 79-180
    anger in, 115-116
    congruence in, 59-60
    delayed responses and, 143-145
    desert journey and, 269
    in discussion groups , 11
    familial rejection and, 72
    gentleness and, 81, 104-105, 118-119, 127-128, 145
    hearing when, 105
    Holy Spirit in, 79
    learning territory by, 148-149
    as ministry, 12, 16
    obstacles to, 58-59
    to oneself, 70
    as path to balance, 233-234
    to prayers aloud, 64, 148, 215
    as priority, 83-84
    in professional exchange, 63
    for questions about God, 163
    resistance to, 208-209
    safe persons in, 196
    safety vs. danger and, 141
    about sleeplessness, 176
    as spiritual assistance, 347
    spiritual guide's perspective on, 82-84
    to survivor needs, 82-84
    survivor's perspective on, 80-82
    therapist's perspective on, 86-88
    unique challenges learned by, 111
    vicarious wounding in, 26, 33, 74, 196, 325
    witnessing evil, 59
Literature, recovery, 44, 75, 97, 175, 183, 199, 200, 223-224
Little deeds with perfection, 106
Little peddler, little pack, 102
Little virtues, 106-107
Liturgical seasons, , 288-289
Live Jesus, 114, 214, 217-218
loneliness
    lost by God and, 129
    prayer in, 215
Lord's Prayer, 259
Losses, 129-131

of childhood, 129, 132
grieving, 131-135
self-discovery versus, 203-204
reconciling self to, 247, 249
therapeutic closure and, 254-255
Lourdes, 305-306, 314-319, 223
Lovability, 105
Love for God, survivor's, 105-106
Loverde, Most Rev. Paul S., 9, 84-85, 281, 401
Lucia de Jesus dos Santos, Sister, 316

Manhattan (New York, NY), 332
Mania, depression and, 117
Manipulation
    by abuser, 237
    secrets in, 98
    by survivor, 150
Mantras, 178-180
Marathon, private, 247
Maria Goretti, Saint, 333
Marian apparitions, 305-306, 314-319, 223
Marian shrine, 311
Marley, Jacob, 263, 265
Marriage Tribunal, 16
Marriages, 161
Mary, 304-310
    apparitions of, 120-131, 305-306, 314-319, 223
    as alternative parent, 307-308
    discipleship as mother, 315
    fidelity of, 308-309
    as first Christian, 305, 308
    God's will and, 214
    interiority of, 241
    Jesus taught faith by, 306-207
    messages from, 318-319
    name of, as prayer, 259
    praise by, 339-340
    protective role of, 315
    triggers related to, 304-205
    as witness to evil, 316
    yes spoken by, 214, 306-307, 308, 316
Mass, 258, 259, 295
    Christmas, 289
    de-sensitizing, 134
    family/friends at, 12
    for healing, 11, 12,32 7
    Philothea and, 253
    survivor's attendance of, 134, 142, 211, 290
    triggers in, 290

Master Craftsman, 128
May altars, 199
McGee, Shenanigans "Mickee," 364
Mealey, O.S.F.S., Mark S., 4-17, 84-85, 208, 345, 401
Media, 299-300, 332
    Catholic, 281
    shaming by, 227
    survivors presented in, 27-28, 58
Medical professionals, 132, 202-203
Medication, 118
Meditation
    for depression, 117-118
    detachment in, 141
    for sleeplessness, 177
    on Eucharist, 344
    ten-day ritual of, 253
    vigilance and, 241
Memories
    backsliding from, 124
    calming and releasing, 155-156
    color of, 50-51
    difficulty believing, 202-206
    emotional torrent in, 100, 124
    feelings sewn into, 202
    gaining focus on, 202
    honesty applied to, 43
    overwhelming impact of, 154
    physical, 230
    reconstructing, 100
    sacred laden with, 32, 88, 132-136, 200, 248
    survivor's misguided sense of guilt in, 130-131, 196, 202, 204, 234, 235, 287, 313, 219, 322-323
    triggered, 134-136
    see also Emotions or feelings; Stories; Triggers
Mental illness
    abuser's opportunity in, 222
    ministry for, 28, 29
    self-regard developed in, 169
    see also specific types and addictions
Mercy, 191, 322-323
    see also God's love
Messiness, 67
    in breaking patterns, 237-238
    in breaking silence, 196
    in decision to heal, 189-190
    as grief thaws, 122
    in reviewing relationships, 216-217
    in seeking "right" listener, 33, 58, 196, 239-240

in setting boundaries, 220
    at starting point, 260
Meyer, Joyce, 358
Midnight Mass, 289
Milk, warm, 175
Mindfulness, 155-156
Miracles, 63-64
Mirror, helpers as, 57-60
Mistakes, 97, 162, 167, 233
    abjections and, 168-170
    by others, 117, 164, 167, 189, 212-213, 216-217, 271
Moderation in all things but ..., 232
Modesty, 227-228
Moment, life changed in one, 292
Monasteries, 241-243
Moncher, Frank, 401, 405
    on first steps, 49-52
    on listening and dialogue, 86-88
    on reconciliation, 254-256
    on turning points, 186-188
Mood disorders, 117-118
Moral conflict, 45, 338, 223, 225
Moral outrage, 112-113
Moses, 69, 70, 270-272
    endangered as baby, 270
Moth, 250
Mother of God, *see* Mary
Mothers
    desert, 144-145
    Mary and feelings toward, 304-305
Mountain, 154
Mourning, *see* Grief and grieving; Losses
Mudd, H. Patricia, 9, 10, 81-82, 83, 401-402
Murder, abuse as, 67-68, 129, 131, 132, 138, 313
Music, 97, 121, 257
Mutuality, 103, 162-163
My Peace I Give to You (Eden, Donovan), 360
Mystics, 91, 153-156

Nativity scene, 313
Nature, 153
    grace building on, 62, 112
    helpful distraction in, 121
    messiness of, 189
Negative thinking, 89
Neglect
    child's, as evil opportunity, 204
    survivor's, of themselves, 242

Negotiation, prayers as, 44
Neighbors, 26
Nests, bird, 220
Neurotic religiosity, 247-248
New Testament, 224-225
Nightmares, 117
Nights, sleepless, 175-177
Nouwen, Henri J.M., 359
Numbness, 119, 122-125
    anger versus, 113
    as distraction, 196
    drug use for, 125-126, 231-232
    learned in childhood, 123
    limited effectiveness of, 123, 183
    recovery from agents of, 124, 231-232
    power versus, 123

Obedience, perversion of, 137
Objectification, 127, 128
Obsession, *see* Habits or compulsions: Worry
Obstacles
    to asking for help, 212-215
    defenses as, 49, 231, 243
    detachment from, 140-142
    to first steps, 31-32, 41-77, 171
    habits as, 153
    misguided sense of sin as, 27, 130, 170, 204-205, 206, 207, 319-322, 323, 324-325
    to psychotherapy, 49-50
    to reconciling with Church, 8
    reducing, 258
    in relating to God, 75-76
    scars as, 184
    timeless truth about, 16
    triggers as, 134-136
    unique to survivors, 76
Off switch, reasoning without, 146
Offense, 95
    see also De-personalizing; Personalizing
Opening up, 237-240
Other shoe dropping, 125
Outrage, moral dimension of, 112-113
Outrunning
    pain, 184
    the world, 150
Over-sharing, inadvertent, 33, 58, 196, 239-240
Overwhelmed, small steps when, 106
Overwork, 175

Pacing, 248, 263, 264, 265
    common courtesies as, 151-152
    delayed responses and, 143-145
    fits and starts, 62, 86, 166, 171, 192, 211, 272
    for forgiveness, 186-187, 192-193, 194, 248, 263, 264, 265, 336
    God's will in, 145, 174
    of grieving, 131, 132-133
    lifelong, 268
    patience needed for, 14
    preserving safety through, 151
    reconciliation later in, 248
    return to Church, 289
    slow, 166, 323
    slowing down, 154-156
    survivor's drive in, 168-169, 174, 265, 287
    therapeutic breaks for, 254-255

Pain
    joy co-existing with, 120
    powerlessness and, 130

Parents
    abuser as, 228
    abuser's manipulation of, 108, 226
    attempts to report by, 99, 125, 195, 235, 245
    baptism and, 252
    before abuse, 138
    complicit, 108
    dismissed by Church authorities, 345
    forgiving, 193
    ideal, loss of, 217
    loss of, 129
    Mary as, 315
    overly scrupulous, 247-248
    protective failure by, 65, 117, 210-211, 218, 226
    teaching triumph of good, 65

Pariah, 223
Parishes, 9, 12
Paschal candle, 251-252
Paschal Mystery, 322-323
Pastors, 28, 34
Patchwork quilt, 41. 61, 62-63, 75, 160, 216
Pathology, abuse as, 55
Patience, 14
    for desert crossings, 268-269
    for learning, 98, 106
    mutual need for, 14, 76
    mutuality developed with, 162
    spiritual guide's, 67, 70, 105, 211
    in survivor ministry, 81-82
    therapist's, 50, 88

Paul, Saint, 117, 174, 337
    cry to praise by, 185
    on joy, 120

Peace
    elusiveness of, 184-186
    remembered abandonment in, 163
    surpassing all understanding, 302, 303-304
    unexpected, 121
    see also Grace

Pediatricians, 26
Penny, dropped unheard, 142, 145
Pentecost, 311
Pep talks, 27, 330
    antidote for, 34
Perceptiveness, survivor's, 107
Perfection, 55, 170
Permission, 166
Persecution, 72
Perseverance, 184
Personalities, 190
    as killed, 67-68, 69, 131, 138, 313

Personalizing
    angry comments, 115-116
    Gospel stories, 63-64
    see also De-personalizing

Personhood, destruction of, 61
Perversion, 136-142
    of faith, 36, 109
    of forgiveness, 137, 276, 288, 336, 338
    of relationships, 161
    salvation history versus, 229
    Truth unaffected by, 55
    see also Abuser; Lies

Peter, Saint, 38, 218-219, 272-277
    Judas versus, 287
    whole families baptized by, 225

Pharaoh, 270
Philothea, 253
Phone calls, unreturned, 156
Phone list, list of numbers, 61, 62, 212
Physicians, 176, 189-190
Pieta, 306, 309
Pity, 65
Playfulness, 69, 129
Pockets, rosary in, 311
Policies, diocesan, 10, 52, 225, 285, 327
Post-traumatic stress, 28, 29, 44, 89, 176, 238, 334

Posture (physical), 89
poverty, spiritual, 105, 185
Power
    of abuser, 21 34 52-53, 66
    over identity, 168-169
    worry mistaken for, 145
Power, O.S.F.S., Joseph F., 359
Powerlessness
    feeling lost as, 129-131
    identity and, 168-169
    numbness versus, 123
    praise in, 185-186
    Savior needed in, 287
    unlearning, 138
    worry versus, 145-146
Practice of Spiritual Direction, The (Barry, Connolly), 360
Praise, 72, 338-341
    in grief, 339
    learning how to, 178-179
    quick fervent, 180
Prayer, 159, 175-177, 212-215, 256-260
    as access to God, 213-214
    agonies in, 256-257
    arguing in, 56
    as practiced presence, 144
    asking for help in, 213
    choosing, 259
    cloistered heart as, 155-156
    community, 72, 252, 296
    as complaint, 55-57, 340
    as conception, 259
    deepening faith, 97
    for deliverance, 52
    demystifying, 259-260
    depression and, 121
    detachment and, 141
    Divine Mercy chaplet, 179
    double-edged sword to, 177
    dry or sterile, 121
    as end in itself, 214
    of expostulation, 56
    as friendship with God, 179-180, 258-259
    first lessons in, 214-215, 257
    for gatherings, 351-355
    gentle companionship during, 118-119
    as heart-to-heart, 133, 141, 214, 241, 258
    imagination and, 156
    Infinite Love in, 213
    insomnia as, 175
    Jesus's invitation to, 201
    Jesus's name as, 176, 177
    Job's, 263
    listening in, 141
    as part of daily life, 259
    power of, 48-49
    praise, 338-341
    quick fervent, 136, 176, 180, 259, 340
    relying on, 151
    to Sacred Heart, 201
    safety preserved in, 148
    sharing aloud, 64, 148, 215
    simplifying life with, 241
    St. Francis's anti-worry, 147
    survivor's interiority and, 143
    survivors' message about, 15
    survivor's special, 349
    survivor's trust in, 213-214
    theodicy issue in, 162-163, 250
    triggers in, 141
    unanswered, 52-53, 257
Prayer services, 11, 327
    attendance at, 15
    family/friends at, 12
    support found in, 73
Pretzel-thinking, 205
Price for healing, 71-73, 98, 223, 323
    of breaking secrets, 98
    family crisis as, 71-72
    rejection by family as, 223
Priest, 26, 34, 37
    abuser as opposite of, 289
    adult survivor's comfort with, 85
    before abuse, 138
    as catalyst for recovery, 289
    guilt by association for, 47, 83, 115, 320
    as inadvertent trigger, 48, 165-166
    info needed by, 33-34, 47
    Jesus as, 252
    mistaken for abusers, 46
    new policies and, 46-47
    psychotherapy and, 49-50
    scandals as hurtful to, 46
    survivor's first encounters with, 28
    survivor's unique clarity about, 289
    teaching triumph of good, 65
    as unique witness to evil, 207-208
    workshops for, 12, 13, 16

Privacy
    burdens hidden in, 14
    denied sense of, 157
    trust withdrawn in, 162
    withdrawal into, 143
Prodigal son, 125
Professional counseling, *see* Psychotherapy
Professionalism, 105, 158-159, 256
Progress
    fits and starts in, 62, 86, 166, 171, 192, 211, 272
    see also Healing; Pacing
Promiscuity, 227, 230
Promised Land, 269-272
Promises, keeping, 105, 183
Protection
    abandonment and, 109-110
    adults responsible for, 13, 210
    before child's abuse, 138
    depression and, 117
    distance as, 123
    enjoyed by abuser, 66
    habits in lieu of, 242-243
    isolation as, 94-95
    rage as, 113
    see also Defense mechanisms; Self-protection
Providence, *see* God's love; Grace
Psalms, 338
Psyche
    fatal option for, 281
    grief delayed by, 131
    isolation's effect on, 94
    managed alone, 125
    opposing sentiments in, 54
    scars in, 67
Psychic dissonance, 53, 117, 207
Psychotherapy, 8, 44, 99, 327
    abjections embraced in, 168
    abuser still active and, 225
    ambivalence about, 49
    backsliding in, 62, 124
    being believed in, 49, 202
    breaks from, 254-255
    Catholics in, 34, 149
    choice leading to, 67
    Christ sought in, 25
    Church reliance on, 55, 98
    common concerns in, 49
    confronting abuser and, 86
    crisis outreach and, 62
    death of old self and, 286
    depression and, 117-118, 119
    detachment and, 140-142
    details reserved for, 33, 58, 196, 239-240
    emotional calm after, 250
    end of, 186-187, 189, 253-55
    false ideas rejected in, 278
    first step in, 43-44
    focus shift in, 75, 187
    family in, 223, 224
    freedom due to, 302
    grace for, 14
    growth in, 111, 112, 254-256
    heavy-lifting period in, 87
    importance of, 70
    in synch with faith inquiry, 62
    insomnia during, 175, 176
    intimacy issues and, 227-228
    as key support, 216
    lead role of, 63
    lifelong tools in, 44, 94
    limited reach of, 55, 183
    listening in, 55
    mantras in, 178
    medical model in, 55
    ministry workshops for, 12, 13, 16, 63
    misconceptions about, 43-44
    moving forward in, 173
    optimistic times in, 186
    prayer for, 48
    present freed from past in, 139
    referrals for, 62, 126-127
    safety developed in, 198-201
    self-discovery beyond, 203
    self-esteem issue in, 128
    self-trust cultivated in, 234
    self-wounding and, 126-127
    sexuality and, 227-228, 230
    sharing as healing in, 49
    spiritual guidance versus, 74-77, 87, 127, 328
    starts/stops in, 43, 87
    suicidal thoughts treated in, 285
    survivor as teacher in, 189
    trepidation about, 49
    triggers managed in, 289
    trust in, 50
    uncharted territory in, 186
    as unnerving, 202
    volition supported in, 186-188

weariness in, 186
workbook for, 16
Punishment, 235-236
Pup, merry little, 134
Putting on the mind of Christ, 214

Quieting practice, 144, 153-156
    insomnia and, 175-176
    in Japanese garden, 237, 238
    Jesus prayer for, 177
    sacred space for, 200, 201
    see also Prayer
Quilt, patchwork, 41. 61, 62-63, 75, 160, 216

Rabbit hole, 146
Rationalization
    for killing Jesus, 16
    Truth versus, 55
    see also Enablers
RCIA, 16
    see also Reconciling with Church
Reactivity, 57-59, 134-136
Reading, 44, 75, 91, 175, 183, 199, 200, 223-224
Rebuke, Eucharist as, 342
Recollection, day of, 47, 82-84
Reconciliation, 32, 247-346
    as continuous, 249
    first steps toward, 11
    forgiveness without, 266
    ongoing, 247
    spiritual guide's perspective on, 251-254
    survivor's perspective on, 249-250
    therapist's perspective on, 254-256
Reconciling with Church, 247-346
    baptism in, 277-280
    Christmas in, 289, 313
    closure in, 250, 253
    Confession in, 324-328
    Creation in, 260-262
    degrees of, 210-211
    Easter, 296-298
    Gethsemane in, 280-284
    versus with God, 210, 251, 253-254
    grieving in, 250
    helpers in, 12, 34, 142, 247-248, 347
    Holy Innocents in, 313
    Holy Saturday in, 294-296
    Holy Thursday in, 288-291
    as impossible for some, 251

    Jesus's baptism in, 313
    Job in, 262-266
    Judas in, 284-288
    as long process, 211
    Lourdes in, 314-319
    pacing in, 258, 289
    Pentecost in, 299-304
    prayer as path for, 256-260, 340
    saints as draw in, 331
    spiritual guide's perspective on, 251-254
    survivor's perspective in, 252-253
    therapist's perspective on, 254-256
    triggers managed in, 250, 251
    truth statements in, 170, 186, 202, 207-208, 209, 278-279, 281, 320, 323
Red Sea, 267
Referrals, 62, 126-127
Relationship with God
    abandonment experience in, 92, 109, 111, 160, 162-163, 209-210, 238, 256-257, 213-214
    abjections in, 170
    as antidote for shame, 279-280
    childhood through adulthood, 164
    Church authority and, 210-211
    in cloistered heart, 155-156
    crisis of faith in, 75
    deepening of, 36, 97, 326
    depression and, 118-119
    detachment helped by, 140-142
    focus of spiritual guidance, 62, 75, 110-111, 112, 140-142, 230, 302
    full self-disclosure in, 240
    grief-stricken prayer in, 257
    grounded in prayer, 213
    healing needed in, 162-163
    Jesus's example in, 283-284
    laughter in, 156
    loss of, 129
    as love story, 228-230
    Mary's help in, 317
    no moderation in, 232
    obstacles to, 75-76
    quiet enjoyment in, 153-156
    reconciling with Church versus, 210, 251, 253-254
    ritualized commitment to, 253-254
    sacred space for, 200-201
    seeking without knowing in, 184-186
    sexuality enriched by, 230

simple conversation in, 258
special care for survivor in, 269
spiritual guide as proxy in, 66, 68, 93, 111
spiritual life as focused on, 258
spiritual sadness in, 119-120
two hearts speaking in, 133, 148, 163, 214, 258, 357
uniqueness in, 139-140
Relationships, 160-166
boundaries in, 91, 95, 156-159
broken, 108, 161, 227
community nature of, 95-96, 152
defense mechanisms in, 49, 66, 231, 243
demeaning, 66
depression and, 118-120
detachment from, 140
God's intention for, 228
God's remaking of, 95
healing relying on, 50
healing shared in, 224
hyper-vigilance reduced in, 241
as key to identity, 160-161
opening up in, 237-240
poor judgment in, 234-236
prayer in context of, 258-259
reconciliation in, 247, 249
self-disclosure in, 33, 58, 196, 239-240
self-reliance and, 212-213
setbacks in, 258
sexual intimacy in, 226-230
shame and, 89
sorting through, 42-43, 68, 160, 162, 216, 254, 255-256
unrealistic expectations in, 170
wounded, 161-162
Relaxing, 201
Release, self-wounding as, 127
Reliability, 26, 66
spiritual guide's need for, 105
survivor's lack of, 81-82
Relief, search for, 27, 119, 257
Religiosity, 247-248
Religious trappings, 207-210
Report
attempts to, 99, 125, 195, 235, 245
see Policies, diocesan
Rescue, unworthy of, 52
Resilience, 37, 323
beauty in, 27

distinctions and, 43
guide's focus on, 139
stories revealing, 346
Resistance
to breaking secret, 68
to Jesus's suffering, 218-219
Responses
delayed, 142-145
learning boundaries and, 158-159
proportionate, 233-234
see also specific responses
Responsibility
for others, 225
for self, 191, 198, 241
Restoration, perfection versus, 167
Restoring Sanctuary (Green), 13, 360
Resurrection, 296-298, 301
abuse as death versus, 292
evil vanquished by, 261-262
storytelling and, 345
Reticence, 26, 233
Re-traumatize, 33, 79, 325
pacing and, 248, 263, 264, 265
sharing inadvertently as, 196
ways to avoid, 26
Retreats, survivor, 11
Revenge, 193-194
Rip tide, psychological, 53
Rituals
hyper-vigilance preserved in, 241
unique to sacraments, 252
as way of life, 250-252
Rock bottom, 286-287
Rock of God's Church, 273
Roles
clear versus confusing, 61
in spiritual guidance, 328
Roman centurion, conversion due to, 224-225
Roman collar, perversion of, 137
Rooms, for prayer, 151, 156
Rosary, 259, 311-314
as current around the world, 312
de-sensitizing, 134
in sacred place, 199
Ryan, John K., 359

Sacraments, 97
associated with childhood, 277-280
de-sensitizing, 142

life passages ritualized in, 252
on Holy Saturday, 295
on Holy Thursday, 288-291
as spiritual practice, 75
rituals unique to, 252
union with God in, 141, 326
as way of life, 250-252
see also Eucharist *and other sacraments*
Sacred
child's danger in, 155
perversion of, 137
as triggers, 32, 88, 134-136, 200, 248
Sacred Heart of Jesus, 201
Sacred space
cloistered heart as, 155-156
creation of, 148
habits for, 154-156
Holy Spirit in, 301
time with God in, 215
Sadness, 117
feeling lost and, 130
prayer and, 147, 180
spiritual, 119
see also Depression; Grief and grieving; Loss
Safety, 61-64, 200
anger and, 116-117
bird nest as, 220, 221
boundaries for, 157-159
busyness versus, 153-156
churches as lacking, 209
cloistered heart as, 156
community actions as, 97
courage to share in, 151-152
discerning, 228
efforts to control versus, 150-152
elusiveness of, 184-186
Eucharist as, 341-342
exile leading to, 68
feelings emerge in, 54
first experience of, 62
forgiveness from afar, 266
grieving in, 133
grooming in, 164
growth in, 110-111
healing effect of, 26, 198
home as, 199-201
imagination in, 201
inviting others in, 238
losing self in Christ, 206

mistakes considered in, 159
phone lists and, 61, 62, 212
prayerful setting as, 74
reconciliation after, 248
redefining, 198-201
saints and, 118
secrets revealed in, 98-99, 100
shame and, 90
survivor events as, 12
survivor's desire for, 166
testing before trusting, 105
therapy as, 50, 88
triggers and, 122, 134-136, 141, 291
trust and, 50
withdrawal into, 143, 144
Saints, 73, 114, 117, 331-335
as cornerstone, 117-118
creed for, 91
Philothea before, 253
quieting practices of, 153-156
sleeplessness and, 177
survivor's connection with, 114, 117-118
as survivors' patron, 313
as witnesses, 332
Salesian bread, 39
Salesian tradition, 47-48
be who you are in, 128, 170
cloistered heart as, 155-156
couper court in, 120-121
detachment, 140-142
as do-able, 191-192
friendship in, 69-70
good balance in, 232-234
introduction to, 359
little deeds in, 106-107
making room for Jesus in, 336-337
see also Francis de Sales, Saint
Salvation
abuse versus, 229
being lost in, 129-131
as love story, 228-230
paradox of grace in, 271
playing out in life, 260-261
psychic dissonance about, 53
survivor's felt unworthiness for, 52
see also God's love; Grace; Holy Spirit, Jesus; Sin
Sanctifier, Holy Spirit as, 251
Sanctuaries, bare, 295

Sand
    carefully combed, 237
    footprints in, 238
Saturday, Holy, 294-296
Savior, 65, 251, 287
    see also Eucharist; God's love; Jesus
Scandal, Catholic child-abuse, 45-46
Scholars, 55
Schools, 34
Scripture, 72, 97, 241, 230, 248
    framework for recovery in, 269
    praise in, 339
    prayer learned in, 214-215
    simplifying life with, 241
    triggers helped by, 135-136
Secondary victimization, 222, 223, 224-225, 306, 309
Secrets, 98-101
Secrets
    avoidance around, 152-153
    bonds broken by, 164-165
    breaking, 28, 71-73, 195-198, 300, 323
    confessional role in, 205, 207
    crisis caused by, 28
    as family wound, 222
    fright upon sharing, 300
    healing as exposing, 71-73
    life complicated by, 240
    normalcy as, 238-239
    reasons to keep, 196
    relief and, 196
    required of accusers, 46
    sick as, 98, 99
    surge of sharing after, 33, 58, 196, 239-240
    threats to secure, 49, 98, 99, 196
    trust broken in, 26
Security clearances, 10
Security, sense of
    abandonment versus, 110
    destruction of, 149-150
    loss of, 129
Seed
    dying to be born, 184
    faith like, 305
Self
    abuse as murder of, 67-68, 129, 131, 132, 138, 313
    death of, as rebirth, 112, 183-184, 286-287
    denial of, 221-222
    fulfilled in intimacy, 230
    full, end of, 182-183
    God's clear view of, 239
    loss of, 204-206
    therapeutic focus on, 187
Self image
    false ideal in, 167
    detachment from, 140-142
    as guilty, 27, 130, 170, 204-205, 206, 207, 319-322, 323, 324-325
    modest, 227-228
    of mystics, 144-145
    survivor's, 90, 143
Self-belief, 202-206
    put on mind of Christ in, 204
    sin and, 27, 130, 170, 204-205, 206, 207, 319-322, 323, 324-325
    see also Belief by others
Self-care, 344
    creating holy space as, 200-201
    difficulty of, 107
    God's role in, 191
    lifelong, 241
    little acts in, 107
    self denial vs. ignoring needs, 221-222
    spiritual guides need for, 76-77
    triggers managed in, 241
Self-destructive behavior
    detachment used for, 123, 124, 140-142
    see also Self-harm and specific behaviors
Self-doubt, 202
    betrayal and, 235
    goodness in, 138
    harming self and, 202, 235-236
    irony in, 235
    sense of guilt and, 323
    trusting others and, 166
    see also Belief by others; Doubt; Self-trust; Trust
Self-esteem, 128, 227-228
Self-harm, 87, 125-128, 329
    abuser's work continued in, 61, 125-126, 128
    decisiveness as, 191
    as numbing, 122, 123
    safety developed after, 198
    self-doubt and, 202, 235-236
    as self-protection, 127
    see also Suicide; Suicidal thoughts
Self-hatred, 89, 90, 127-128, 174
    breaking silence and, 195

detaching from, 243
amily member's feeling of, 223-224
grace and, 60
hurt and, 167
hushed, 342
paralysis in, 205
see also Self-harm
Self-help programs, 207, 209-210
Self-protection
  anger as, 113, 115, 231
  hiding as, 60, 231, 238-239
  hurting others by, 190
  self-wounding as, 127
  sudden assertion of, 158-159
  vigilance developed for, 80, 145-146, 165, 240-241
  walls needed in, 220-221
  see also Defense mechanisms; Safety
Self-recrimination, 52-53, 205
Self-reliance, 212-213
Self-trust, 234-237
  hard won, 234, 235
  poor judgment and, 234-235
  see also Healing; Self-care; Trust
Seminarians, 12, 13, 75
Serenity prayer, 178
Service, call to
  Catholic's, 17, 23, 26-29
  survivor's, 114, 193, 301-302, 338
Setbacks, 191, 258
Sexuality
  abuse mistaken for, 226-227
  as de-humanizing tool, 228, 230
  promiscuous, 122, 123
  rediscovering healthful, 230
  too-early exposure to, 227, 230
Shadow, grief's, 132
Shalom, 301, 303
Shame, 29, 52-53, 89-93, 239
  body, 227
  breaking silence and, 195
  confession and, 326, 327
  culture of, 227
  distance from, 59
  eating habits and, 344
  at end of self, 183
  faith and, 91
  grace and, 60
  guilt versus, 279-280
  hiding from, 57-58
  Holy Spirit versus, 194
  hushed, 342
  as identity, 190-191, 192-193
  isolation due to, 93, 94
  Jesus's experience of, 91-92
  mistakes triggering, 159
  near sacraments, 278-280
  new creation from, 277-278
  as normal reaction, 86
  not reinforcing, 105
  physical, 89
  powerlessness of, 130
  reflecting Jesus versus, 174
  secrets kept in, 99, 100
  self-indictment and, 205
  sharing stories and, 75
  sin and, 319-320
  survivor's power to hurt and, 167
  variations of, 89
  walls to contain, 220-221
  see instead Beauty; Creativity; Freedom; Gift; God's love; Holy Spirit; Jesus; Joy
Sheen, Fulton J., 359
Shell, broken, 184
Shepherds, 312
Shore, washing up on, 339
Shroud, 256
Shutting down, 142-143, 227, 240
Siblings
  self-blame among, 226
  some also abused, 222, 223
  see also Family and family members; Help and helpers; Support network
Sick and tired of...., 184
Signs, absence of, 257
Silence
  breaking, 195-198, 222, 235, 236-237
  sharing impulses after, 33, 58, 196, 239-240
  safety in, 198
  shame versus solitude and, 196
  threats to secure, 49, 98, 99, 196
Simon of Cyrene, 329, 330, 331
Simplicity, 66
Simplifying life, 240-243
Sin, 75, 319-324
  as it stands before God, 325
  bearing another's, 130-131, 196, 202, 204, 234, 235, 287, 313, 219, 322-323

confession of abuse, 205, 207, 322
Cross of Jesus and, 293
detachment from, 140
estrangement as, 250
grappling with, 169-170
happy, 320, 322
Jesus's help rejected in, 287
misguided sense of, 27, 130, 170, 204-205, 206, 207, 319-322, 323, 324-325
original, 229
paradox of, 169
priests as holding bound, 207-208
secrets released versus, 100-101
spiritual guidance after, 102
spiritual sadness versus, 119
survivor's, 169-170, 190, 320
water washing away, 251-252
Sisters, 26
at prayer services, 15
seeking to help, 47
survivor's confiding in, 28
workshops for, 12, 13, 16
Sisters of the Visitation, 241
Sleeplessness, *see* Insomnia
Sleeplessness, 332
Social media, 24
Social workers, 34
Soldiers, 134
Solidarity, 9, 312
Solutions, 183, 330
pep talks as, 27, 34, 330
wish for easy, 324-325
Song of Songs, 228-230
Sorrow, 118
joy co-existing with, 120
see also Depression; Grieving
Space, personal, 156-159
see also Boundaries; Safety
Space in between, 294
Speaking heart to heart, 141, 148, 258
Spirit, human, high point of, 120
Spiritual direction, spiritual guidance versus, 69
Spiritual guide
best teacher for, 159
as bridge, 165-166
boundaries needed by, 158-159
debate not role of, 148
core competence of, 76
deepening faith of, 76-77

divine reunion facilitated by, 62, 75, 110-111, 112, 140-142, 230, 302
as early witness, 131
forgiveness as challenging for, 266
God as guide for, 60, 67
God's words at baptism repeated by, 314
gratitude for role as, 341
Holy Spirit and, 64, 193, 308
important message from, 125
individuality encouraged by, 121
Jesus as model for, 114
as key support, 216
making room for Jesus in, 337-338
Mary presented by, 310, 316
no playbook for, 48
obstacles to listening, 58-59
personal growth of, 145, 148
praying aloud and, 64, 148, 215
as proxy for Church, 323
as proxy for God, 66, 68, 93, 111
as proxy for Higher Power, 123-124
quick call for guidance by, 136
realistic goals clarified by, 119-120
as reflection of survivor, 139
repetitions by, 175
revealing self, 117-118
saints help for, 334
self-care for, 92-93
survivor's cross not owned by, 329, 330-331
survivor's depth important to, 143-145
survivor's imitation of, 114-115
topics important to, 33
undergoing testing, 147
vigilance for triggers, 248-249, 290-291
Spiritual practices
cloistered heart, 155-156
couper court, 120-121
detachment, 140-142, 243-244
disciplines desire for, 213
losing self in Christ, 206
mantras, 179-180
praise, 339
prayer, 213-215
quieting practices, 153-156
spiritual retirement, 180
sun of all, 141
see also Prayer
Spontaneity
in intimacy, 228

loss of, 69, 129
self-image opening to, 143
Spouses, 49-50
Spring, 122
St. Peter's Square (Rome, Italy), 80
Stabilizing, 87, 94, 105, 118
Stations of the Cross, 289
Statues, 199
Still small voice, 154, 155
Stone, giant immovable, 15-16, 292, 294
Stories
    in breaking silence, 100, 195-198
    believing one's own, 202-205
    choices about, 345
    confession versus, 326-327
    difficulty telling, 58-59
    faith as nature of, 345
    of family members, 223-224
    God revealed in, 29
    healing effects of, 70, 209, 346-347
    as insights into helping, 148-149
    lies versus, 64-65
    listener's role in, 74, 100-101, 196
    listeners chosen for, 59, 74, 187-188, 324-325
    as nature of faith, 345
    personal crucifixion in, 163-164, 346
    recoiling from, 208
    rejection of, 325
    resistance to, 196
    reticence in recounting, 50-51, 59
    at start of guidance, 149
    strange reactions to, 57-58
    survivor's faith in, 149
    survivor's voice in, 70
    unheard, 344-345
Strangers, 26
Stress, post-traumatic, 28, 29, 44, 89, 176, 238, 334
Stubborn, *see* Tenacity
Success, measurements of, 145
Suicidal thoughts, 125-128
    commonality of, 284-285
    criticism and, 89
    death to self versus, 285-288
    at end of self, 183-184
    as escape, 285
    God's new creation versus, 285
    ideas leading to, 44
    reaching for help in, 285
    support list for, 61, 62, 212

    see worldwide web for hotlines
Suicide, 28, 284
    abuser's work finished in, 61, 125-126, 128. 285
    Judas's guilt and, 264-288
    spiritual, 281
    see also Self-harm; Suicidal thoughts
Suicide hotlines, 127
Sun of all spiritual exercises, 141
Support system, 215-219
    acceptance in, 216
    alienated members in, 72
    alternatives for, 71-72
    blind spot in, 157
    boundaries in, 95
    breaking secrets and, 98, 196
    caricature rejected in, 173
    child's need for, 218
    dangerous people and, 216
    diversity in, 75, 235
    emotions observed in, 221-222
    families as, 222-226
    for family members, 224
    grief unfreezing and, 122
    healing shared in, 224
    importance of, 215
    independence learned in, 110
    isolating from, 87
    needs explored in, 221-222
    options for, 72-73
    other survivors in, 4, 216, 347
    as patchwork, 41, 61, 62-63, 75, 160, 216
    reconciliation in, 247, 249
    storytelling and , 347
    survivor events and, 12
    survivor's confession and, 326
    waiting to help, 221-222
    walls in, 220-221
    see also Angels; Family and family members; Friends and friendship; God; God's love; Grace; Help and helpers; Holy Spirit; Jesus; Psychotherapy; Saints; Spiritual guide
Surgery, 203, 216, 311
Surrender
    as annihilation, 227, 284
    confusion about, 137, 226-227, 284
    courage needed for, 107-108
    at end of self, 183
    exhaustion and, 182-183
    forgiveness as, 266

Jesus's versus victim's, 283-284
Mary's, 305
Mary's versus victim's, 307
perversion of, 137
Survivor ministry, 364
   before 2002, 8
   bishop's commitment to, 84-85
   choice in, 11
   Church relationships among, 84
   commitment shown in, 81
   confronting abuser and, 86
   diocesan coordinators in, 15, 62, 127, 285, 327, 347
   early lack of, 46
   emergency support from, 127
   first encounter with, 80-82
   gentleness in, 81
   gifts of, 85
   inclusive , 11
   listening as, 12, 16
   options offered by, 81
   partnership in, 10-11
   past vs. current, 44
   prayer for, 48
   readiness in, 81
   spiritual guidance in, 47-48
   support system in, 72-73
   testing before trusting, 101-102
   truth statement needed in, 170, 186, 202, 207-208, 209, 278-279, 281, 320, 323
   USCCB Charter and, 8-9
Survivors, 171
   arc of victims to, 68
   bearing another's guilt, 130-131, 196, 202, 204, 234, 235, 287, 313, 219, 322-323
   chain-like burdens of, 265
   confessional impulses of, 324-325
   drive of, 168-169, 174, 265, 287
   lead taken from, 100, 135-136
   miracle of, 210
   others healed by, 224-225
   patron saints for, 313
   range of faith responses among, 210-211
   special feast day for, 295-296
   special gifts from, 187-188, 341
   support among, 4, 216, 347
   thriving, 148-149, 171-172, 251
   see also Beauty; Choice; Creativity; Freedom; Gift; Hope; Joy *and so forth*

Symbols, 250, 252

Tabernacles, survivor as, 124
Talent, consumed, 150-152
Teachers, 108
   abusers as, 26
   before child's abuse, 138
   failed protection by, 65, 218
   teaching triumph of good, 65
Tectonic shifts, 244
Teeth, brushing, 70
Temper, 113
Temple, torn curtain of, 292
Temptation
   of Jesus, 261
   to despair, 44
   to remain in past, 205
Tenacity, 27, 28, 105
   despite limitations, 184
   faith and, 48
   of family members, 223
   reconciling with Church and, 211
   reconciliation and, 247
   resistance versus, 42
Theodicy issue, 57, 185, 162-163, 250, 282-283
Therese of Lisieux, Saint, 332
Thibert, V.H.M., Peronne Marie, 359
Threats, 49, 98, 99, 196
Threshold for pain, 126
Thriving, step in recovery, 148-149, 171-172, 251
Thursday, Holy, 288-291
Tobias, 173
Tradition, 177
Transparency, 59-60, 66
Trauma
   post-, stress syndrome, 28, 29, 44, 89, 176, 238, 334
   re-, 26, 33, 79, 196, 248, 263, 264, 265, 325
   secondary, 222, 223, 224-225, 306, 309
   vicarious, 26, 33, 74, 196, 325
   see also Abuser; Child victims; Lies; Wounds
Treatise on the Love of God (Saint Francis de Sales), 339-340, 359
Trial and error, 97, 121, 223
Triggers
   12-Step program and, 210
   abandonment as, 177
   backslides temporary after, 124
   before psychotherapy, 290

boundaries and, 219-220
Church affiliation as, 48
de-sensitizing, 134-136, 250
desire in overcoming, 102-103
disappointment as, 160
Eucharist as, 141
gentle responses to, 291
Holy Saturday and, 296
Holy Spirit as soothing, 291, 278, 313
Holy Thursday and, 288-291
in Jesus's struggle, 282
liturgical seasons as, 288-289
mantras for, 178
natural shortfalls as, 161-12
others' spiritual steps as, 253
others' stories as, 11, 345, 346
prayer as, 141
priestly garb as, 83
priests as, 48, 165-166
reconciliation and, 211, 248, 249-251
recurring grief as, 132-133
regrouping after, 291
sacred associations as, 32, 88, 134-136, 200, 248
safe places and, 122, 134-136, 141, 291
sexual intimacy as, 227
shame and, 159
sudden changes due to, 159
unexpected nature of, 290-291
weakening of, 142
Trinity, 93-94, 96-97, 251-252
Trust, 7, 26, 27, 101-108, 129, 138
anger and, 116
abandonment and, 108, 109-110
abuser's perversion of, 26, 137, 237
burning to speak, 65
Church outreach and, 8
control ceded with, 152
courage in developing, 162-163
crucial for healing, 50
in grooming process, 164
hurting others and, 190
Jesus, for God, 53-54, 283
mistakes and, 159
numbing versus, 124
in prayer, 213-214
safe places and, 50
self-, recovering, 101-102, 246-249
slow development of, 51-52, 103-104, 146, 187
spiritual guidance and, 66-67

survivor's sense of fault and, 13-14
in therapy, 88, 189
waxing and waning of, 166
worry supplanted by, 146-149
see also Self-trust
Truth
breaking secrets and, 98-101
importance of, 66
liberating power of, 99-100
repeating statements of, 170, 186, 202, 207-208, 209, 278-279, 281, 320, 323
repression of, 131
seeping into adulthood, 125-126
survivor's avoidance of, 153
taken personally by survivor, 128
tentative hope in, 183
unperverted, 55
worth the price, 73
Try, try again, 124, 191
TSA checkpoints, 178
Tumor, 216, 203
Turning points, 32, 181-245
affirming boundaries as, 219-222
asking for help as, 212-215
breaking silence as, 195-198
endurance course and, 181
finding balance as, 231-234
opening up as, 237-240
reaching out as, 185-186
reconciliation as, 210-211, 248
redefining safety as, 198-201
relating to family as, 222-226
sharing prayer insights in, 215
simplifying life as, 240-243
spiritual guide's perspective on, 184-186
survivor's perspective on, 182-184
therapist's perspective on, 186-188
trusting self as, 234-237
Turtles, 94

Ugly, feeling, 57
Uncles, 26, 108
Uncreated Grace, 279
Unlearning, 137-140
building a support while, 216
dependence vs. independence, 110, 111
replacing falsehoods in, 141-142
Salesian detachment and, 140-142
Unpredictability, 150-152

Upheaval, healing beginning as, 42
USCCB (United States Conference of Catholic Bishops), 8-10, 24-25
USCCB.org, 361

Vague longing, 61
Veronica, Saint, 27, 29, 58, 79
Vessels, earthen, 38-39, 170, 270-272
Via Dolorosa, 58, 224
Viaticum, 295
Vicarious trauma, 26, 33, 74, 196, 325
Victim, 58
    being survivor versus, 171
    choice versus, 195-196
    as identity, 190-191, 192-193
    re-wounding of, 26, 33, 79, 196, 248, 263, 264, 265, 325
    secondary, 222, 223, 224-225, 306, 309
    spiritual sadness in, 119
    vicarious, 26, 33, 74, 196, 325
    see also Child victims; Survivors; Stories; Triggers; *and all that Jesus reflects as a victim*
Victim Assistance Coordinators, 15, 62, 127, 285, 327, 347
Victim Assistance programs, *see* Survivor ministry
Vigil light, 342
Vigilance, hyper-, 80, 145-146, 165, 240-241
Virginity, loss of, 129
Virtue
    balance as, 232
    desired by survivor, 117
    detachment and, 140
    habit through repetition, 233-234
    heroic, 334-335
    as spiritual practice, 75
    St. Francis on, 106-107, 114
Visit to church, 134
Visitation, 241
Voice
    minister's, 81
    other's, internalizing, 278
    price of gaining, 144
    rediscovery of, 70
    restoring, 98
    see also Belief by others; Stories
Voice, still, small, 154, 155
Volunteers, *see* Child protection programs
Vulnerability, 138, 187
    as abuser's advantage, 164
    disruption creating, 150-152
    guarding against, 150, 151-152
    in sleeplessness, 176-177
    therapeutic breaks and, 254

Walls, boundaries versus, 156, 220-221, 239
Washing of feet, 289, 290
Water
    bird nests near, 220
    original sin and, 251-252
    walking on, 218-219, 272-277
    working with currents in, 339
Weakness
    fear of, 133
    God's power and, 117
    of spiritual guide, 38-39
    St. Peter's, 38
    trigger for past, 160, 161-162
Websites of interest, 11-12, 360-361
Weddings
    abuser at, 71
    ancient Jewish, 229
    Cana, 308
Weeping, 117
Wells, deep, 142, 143-144
What Would Jesus Do?, 218
Whispers, 74, 98, 99, 154, 155
Why me?, 52-54
Why, God?, 54-57
Will power, 117, 266
Wind, 154
Window-dressing, 10
Windows, 46
Wisdom, 144, 235-236
Wise men, 312
Withdrawal, 231
    balance versus, 233
    delayed responses in, 143
    from intimate relationships, 227-228
    pacing and need for, 143-144
    triggers for, 291
    see also Detachment; Isolation
Wonder, 138, 270
Words
    bishop's, 85
    deceitful, 66
    perversion of, 65
    truthful, 69
    The, *see* Jesus

unsure of, 66
Wordsworth, William, 153
Work, 232
Worldwide Web, 80
Worry, 145-149
Worthlessness, 53, 66
Wounds
   borne by survivor's siblings, 222, 223, 224
   crisis re-sparking, 43
   desire for faith despite, 102-103
   factors in, 139
   faith pursued with, 209
   as familiar, 72
   inflicted in youth, 76
   of Jesus versus survivor, 126
   many levels of, 138
   others wounded by, 190
   professional help for, 76
   pushing on fresh, 265
   Resurrected, 298-301
   re-, 26, 33, 79, 196, 248, 263, 264, 265, 325
   secondary, 222, 223, 224-225, 306, 309
   secrets as source of, 98, 222
   self re-created and, 260-261
   self-indictment as, 205
   self-love and, 107
   shared in families, 222-226
   in survivor's identity, 167
   vicarious, 26, 33, 74, 196, 325
   in wounded world, 261
Wright, Wendy M., 359
Writing, 100

Yes, Mary's *Fiat*, 214, 306-307, 308, 316

ACKNOWLEDGMENTS

Together we would like to thank Most Reverend Paul S. Loverde, Bishop of the Arlington Diocese, Virginia, under whose pastoral care many survivors of abuse by clergy and others have been able to return to the Church for support in a new life and, with him, Rev. Mark S. Mealey, O.S.F.S., J.C.D., General Vicar and Moderator for the Curia in the Arlington Diocese, who have played crucial roles as spiritual guides for the diocesan Program for Victim Assistance. Fr. Mealey, in fact, requested we compile this work, originally conceived as a manual in diocesan training for offering spiritual counsel to abuse survivors.

We also thank Frank J. Moncher, Ph.D., for contributing several essays to this book to interject the point of view of psychologist and to help make clear the distinction between therapeutic counseling and spiritual guidance.

A particularly special note of thanks goes to Mrs. Pat Mudd, social worker and Victim Assistance Coordinator of the Arlington Diocese, who, with Fr. Mealey, and later with Ms. Adlin deCardi, developed the extensive and diversified victim outreach program and related training which brought Fr. Lou and Teresa's work together.

We are grateful to survivors, therapists, social workers, and others in survivor ministry in the Catholic Church who have reviewed this manuscript at various stages of its development to help us make these pages the most useful to survivors, their families and friends, therapists, and Catholics who wish to support their healing process.

Fr. Lou: For my part, I would like to thank adult survivors who have invited me into their days of reflection and programs of recovery. I have received so much more than I have given!

Teresa: *I offer a word of gratitude to fellow survivors who uplift me, to my parents who offered me unconditional love and gave me faith, to my inspiring sisters, and to my companion K9s, Jeepers and Shenanigans St. Michael McGee.*

AUTHORS

Rev. Lewis S. Fiorelli, O.S.F.S.

Fr. Lou has taught dogmatic theology and Salesian spirituality at De Sales School of Theology and at other theological schools in the Washington area. He has served as the tenth Superior General of the Oblates (1994-2006), now serves as chaplain to several Salesian lay groups, is the Auxiliary Religious Assistant to the monasteries of the Order of the Visitation in the United States, and, since 2007, has served as General Formation Coordinator for the Oblate Congregation. Fr. Lou's academic *bona fides* include undergraduate studies in philosophy and modern languages at Catholic University and Niagara University, theology at the University of Fribourg in Switzerland and at the Catholic University in Washington, DC, with his doctorate in systematic theology. Currently a member of the Pastoral Team at Our Lady of Good Counsel in Vienna, Virginia, Fr. Lou extensively travels the country giving retreats and workshops in both the spirituality of St. Francis de Sales and in spiritual direction. Among scholarly works he has written or edited about St. Francis de Sales are included articles for most Catholic magazines, as well as a rich series on *The Sermons of St. Francis de Sales* as well as a *Spiritual Directory of St. Francis de Sales: Reflections for the Laity*.

T. PITT GREEN

Teresa is a survivor of sexual child abuse by clergy for over a decade. Her recovery program includes fifteen years of professional counseling, thirty-plus years of 12-step program work, and immersion in recovery literature. Green is a pseudonym for a survivor who works with the Arlington, Virginia, diocese in one of the United States Catholic Church's leading programs to promote healing and reconciliation among adult survivors of abuse by clergy and of all child abuse. She has been part of a team offering guidance to other dioceses—from the United States through Europe—finding new ways to integrate healing and reconciliation in the lives of survivors and their families, but also in the larger Church. She is grateful for ever-increasing opportunities to speak to survivors, their families, and support persons, bishops and priests, seminarians, nuns and other religious, to all lay ministries, secular counseling groups, and other faiths seeking to tap the Catholic experience to shore up their child protection and victim support work. Her book, *Restoring Sanctuary*, chronicles encounters with people who helped her "keep the faith" over several decades. Teresa's educational background is in literature, history, and rhetoric. Green operates her own business.

Frank J. Moncher, PhD

Frank is a licensed clinical psychologist in Virginia and Washington, DC, currently employed by the Diocese and Catholic Charities of Arlington as a psychological consultant and Director of Catholic Integration and Training. In these roles he provides consultation to a variety of ministries, supervises trainees, and provides psychotherapy and evaluations. He received his bachelor's degree in psychology from Kent State University and his PhD in Clinical-Community Psychology from the University of South Carolina, Columbia. After working several years in the Department of Psychiatry at the Medical College of Georgia in adolescent psychology, Frank joined the faculty of the Institute for the Psychological Sciences in 2000. His teaching and research interests include the integration of Catholic thought into psychotherapy, child, and family development issues, and the evaluation of candidates for the priesthood, permanent diaconate, and religious life. He has published and presented on these topics nationally and internationally. A proud husband and father of three young children, he and his family reside in Alexandria, Virginia.

You Are Invited.

This book has been written as a gift—to you, to others, and to the Church. In that spirit, if you find merit in these pages, please feel free to offer it as a gift to any Catholic survivor of child sexual abuse, to any Catholic priest, pastor, deacon or sister dear to you, or to anyone whom you know ministers to survivors either in diocesan ministries or as a health care professional. They will find additional resources for their work at the website below.

Also, please feel free to share your impressions, suggestions and ideas with the authors via the Contacts page on the website below.

We are particularly interested in suggestions for Scripture verses or quotations from saints and other inspiring people of faith. If and when a second edition is published, we may include your submission. Use the Submission form on the website below to help make any next editions even better.

www.restoringsanctuary.org

CPSIA information can be obtained
at www.ICGtesting.com
Printed in the USA
FFOW01n1821070318
45505178-46236FF